Book Lovers' London

Lesley Reader

Book Lovers' London

Lesley Reader

Book Lovers' London

Written by Lesley Reader
Photography by Metro
Main cover photograph by Natalie Pecht
Edited by Andrew Kershman
Design by Susi Koch & Lesley Gilmour
Maps by Lesley Gilmour

Published 2006 by
Metro Publications
PO Box 6336
London
N1 6PY

Printed and bound in India by Replika Press Pvt. Ltd.

© 2006 Lesley Reader

British Library Cataloguing in Publication Data.
A catalogue record for this book is available from the British Library.

ISBN 1 902910 26 5

Jarndyce

Acknowledgments

My continued thanks to Metro who do all the boring bits while I have the fun. Also to the booksellers who welcomed me into their shops both big and small and found time to answer endless questions.

For Yau Sang Man - with love.

Contents

Arthur Probsthain

Introduction

During the course of my research for this new edition I had the pleasure of visiting the British Library on several occasions. It was in this modern, marble clad environment that I discovered more about the history of bookselling in London, the first recorded bookshop being that of William Caxton established in the late fifteenth-century. My thoughts were, as always, as meandering as the River Thames as I wondered how a fifteenth-century bookshop might differ from its twenty-first-century descendent. Having now visited every contemporary bookshop in London I realise that such a comparison is impossible because the label 'bookshops' now covers an almost infinite variety of establishments. At one end of the spectrum there are the hushed antiquarian bookshops displaying beautiful leather bound tombs; at the other end are the book supermarket-cafés offering piles of the latest publications, CD's and magazines to the sound of pop music. The bookshop chains are of course well organised and offer some great deals on the best-sellers, but it is the independent book-shops that make a lasting impression, reflecting the interests and foibles of the individual proprietors. Order and efficiency are all well and good, but for me the charm of a cluttered, second-hand bookstore – with the possibility of discovering a little gem amongst the tottering piles – comes closest to the perfect book buying experience.

London's literary diversity includes far more than the new, second-hand and antiquarian bookshops and, as with the earlier editions, I have included chapters on charity shops, markets, book fairs, auctions and of course the main book websites. There are also many ways to enjoy literature without shopping for books and I have again included details of museums, art galleries, libraries, literary walks, events and festivals which offer opportunities to enjoy books in a broader sense. Whichever aspect of London's book world you decide to explore I wish you luck.

Bloomsbury Map

Charing Cross Road Map

TOTTENHAM COURT RD

OXFORD ST   NEW OXFORD ST

SOHO   ST GILES HIGH ST

DEAN ST   WARDOUR ST   FRITH ST   GREEK ST   DENMARK ST

SOHO SQ

CHARING CROSS RD

ST GILES   NEAL ST   ENDELL STREET   GARDENS

OLD COMPTON ST   SHORTS ST

SHAFTESBURY AVENUE   EARLHAM ST   WEST ST   MONMOUTH ST   SHELTON STREET   LONG ACRE   BOW ST

LISLE ST   JAMES ST   COVENT GARDEN   RUSSELL ST

WHITCOMB ST   LEICESTER SQUARE   ST MARTIN'S LANE   GARRICK ST   KING ST   BEDFORD ST   TAVISTOCK ST

CECIL COURT   CHANDOS PLACE   STRAND

TRAFALGAR SQUARE

COCKSPUR ST   CHARING CROSS

Mayfair Map

New Bookshops

Daunt Books

A

Abbotts

⌑ 135 George Lane,
   South Woodford, E18 1AN
☎ 020 8989 6164
✆ 020 8989 6164
🚌 South Woodford LU
🕐 Mon-Fri 9am-5.30pm, Sat 9am-5pm

A short walk from South Woodford tube station, this shop is mainly a stationers and art suppliers but also stocks some general fiction, reference, local interest and children's titles, as well as guide books and maps.

Africa Book Centre

⌑ 33 King Street, WC2E 8JT
☎ 020 7240 6649
✆ 020 7497 0309
🖝 www.africabookcentre.com
🚌 Covent Garden LU
🕐 Mon 1pm-6pm, Tues-Sat 10.30am-6.30pm

Situated on the ground floor of the Africa Centre, this bookshop is jam packed with books about Africa's history, politics, literature, languages and development. The stock includes many publications unavailable elsewhere. African fiction, poetry and drama are especially well represented and there's a good choice of books for children. The shop runs a monthly reading group as well as regular events linked to books. Magazines, CDs and African crafts are also sold here. For those interested in keeping up with what's being published about Africa, The Book Review is available by subscription. Customers can alternatively sign up for a weekly e-mail of new publications.

Agape Arabic Christian Centre

⌑ 11 Porchester Road, W2 5DP
☎ 020 7221 4355
🖝 www.agapecentre.org
🚌 Bayswater, Royal Oak & Queensway LU
🕐 Mon-Sat 10am-8pm

Christian books in Arabic and English plus videos, audio tapes and CDs. The bookshop incorporates a large coffee shop for thirsty browsers and the centre holds English and Arabic language and culture classes.

Ian Allan

⌨ *45-46 Lower Marsh, SE1 7RG*

☎ *020 7401 2100*

✆ *020 7401 2887*

✍ *www.ianallanpublishing.co.uk*

✍ *waterloo@ianallanpublishing.co.uk*

🚌 *Waterloo LU/Rail*

🕐 *Mon-Fri 9am-5.30pm, Sat 9am-5pm*

Located just behind Waterloo Station, this is a specialist shop for books on transport worldwide. As well as its own range of transport titles, Ian Allen also stocks a huge selection of books from other specialist and general publishers with comprehensive sections on road, rail and sea transport, aviation as well as military history, transport, equipment and uniforms. The shop also sells magazines, DVDs, videos and models and offers a mail order service.

All Flutes Plus

⌨ *60-61 Warren Street, W1T 5NZ*

☎ *020 7388 8438*

✆ *020 7388 7438*

✍ *www.allflutesplus.co.uk*

🚌 *Warren St LU*

🕐 *Mon-Fri 10am-6pm, Sat 10am-4.30pm*

A shop devoted to flutes, sheet music, tutors and reference books about the instrument. There's also a good range of accessories such as music stands, carrying cases and metronomes. The shop has many leaflets advertising concerts, summer schools and anything else of interest to flautists.

Al Saqi Books

⌨ *26 Westbourne Grove, W2 5RH*

☎ *020 7229 8543*

✆ *020 7229 7492*

✍ *www.alsaqibookshop.com*

🚌 *Bayswater LU*

🕐 *Mon-Sat 10am-6pm (until 7pm in summer)*

Specialist publisher and bookseller selling Arabic and English books on all aspects of the Middle East and Central Asia. Children's books are also well represented, as are Arabic language learning materials. Readers can join a mailing list for regular updates on new books.

J Alsenthal

⌨ *11 Ashbourne Parade, Temple Fortune,*
Finchley Road, NW11 0AD

☎ *020 8455 0501*

🚇 *Golders Green LU*

🕐 *Mon-Thurs 9am-6pm, Fri 9am-2pm (varies – ring to check)*
Sun 9.30am-2pm

A Jewish religious goods store with a large range of religious volumes in Hebrew and English on Jewish scripture, philosophy and life plus a selection of Jewish fiction.

Antonym Bookshop

⌨ *58 Chetwynd Road, NW5 1DJ*

☎ *020 7267 3131*

✆ *020 7485 8462*

✎ *www.antonymbookshop.seekbooks.co.uk*

🚇 *Tufnell Park LU*

🕐 *Mon-Sat 10-6pm*

An excellent, welcoming shop located in the Dartmouth Park area, home to literary figures such as Margaret Forster, Julian Barnes, Amanda Craig and Tracy Chevalier. The carefully selected and well-displayed stock reflects an interest and enormous strength in serious literature as well as associated arts subjects. In addition there's a permanent bargain section and a community notice board.

Argent's Printed Music

⌨ *20 Denmark Street, WC2H 8NE*

☎ *020 7379 3384 or Freephone 0800 515814*

✎ *mip23@dircon.co.uk*

✆ *020 7240 4159*

🚇 *Tottenham Court Road LU*

🕐 *Mon-Fri 9am-6pm, Sat 10am-6pm, Sun 11am-5pm*

Packed with a huge range of printed music of all types: classical, popular, jazz, blues and folk, and for all levels of ability. There are instrumental tuition courses for those who want to learn as well as books and DVDs about music. A notice board advertises classes, bands looking for members and musicians looking for work.

Astrology Shop

Artwords

- 65A Rivington Street, EC2A 3QQ
- 020 7729 2000
- 020 7729 4400
- www.artwords.co.uk
- Liverpool Street or Old Street LU/Rail
- Mon-Sat 11am-7pm

Specialists in newly published material on contemporary art, art theory, architecture, graphic design and photography. It's ideally suited in artsy Shoreditch and there are enough galleries and cafés in the area to while away a pleasant few hours. If you're here at the right time have a look at the highly original bookartbookshop nearby (see p.21) and their other store (see below).

Artwords Bookshop at The Whitechapel Gallery

- 80-82 Whitechapel High Street, E1 7QX
- 020 7247 6924
- 020 7729 4400
- Aldgate East LU
- During exhibitions Tues-Sun 11am-6pm, Thurs 11am-9pm
  Between exhibitions Thurs-Fri 11am-5pm

This branch offers a great selection of books on art from the 1960's onwards. Stock includes books on art theory, architecture, graphic design and photography plus tapes, CDs, DVDs and videos by and about artists. There's always a big display of material that relates to current shows and a consistently fine selection of art magazines and postcards. A few bargain books are usually available.

Astrology Shop

- 78 Neal Street, WC2H 9PA
- 020 7813 3051
- 020 7813 3052
- www.londonastrology.com
- Covent Garden LU
- Mon-Sat 11am-7pm, Sun 12noon-6pm

Specialist shop dealing with all aspects of astrology. There's a wide selection of serious books, periodicals and magazines covering many astrological traditions including the Indian and Chinese as well as more light hearted items such as fun gifts and cards. The shop also offers a personal horoscope service.

Atlantis Bookshop

- 49A Museum Street, WC1A 1LY
- 020 7405 2120
- www.theatlantisbookshop.com
- Holborn or Tottenham Court Road LU
- Mon-Sat 10.30am-6pm

This shop carries an expansive collection of new and second-hand titles on astrology, witchcraft, magic and myth, healing and associated subjects as well as Tarot cards. Established in the 1920's, Atlantis prides itself on being the oldest independent occult bookshop in the area. Browsing here is fascinating, with plenty to interest readers new to the field as well as serious students.

Avalon Comics

- 143 Lavender Hill, SW11 5QJ
- ☎ 020 7924 3609
- ✆ 020 7801 9152
- ✍ www.avaloncomics.co.uk
- 🚌 Clapham Junction Rail
- 🕐 Mon, Tues, Thurs 10am-5.45pm, Wed 10am-5.30pm, Fri 10am-6pm, Sat 9.30am-5.30pm, Sun 11am-3.30pm

Comic dealer specialising in new American comics. The extensive stock includes around 40,000 back issues and unusual associated merchandise, models, toys and kits. Look out for the Dalek Cookie Jar if you are a fan.

B

Banana Bookshop

- 42 The Market, Covent Garden, WC2E 8RA
- ☎ 020 7836 0561
- ✆ 020 7836 0561
- 🚌 Covent Garden LU
- 🕐 Mon-Sat 10am-8pm, Sun 11am-6pm

Located inside the main market area, this shop stocks discounted books covering most popular subjects including a decent selection of children's titles. The stock extends over two floors with plenty of book bargains as well as a good selection of puzzles, toys, stationery and CDs.

Barbican Chimes Music

- Cromwell Tower, Silk Street, Barbican, EC2Y 8DD
- ☎ 020 7588 9242
- ✆ 020 7628 1080
- ✍ www.chimesmusic.com
- 🚌 Barbican LU
- 🕐 Mon-Fri 9am-5.30pm, Sat 9am-4pm

This is the sister shop to Kensington Chimes (see p.82) and is situated close to The Guildhall School of Music and Drama and the Barbican. The shop stocks music scores and courses for all instruments and levels as well as books about every aspect of music. Classical and modern music on CD and attractive gift items complete the ensemble.

The Bargain Bookshop

- 135 Station Road, North Chingford, E4 6AG
- ☎ 020 8524 9002
- 📠 020 8559 3432
- 🖳 www.bookservice.biz
- 🚆 Chingford Rail
- 🕐 Mon-Sat 9.30am-5.30pm
  (From Easter to Christmas Sun 11am-3pm)

Just a few minutes walk from Chingford Station, this shop offers a beguiling mix of discounted and full price new books, greetings cards and videos with a particularly strong children's section. This is a super local shop with a lovely atmosphere. There's a great music shop next door and a few doors down Café Delice is a lovely spot to read your purchases over a coffee.

BBC Shops

- 🖳 www.bbcshop.com

Full of BBC merchandise (particularly DVDs, CDs and tapes), but with a good selection of books linked to specific radio and television programmes, including some highly glossy cookery, gardening, history and nature titles. The stock also includes magazines and language courses along with books on media, politics, current affairs and anything with a tie-in to a radio or television programme.

- Bush House, Strand, WC2B 4PH
- ☎ 020 7557 2576
- 🚆 Charing Cross LU/Rail, Covent Garden LU
- 🕐 Mon-Fri 10am-6pm, Sat 10am-5.30pm, Sun 1pm-6pm

And:

- 50 Margaret Street, W1W 8SF
- ☎ 020 7631 4523
- 🚆 Oxford Circus LU
- 🕐 Mon-Fri 9.30am-6pm, Sat 10am-5.30pm, Sun 12noon-5pm

This shop may move in the future when the redevelopment of Broadcasting House is completed, but will remain in the vicinity.

Beaumonts

🖃 *60 Church Road, SW13 0DQ*

☎ *020 8741 0786*

🚌 *Barnes Common Rail*

🕐 *Mon-Sat 9.30am-5.30pm*

    (Ring for details of Sunday opening in December)

A short walk from Barnes Common, this general local shop sells an interesting range of new fiction and non-fiction titles in all subject areas with a particularly good children's section. In addition to the books they also stock a range of art materials, audiobooks, stationery and greetings cards. There's plenty of local information on offer on their notice board and a lovely little Italian deli next door.

Beautiful Books

🖃 *24 Brixton Station Road, SW9 8PD*

☎ *020 7738 3302*

✆ *020 7274 4223*

✉ *service@beautifulbooks.freeserve.co.uk*

🚌 *Brixton LU/Rail*

🕐 *Mon-Sat 10am-5pm (Wed closes at 2pm)*

An extensive array of books and audio-visual material on all aspects of Christianity including a good selection for children. It's located underneath the railway arches in the heart of the Brixton Market area.

BEBC Bookshop

🖃 *1 Yarmouth Place, W1J 7BU*

☎ *020 7493 5226*

✆ *020 7493 5226*

✉ *www.bebc.co.uk*

🚌 *Green Park LU*

🕐 *Mon-Fri 10am-1.30pm & 2pm-6.30pm*

Located in the entrance hall of International House (which specialises in training English language teachers), this bookshop sells course materials, dictionaries and theoretical and practical books for anybody teaching or learning English.

Beckett's

- 6 Bellevue Road, Wandsworth Common, SW17 7EG
- ☎ 020 8672 4413
- ✍ Beckbooks@aol.com
- 🚌 Wandsworth Common Rail
- 🕐 Mon-Sat 9.30am-5.30pm, Sun 10.30am-5pm

Located in a row of stylish shops and coffee bars overlooking Wandsworth Common. The area is fabulous in the summer but bleak in the winter, which is when this small but well-stocked bookshop lights its welcoming open fire. There are big and small chairs for big and small browsers and the wide-ranging selection of books is thoughtfully displayed and supplemented by an appealing range of greetings cards and audio books. For foodies, Chez Bruce – the famous gourmet restaurant – is almost next door.

Chris Beetles

- 8 & 10 Ryder Street, St James's, SW1Y 6QB
- ☎ 020 7839 7551
- ✆ 020 7839 1603
- ✍ www.chrisbeetles.com
- 🚌 Piccadilly Circus LU
- 🕐 Mon-Sat 10am-5.30pm

Modern security mean you have to ring the bell to get in but don't let that worry you, this gallery doesn't have the snobbish attitude of many. The gallery specialises in illustrations, cartoons and watercolours (they have more than 15,000 of these) and stages an annual 'Illustrators' show from early November through to the New Year as well as other exhibitions through the year. They publish and sell their exhibition catalogues – fascinating and almost works of art in their own right – and now have more than fifty on the backlist at prices from £3 for small pamphlets to £200 for superbly produced limited editions. Featured artists include Thelwell, Mervyn Peake, Mabel Lucie Atwell, Michael Foreman and Quentin Blake among many others.

Whilst you can wander in just to look at the books it is also worth having a peek at the art which includes the largest stock of British watercolours in the country, much of it stored in huge boxes downstairs. With prices from £100 it's perhaps less prohibitive than you'd think. There are also posters for sale if you don't need an original.

Blackwell's

✍ *www.blackwell.co.uk*

Founded in Oxford over a century ago, the Blackwell's chain now has more than 70 academic, professional and specialist shops in the UK with eight in London Their branches retain a serious academic emphasis but even the general stock gives prominence to heavyweight and literary titles above the more popular genres. Incidentally, all book lovers should visit the original Blackwell's in Oxford – The Norrington Room downstairs in particular shouldn't be missed. Branches at:

Charing Cross Road

▱ *100 Charing Cross Road, WC2H 0JG*

☎ *020 7292 5100*

✎ *020 7240 9665*

🚇 *Leicester Square or Tottenham Court Road LU*

🕐 *Mon-Sat 9.30am-8pm, Sun 12noon-6pm*

Set in the capital's bookselling heartland, Blackwell's flagship store offers over sixty thousand titles covering all subjects but with particular strengths in history, philosophy, finance, fiction, medical and computing. The shop is confusing to navigate, but it's still well worth visiting.

Business and Law Bookshop

▱ *243-244 High Holborn, WC1V 7DZ*

☎ *020 7831 9501*

✎ *020 7405 9412*

🚇 *Holborn LU*

🕐 *Mon-Fri 9am-6pm (Wed from 9.30am, Thurs to 6.30pm), Sat 10am-4pm*

Specialising in law and all aspects of business including accountancy, management, banking, tax, investment, human resources management and computing with 30,000 titles in stock.

London Business School

▱ *18-22 Park Road, NW1 5SH*

☎ *020 7723 6953*

✎ *020 7723 7017*

🚇 *Baker Street LU*

🕐 *Mon-Fri 9.30am-6pm, Sat 10.30am-5pm*

This shop covers business and finance but there is also a limited general range of books

South Bank University

⌖ 119-122 London Road, SE1 6LF

☎ 020 7928 5378

✆ 020 7261 9536

🚌 Elephant & Castle LU/Rail

🕐 Mon-Fri 9am-6pm (Wed from 9.30am), Sat 11am-5pm

Ten minutes walk north of Elephant & Castle shopping centre, just next to South Bank University. This branch concentrates on books related to the university's courses with sections on law, business, management, marketing, education, psychology, research and health and features an especially extensive range of computing books.

Guy's Hospital

⌖ Bowland House, St Thomas Street, SE1 9RT

☎ 020 7403 5259

🚌 London Bridge LU/Rail

🕐 Mon-Fri 9.30am-5.30pm

Medicine, physiotherapy and dentistry.

King's College

⌖ First Floor, Macadam Building, Surrey Street, WC2R 2NS

☎ 020 7240 9723

✆ 020 7240 2997

🚌 Temple LU

🕐 Mon-Fri 9.30am-5.30pm

General academic bookshop with good sections on law, business, management, philosophy, history, war studies, literature, geography, computing, engineering, chemistry, physics and the life sciences.

London Metropolitan University

⌖ Ladbroke House, 62-66 Highbury Grove, N5 2AD

☎ 020 7314 4215

🚌 Highbury & Islington LU/Rail

🕐 Mon-Fri 10am-4pm

and

⌖ 158 Holloway Road, N7 8DD

☎ 020 7700 4786

✆ 020 7700 7687

🚌 Holloway Road LU

🕐 Mon-Fri 9am-5.30pm (Wed opens 9.30am), Sat 11am-5pm

Near the campus of London Metropolitan University, a couple of minutes walk from Holloway Road tube station, this branch mainly sells books related to courses at the university as well as a decent general fiction section and some second-hand books and CDs.

Blenheim Books

⌨ *11 Blenheim Crescent, W11 2EE*

☎ *020 7792 0777*

✐ *www.blenheimbooks.co.uk*

🚌 *Ladbroke Grove LU*

🕐 *Mon-Sat 9am-6pm, Sun 12noon-5pm*

This lovely shop justifiably bills itself as an 'Inspiration for designers, architects and gardeners'. The shelves bow under the weight of fabulous volumes, many of them difficult to find elsewhere, and there is an extremely good selection of children's books. One of the best things about this delightful shop is the staff who are consistently helpful and well-informed with a particularly detailed knowledge of gardening and design. This is one of the trinity of great bookshops that makes Blenheim Crescent a required destination for all book lovers (see Books for Cooks, p.30 and The Travel Bookshop, p.147).

Bolingbroke Bookshop

⌨ *147 Northcote Road, Battersea, SW11 6QB*

☎/✆ *020 7223 9344*

✐ *bolingbroke_bookshop@hotmail.com*

🚌 *Clapham Junction Rail*

🕐 *Mon-Sat 9.30am-6pm, Sun 11am-4pm*

This is a brilliant, well-stocked local shop in the popular shopping/dining enclave of Northcote Road. Despite not being of modest proportions by modern standards, there's an impressive general stock in all subjects with new publications prominently displayed, seats for browsing and a child-friendly section as well. There are numerous places to get a coffee or food in this neck of the woods and the market is always worth a visit at the weekend.

bookartbookshop

- 17 Pitfield Street, N1 6HB
- 020 7608 1333
- www.bookartbookshop.com
- Old Street LU/Rail
- Wed-Fri 1pm-7pm, Sat 1pm-6pm

Situated in the art hub that is Shoreditch, this is a great little shop selling artists books and small press publications and London's only specialist artists' bookshop. The range of books is wide and it's refreshing to see a shop that is intent on displaying some of the more innovative examples of book design. Be sure to pay a visit to Artwords (see p.12) which is just around the corner.

Bookcase

- 268 Chiswick High Road, W4 1PD
- 020 8742 3919
- Turnham Green LU
- Mon-sat 9.30am-7pm, Sun 11am-5pm

The only remaining shop of what was once a Londonwide discount chain. They are strong in all areas, offer large discounts, displayed their stock well and have a genuine bargain table outside. The widest choice is available in art, design, photography, history, cookery, fiction and children's books. The large, glossy coffee-table volumes are especially alluring. Bookcase also sell a selection of bargain music CDs.

Bookends

- 108 Charing Cross Road, WC2H 0BP
- 020 7836 3457
- www.bookspostfre.com
- Leicester Square LU
- Mon-Fri 9am-7pm, Sat 9.30am-6.30pm, Sun 10am-4pm

The only branch of this discount book chain situated in the heart of the Charing Cross Road bookselling community. The stock changes regularly, prices are extremely reasonable and there's a good spread of popular, mainstream and more academic titles.

Book Ends Papercrafts

⌨ *25/28 Thurloe Place, SW7 2HQ*
☎ *020 7589 2285*
✎ *www.bookendslondon.co.uk*
🚇 *South Kensington LU*
🕐 *Mon-Fri 9am-6.30pm, Sat 10am-6pm, Sun 2pm-6pm*
    (Closed on Sundays in June, July & August)

An unusual and enticing shop, about five minutes walk from South Kensington tube station with an inspiring range of books about and materials for all arts and papercrafts including origami, modelling, stencilling, découpage and paper dolls. They also stock a range of art and design source books and children's books on all subjects. A brilliant place to look for unusual gift ideas.

Bookhouse

⌨ *24 Torrington Place, WC1E 7HJ*
☎ *020 7436 3286*
✆ *020 7436 4614*
🕐 *Mon-Sat 10am-7pm, Sun 12noon-6pm*
🚇 *Goodge Street LU*

Located just around the corner from furniture store Heal's, this is a good discount shop. The emphasis is quite serious and literary with extensive selections of glossy art and design, fiction, history, music and biography but with most subject areas covered including gardening, travel and children's books.

Book House Nasherketab

⌨ *157 North End Road, W14 9NH*
☎ *020 7603 6936*
🚇 *West Kensington LU*
🕐 *Mon-Sat 9am-7pm*

A bookshop specialising in Islamic books.

Bookmarks

🗔 *1 Bloomsbury Street, WC1B 3QE*

☎ *020 7637 1848*

🖋 *020 7637 3416*

✎ *www.bookmarks.uk.com*

🚌 *Tottenham Court Road LU*

🕐 *Mon 12noon-7pm, Tues-Fri 10am-7pm, Sat 10am-6pm*

A Socialist bookshop and publisher with mostly new but also a few remaindered and second-hand books on general subjects as well as politics, Socialist thinkers and philosophy, history and labour issues. They also stock a selection of Labour Research Department booklets and boast an excellent international section, a good range of magazines and periodicals, and children's books. The centrepiece of the shop is a scale model of Tatlin's epic but never realised monument to the 3rd international (otherwise known as "Tatlin's Tower"). The Bookmarks Review of Books is published four times a year to keep readers up to date with publications of interest.

Books etc

🖱 *www.booksetc.co.uk*

Books etc currently have 35 stores in the UK including eight airports branches. The shops are bright, airy and well laid out, have a lively atmosphere and some have in-store coffee bars. Branches at:

Broadgate
🏠 *30 Broadgate Circle, EC2M 2BL*
☎ *020 7628 8944*
✉ *020 7256 8590*
🚇 *Liverpool Street LU/Rail*
🕐 *Mon-Fri 8am-7.30pm*

A small shop with a reasonable general stock as well as titles on finance, business and computers to browse. The shop occupies a prime site overlooking the small ice skating rink in the centre of Broadgate Circus – lively and bustling at lunchtimes, especially in the summer.

Canary Wharf
🏠 *Cabot Place East, Canary Wharf, E14 4QT*
☎ *020 7513 0060*
✉ *020 7513 0156*
🚇 *Canary Wharf LU/DLR*
🕐 *Mon-Fri 8.30am-7pm, Sat 10am-6pm, Sun 12noon-6pm*

A medium-sized store located in the heart of the Canary Wharf shopping complex.

Jubilee Place
🏠 *Canary Wharf, E14 5NY*
☎ *020 7719 0688*
✉ *020 7715 9664*
🚇 *Heron's Quay DLR*
🕐 *Mon-Fri 9am-7pm, Sat 10am-6pm, Sun 11am-5pm*

Cheapside
🏠 *70-72 Cheapside, EC2V 6EN*
☎ *020 7236 0398*
✉ *020 7236 0402*
🚇 *Bank LU*
🕐 *Mon & Wed-Fri 8.30am-6.30pm, Tues 9am-6.30pm*

Smaller than the major London Wall branch but still occupying two floors, with bags of display space, a good general stock, and excellent greetings cards. It's about ten minutes west of Bank tube station.

Cowcross

- 9-13 Cowcross Street, EC1M 6DR
- ☎ 020 7608 2426
- ✆ 020 7608 2436
- 🚌 Farringdon LU/Rail
- 🕐 Mon-Fri 8.30am-8pm, Sat 10am-6.30pm

Covent Garden

- 26 James Street, WC2E 8PA
- ☎ 020 7379 6947
- ✆ 020 7497 9342
- 🚌 Covent Garden LU
- 🕐 Mon-Sat 10am-10pm, Sun 12noon-6pm

A two storey branch with the usual quality selection. It can get pretty packed here although they still have space for some displays, cards and gifts.

Finchley Road

- Unit 5, Level 1, O2 Centre, 255 Finchley Road, NW3 6LU
- ☎ 020 7433 3299
- ✆ 020 7794 9390
- 🚌 Finchley Road LU
- 🕐 Mon, Wed-Sat 10am-10pm, Tues 10.30am-10pm,
  Sun 11.30am-6pm

A large shop with an extensive range of books on all subject areas. It has a large Jewish and local history section and a particularly good children's area. There's a Costa Coffee next door.

Fleet Street

- 176 Fleet Street, EC4A 2EN
- ☎ 020 7353 5939
- ✆ 020 7583 5648
- 🚌 Chancery Lane LU
- 🕐 Mon-Fri 8.30am-6.30pm

In keeping with its city location at the corner of Fleet Street and Fetter Lane, this branch features sections on business and computing, in addition to the usual general stock. There is also a good selection of talking books and greetings cards.

Hammersmith
- 28 Broadway Shopping Centre, W6 9YY
- ☎ 020 8746 3912
- ✆ 020 8746 3676
- 🚇 Hammersmith LU
- 🕐 Mon-Fri 8am-8pm, Sat 9am-7pm, Sun 11.30am-6pm

In true Books etc style, they manage to pack a huge selection into a small space at this branch. They are especially well-stocked with computer, fiction and travel books.

High Holborn
- 263 High Holborn, WC1V 7EZ
- ☎ 020 7404 0261
- ✆ 020 7404 5187
- 🚇 Holborn LU
- 🕐 Mon-Fri 9am-7pm

King William Street
- 47-51 King William Street, EC4R 9AF
- ☎ 020 7929 1414
- ✆ 020 7929 1292
- 🚇 Monument LU
- 🕐 Mon-Fri 8.30am-7.30pm

London Wall
- 54 London Wall, EC2M 5RA
- ☎ 020 7628 9708
- ✆ 020 7628 9643
- 🚇 Moorgate LU
- 🕐 Mon-Wed & Fri 8.30am-6.30pm, Thurs 8.30am-6pm

Probably the biggest City branch of this chain, it carries a huge range of titles plus plenty of cards, spoken word tapes and gifts.

Oxford Street
- 421 Oxford Street, W1C 2PQ
- ☎ 020 7495 5850
- ✆ 020 7495 5851
- 🚇 Bond Street LU
- 🕐 Mon-Wed, Sat 9.30am-8pm, Thurs & Fri 9.30am-8.30pm,
  Sun 12noon-6pm

Located at the Marble Arch end of Oxford Street, opposite Selfridges, this is a spacious branch with an excellent stock.

Shepherd's Bush
- 🖳 Units 4/6, West 12 Shopping Centre, W12 8PP
- ☎ 020 8749 8983
- ✆ 020 8749 8358
- 🚌 Shepherd's Bush LU
- 🕐 Mon-Sat 10am-10pm, Sun 12noon-6pm

Victoria Street
- 🖳 66 Victoria Street, SW1E 6SQ
- ☎ 020 7931 0677
- ✆ 020 7233 5579
- 🚌 Victoria LU
- 🕐 Mon-Fri 8.30am-7pm, Sat 9.30am-6pm, Sun 12noon-6pm

A large and well stocked branch just 5 minutes walk from Victoria Station, with a particularly good children's section. It is especially busy with local office workers at lunch-time.

Victoria Place
- 🖳 Unit SU14, Victoria Place Shopping Centre, SW1W 9SJ
- ☎ 020 7630 6244
- ✆ 020 7233 5696
- 🚌 Victoria LU
- 🕐 Mon-Fri 8am-8pm, Sat 9am-8pm, Sun 11am-6pm

Ideal for travellers and commuters, this branch can be found in the high level shopping centre that leads from the station concourse towards the coach station. It's jam-packed with books and includes a good children's section plus magazines and gifts.

Wandsworth
- 🖳 Southside Shopping Centre, SW18 4TF
- ☎ 020 8874 4597
- ✆ 020 8874 0708
- 🚌 Wandsworth Town
- 🕐 Mon-Sat 9am-10pm, Sun 11am-5pm

Located in the gleaming, newly renovated Southside Shopping Centre - there are eateries just up the escalator.

Whiteleys

⌗ *Unit F, Whiteleys of Bayswater, Queensway, W2 4YQ*
☎ *020 7229 3865*
✉ *020 7221 2393*
🚉 *Queensway & Bayswater LU*
🕐 *Mon-Sat 10am-10pm (Tues from 10.30am), Sun 12.30pm-6pm*

This shop has a great atmosphere and a staff with genuine enthusiasm for books that is really refreshing. Located on the first floor of the shopping centre, the branch is all on one level, large and extensively stocked with a particularly large children's section.

Wimbledon

⌗ *Unit 6, 15-29 The Broadway, SW19 1PS*
☎ *020 8946 1412*
✉ *020 8879 7953*
🚉 *Wimbledon LU/Rail*
🕐 *Mon, Wed-Fri 9.30am-8pm, Tues 10am-8pm,*
   Sat 9am-7pm, Sun 11am-5pm

Good-sized store with a coffee shop.

Books Ink

Two discount bookshops from the Stoke Newington Bookshop stable. They offer a good range at fair prices and are especially strong on fiction, cookery, health, new age and children's titles. Greetings cards and stationery are on sale as well.

⌗ *153 Stoke Newington High Street, N16 ONY*
☎ *020 7249 8983*
✉ *020 7249 6110*
🚉 *Stoke Newington Rail*
🕐 *Mon-Sat 10am-5pm*

and

⌗ *134 High Street, Walthamstow, E17 7JS*
☎ *020 8520 8551*
🚉 *Walthamstow LU*
🕐 *Mon-Sat 9.30am-5.30pm*

Books of Blackheath

⌨ *11 Tranquil Vale, SE3 0BU*

☎ *020 8852 8185*

🚌 *Blackheath Rail*

🕐 *Mon-Fri 9.30am-5.30pm, Sat 9.30am-5pm, Sun 10am-4pm*

A local, general bookseller in the heart of the village close to the station, shops and pleasant eateries which abound in Blackheath. Upstairs houses the sale books with plenty of bargains, many of them at half-price. In good weather take a picnic up onto the heath itself which is nearby. If you fancy a longer walk, it's a couple of miles across the heath and Greenwich Park to get down to the riverside, and the book-buying and weekend market joys of Greenwich.

Bookseller Crow on the Hill

⌨ *50 Westow Street, Crystal Palace, SE19 3AF*

☎ /✆ *020 8771 8831*

✍ *www.booksellercrow.com*

🚌 *Crystal Palace Rail*

🕐 *Mon-Fri 9am-7.30pm, Sat 9am-6.30pm, Sun 11am-5pm*

Just up the road from the large Safeway/Morrisons supermarket, this is an excellent local bookstore which, although small, has room for a quality, well-selected stock, which is always thoughtfully displayed. They have a garden bench, small table and chairs for browsers and especially choice displays of fiction, children's books, travel, art titles and American imports. Crystal Palace has an abundance of excellent cafés and restaurants to suit every taste and pocket – alternatively a picnic in Crystal Palace Park is no bad way to round off a book-buying spree. Combine a trip here with a visit to Haynes Lane Market (see p.242).

Books For Cooks

⌧ *4 Blenheim Crescent, W11 1NN*
☎ *020 7221 1992*
✎ *020 7221 1517*
🖰 *www.booksforcooks.com*
🚌 *Ladbroke Grove LU*
🕐 *Tues-Sat 10am-6pm (Closed three weeks in August and
10 days at Christmas, ring to check)*

Opened in 1983, this shop, just off Portobello Road, is possibly the most famous dedicated cookery bookshop in the world. It has more than eight thousand titles on its shelves, has won numerous awards, is reviewed regularly in the press and is visited by foodies from all over the world. The shop sells books on all aspects of food: from specialised professional manuals to family cookbooks. There is a delightful café/restaurant at the back of the shop where a rota of chefs prepare divine meals based on recipes from the books on the shelves. The demonstration kitchen upstairs is the scene for regular workshops and there is also an Italian Cookery School in Tuscany for enthusiasts. This really is a remarkable place but very small and terribly packed at week-ends – go early in the day during the week for really relaxed browsing.

Books For Life

⌧ *Bethnal Green Mission Church,
305 Cambridge Heath Road, E2 9LH*
☎ *020 7729 4286*
✎ *020 7739 5079*
🖰 *book@bgmchurch.plus.com*
🚌 *Bethnal Green LU*
🕐 *Mon-Fri 9.30am-5.30pm, Sat 9.30am-12.30pm*

Located just off the entrance hall of the church, this shop is well-stocked with magazines, books, DVDs, CDs and videos covering almost every aspect of Christian life and worship. The stock extends over two storeys and includes a few non-English bibles. The church is just opposite the Museum of Childhood.

Bookshop in the Crypt

⌧ *St Martin's in the Fields, Duncannon Street, WC2N 4JH*

☎ *020 7766 1122*

🚌 *Charing Cross LU/Rail*

🕐 *Mon-Wed 10am-7.30pm, Thurs-Sat 10am-10pm, Sun 12noon-7pm*

This central London church in Trafalgar Square holds regular services but also stages concerts, and has a brass-rubbing centre in its crypt with an attached restaurant and bookshop. Alongside an excellent range of gifts and cards the shop also has a selection of books on Christianity, comparative religion and history.

The Bookshop Dulwich Village

⌧ *1d Calton Avenue, SE21 7DE*

☎ *020 8693 2808*

✎ *bookshopdulwich@btconnect.com*

🚌 *North Dulwich Rail*

🕐 *Mon-Sat 9am-5.30pm, Sun 11am-5pm*

Located in the heart of Dulwich Village (the Dulwich Picture Gallery is ten minutes walk away and the excellent Crown and Greyhound pub is just around the corner), this small two-storey shop is a reliable local bookseller. The stock is well selected and displayed with an extensive range of travel and children's books among a solid general selection, some attractive greetings cards, interesting audio books, and a plethora of adverts for local events and groups. Au Ciel patisserie and chocolate shop is a couple of doors away and an excellent place to recuperate from the book-buying.

Bookstop

⌧ *375 Upper Richmond Road West,*
    East Sheen, SW14 7NX

☎/✉ *020 8876 1717*

🚌 *Mortlake Rail*

🕐 *Mon-Sat 9.30am-6pm (Sunday opening in December – ring for details)*

An appealing local shop in the East Sheen shopping area offering a general stock of new books in all subject areas. The books are well-displayed and there are especially strong children's, fiction and travel sections plus some gifts, greetings cards and audiobooks. The ordering service is speedy and reliable.

Bookthrift South Kensington Bookshop

📖 *22 Thurloe Street, SW7 2LT*

☎ *020 7589 2916*

✆ *020 7589 0522*

✎ *www.bookthrift.co.uk*

🚌 *South Kensington LU*

🕐 *Mon-Fri 10am-8pm, Sat 11am-7pm, Sun 12noon-7pm*

The only London branch of a small discount chain which has branches across the country. They offer a good general range of fiction and non-fiction at reasonable prices but are especially strong on history and large format, glossy art, design, architecture and photography titles – all very much in keeping with their location a few minutes walk from the Victoria and Albert Museum. They've also plenty of poetry titles – unusual for a discount shop.

Book Warehouse

An established London discount chain with six London branches offering long opening hours, plenty of choice across all subject areas and a rapid turnover of stock. They are especially good on glossy, coffee-table books on art, architecture, design, photography, cookery and gardening but are worth a visit for more or less any topic. There are also bargain CDs plus cards and stationery. Branches at:

- 📖 *38 Golder's Green Road, NW1 8LL*
- ☎ *020 8458 0032*
- 🚌 *Golders Green LU*
- 🕐 *Daily 10am-9.30pm (Fri closes at 8pm)*

- 📖 *72-74 Notting Hill Gate, W11 3HT*
- ☎ *020 7727 4149*
- 🚌 *Notting Hill Gate LU*
- 🕐 *Mon-Sat 8.30am-10pm, Sun 10am-10pm*

- 📖 *295A Regent St, W1B 2HL*
- ☎ *020 7636 6011*
- 🚌 *Oxford Circus LU*
- 🕐 *Mon-Fri 8.30am-9pm, Sat & Sun 11am-8pm*

- 📖 *120 Southampton Row, WC1B 5AB*
- ☎ *020 7242 1119*
- 📠 *020 7404 5636*
- 🚌 *Russell Square LU*
- 🕐 *Mon-Fri 8.30-10pm, Sat 9am-10pm & Sun 10am-9pm*

- 📖 *41 Strutton Ground, SW1 2HY*
- ☎ *020 7976 0577*
- 🚌 *St James's Park LU*
- 🕐 *Mon-Fri 10am-7pm*

- 📖 *158 Waterloo Rd, SE1 8SB*
- ☎ *020 7401 8528*
- 🚌 *Waterloo LU/Rail*
- 🕐 *Mon-Sat 8.30am-8pm, Sun 11am-7pm*

bw! A Bookworld Shop

- *Unit 12, Ealing Broadway Centre, W5 5JY*
- ☎ *020 8840 7355*
- ✐ *www.bbwbooks.co.uk*
- 🚇 *Ealing Broadway LU*
- 🕐 *Mon-Fri 8.30am-8pm, Sat 8.30am-7.30pm, Sun 10am-6pm*

The only London branch of this nationwide discount bookshop chain, is located in the shopping centre a few minutes walk from Ealing Broadway tube station. They have an excellent, mixed stock of both fiction and non-fiction with a particularly impressive selection for children and a pleasant kid's reading area. There's also a selection of art and craft materials on sale.

Bookworm

- *1177 Finchley Road, NW11 0AA*
- ☎ *020 8201 9811*
- ✆ *020 8201 9311*
- ✐ *www.thebookwormuk.com*
- 🚇 *Golders Green LU (then bus)*
- 🕐 *Mon-Sat 9.30am-5.30pm, Sun 10am-1.30pm*

A lovely little shop specialising in books for children and young adults, packed with an extensive and interesting stock. A regular newsletter advertises events held in the shop such as parties involving favourite characters and visits by authors. There are storytimes at 2pm every Tuesday and Thursday for 2-5 year olds.

Boosey and Hawkes @ Brittens Music

- *16 Wigmore St, W1U 2RF*
- ☎ *020 7079 5940*
- ✆ *020 7079 5947*
- ✐ *www.brittensmusic.co.uk*
- 🚇 *Oxford Circus LU*
- 🕐 *Mon-Sat 10am-6pm*

Sheet music specialists catering for all instruments, levels and tastes and especially strong in choral music. They also stock a small selection of theory and reference books, as well as musical gifts, CDs, cabinets, stands and metronomes. The instrument showroom is downstairs.

Borders

✍ *www.borders.co.uk*

Operating more than 30 stores in the UK, the Borders shops are characterised by a large and impressive book stock (expect more than 100,000 titles per store) plus music, a café, magazines, stationery and a generally buzzy, lively atmosphere. The shops also have a packed programme of book signings, readings, music and children's events. There are several branches in London:

203 Oxford Street, W1D 2LE
☎ *020 7292 1600*
✆ *020 7292 1616*
🚇 *Oxford Circus LU*
🕐 *Mon-Sat 8am-11pm, Sun 12noon-6pm*

This is an extremely busy shop. The café overlooks Oxford Street – getting a seat can be a challenge. The queues at the tills and information counters can be annoying and there aren't really enough seats for browsing outside the café, but if you like your bookshops with buzz and excitement this is certainly the place to go. For a more peaceful experience visit either early or late.

122 Charing Cross Road, WC2H 0JR
☎ *020 7379 8877*
✆ *020 7836 9486*
🚇 *Tottenham Court Road LU*
🕐 *Mon-Sat 8am-11pm, Sun 12noon-6pm*

Not quite as huge as the Oxford Street shop but still bustling, well-stocked and with plenty happening. This branch has the advantage of being in the heart of book-buying London. The coffee shop on the first floor is always busy.

N1 Centre
🏠 *Islington, N1 0PS*
☎ *020 7226 3602*
✆ *020 7704 1081*
🚇 *Angel LU*
🕐 *Mon-Sat 9am-11pm, Sun 12noon-6pm*

Situated in the heart of Islington's new shopping complex, this Borders extends over 2 storeys and holds a huge stock. They also have a Café on the first floor.

Gallions Reach Shopping Park

⌨ *Beckton, E6 7ER*

☎ *020 7476 7571*

✆ *020 7476 7489*

🚌 *Gallions Reach DLR or Beckton DLR and bus*

🕐 *Mon-Sat 9am-10pm, Sun 11am-5pm*

Brent Cross Shopping Park

⌨ *Tilling Road, Brent Cross, NW2 1IJ*

☎ *020 8452 9245*

✆ *020 8450 4797*

🚌 *Brent Cross LU*

🕐 *Mon-Sat 9am-10pm, Sun 11am-5pm*

Across the bridge in the shoppping park rather than the Brent Cross Shopping Centre, this is the newest London Borders and has all the usual features. An ideal haven if the shopping gets too much.

Borders Express

⌨ *Unit 3, Fulham Broadway Retail Centre, Fulham Road, SW6 1BH*

☎ *020 7386 5451*   ✆ *020 7386 5286*

🚌 *Fulham Broadway LU*

🕐 *Mon-Sat 9am-10pm, Sun 12noon-6pm*

The Borders Express stores are smaller than the standard Borders with about a third of the usual book stock, no café and compact selections of music, DVDs, newspapers and magazines. Still, with about 30,000 titles there's still plenty from which to choose.

British Geological Survey

⌨ *London Information Office,*
   Natural History Museum Earth Galleries - Gallery 50,
   Cromwell Road, SW7 2DE

☎ *020 7589 4090*

✆ *020 7584 8270*

✎ *www.bgs.ac.uk*

🚌 *South Kensington LU*

🕐 *Mon-Fri 10am-5pm (ring to check before making a journey)*

The Office sells Survey publications including geological maps, guides, popular and academic books and posters. While many of the books are highly academic, a surprising number are of interest to general readers and anyone who enjoys the countryside.

Borders

37

British Bookshops/Sussex Stationers

- 530 Oxford Street, W1C 1LP
- 020 7355 1391
- Marble Arch LU
- Mon-Fri 9.30am-7pm (Thurs until 8pm),
  Sat 9.30am-7pm, Sun 12noon-6pm

This is the only central London representative of this nationwide discount chain, which has around fifty shops across the country. However, there are also branches in Harrow, Croydon and Kingston if you live outside central London. There is a large stock covering all general subject areas and they are especially strong on discounted current bestsellers.

British Museum Bookshop

The British Library Bookshop

⌨ *96 Euston Road, NW1 2DB*

☎ *020 7412 7735*

✆ *020 7412 7172*

✍ *www.bl.uk*

🚇 *King's Cross/St Pancras LU & Rail*

🕐 *Mon 10am-6pm, Tues 9.30am-8pm, Wed-Fri 9.30am-6pm,
Sat 9.30am-5pm, Sun 11am-5pm*

The bookshop attached to the British Library has a top class range of more than five thousand titles about all aspects of the history and the making of books and subjects related to the library. In addition to guides and catalogues on the collections there are interesting sections on bookbinding and bookcrafts, calligraphy and scripts, cartography, music, history, religion and Oriental culture plus a good selection of children's books. There is also a large stock of gift items, particularly stationery, and greetings and postcards. The bookshop stages regular events. See p.298 for a description of the amazing exhibitions in the Library and p.249 for details on using the library. The café and restaurant are located next to a glass tower, several storeys high, in which the King's Library (collected by King George III) is displayed. Leatherbound volumes soar skywards as you sip your coffee – splendid.

The British Museum Bookshop

⌨ *Great Russell Street, WC1B 3DG*

☎ *Museum switchboard 020 7636 1555
Direct number 020 7323 8587*

✆ *020 7580 8699*

✍ *www.thebritishmuseum.co.uk*

🚇 *Russell Square LU*

🕐 *Mon-Wed & Sat 9.30am-6pm, Thurs & Fri 9.30am-8pm,
Sun 12noon-6pm*

The bookshop is situated in the Great Court, the beautiful heart of the museum. It stocks books on all the topics most relevant to the museum's collections: ancient cultures both European and Oriental, religion, the decorative arts, the history of medicine and history. There are plenty of titles for the general reader alongside more weighty tomes and there are children's books as well. Climb up the central building in the Great Court to reach the Court Restaurant, the most relaxing spot in the museum for rest and refreshment. All profits from the bookshop go towards the museum's support.

Brook Green Bookshop

- 72 Blythe Road, W14 0HB
- 020 7603 5999
- 020 7603 5655
- brookgreenbooks@btconnect.com
- Olympia LU
- Mon-Sat 9.30am-6.30pm (longer opening hours from mid-May to end-July and Sept to Christmas – ring for details)

This stores speciality in children's books is supplemented by the latest releases in adult fiction and non-fiction plus a large cookery section. They have an estimated 15,000 children's titles covering birth to 16 years of age and are especially proud of the non-fiction sections. They host plenty of events that are likely to appeal to very young children.

Building Centre Bookshop

- 26 Store Street, WC1E 7BT
- 020 7692 4040 / 0845 330 1355
- 020 7636 3628
- www.buildingcentre.co.uk
- bookshop@buildingcentre.co.uk
- Goodge Street or Tottenham Court Road LU
- Mon-Fri 9.30-6pm, Sat 10am-4pm

Located on the ground floor of The Building Centre, this bookshop is the UK's largest specialist bookshop dedicated to construction, architecture, design and home renovation. A combination of technical, academic and illustrated books are in stock for amateurs and building professionals. The Bookshop also stocks all the specialist construction related contracts, building regulations and BSI publications. Subject areas covered include, architecture, design, construction, surveying, property law and management, building services, civil and structural engineering, interior design, home improvement and self-build.

Calder Bookshop
⌨ *51 The Cut, SE1 8LF*
☎ *020 7620 2900*
✎ *www.calderpublications.com*
🚌 *Waterloo LU*
🕐 *Mon-Sat 9am-7pm*

Across the road from the Young Vic theatre, this is an attractive shop specialising in literature, including poetry and the performing arts but with good sections of crime fiction, history, politics, biography and current affairs as well. Literary, artistic, and political readings and discussions are held here every Thursday evening (except August). This is definitely a shop that deserves to be better known.

Call to Islam Bookshop
⌨ *318 Hoe Street, E17 9PX*
☎ *020 8520 1618*
✆ *020 8520 1618*
✎ *www.calltoislam.co.uk*
🚌 *Walthamstow LU*
🕐 *Mon-Sat 10am-7pm & Sun 10.30-6pm*
   (Closed for 10 to 15 mins during prayer times)

Islamic bookshop selling a variety of books in English and Arabic about the religion and history of Islam and all issues related to Islamic life.

Camberwell Bookshop see Wordsworth p.162

Camden Arts Centre
⌨ *Arkwright Road, NW3 6DG*
☎ *020 7472 5500*
✆ *020 7472 5501*
✎ *www.camdenartscentre.org*
🚌 *Finchley Road LU*
🕐 *Tues, Thurs, Fri-Sun 10am-6pm, Wed 10am-9pm (closed Monday)*

Although small, this bookshop based in the CAC's reception area does stock a reasonable range of books on art and critical theory as well as artists' monographs and exhibition catalogues.

Camden Lock Books

⌨ *Old Street Station, 4 St Agnes Wells, EC1Y 1BE*

☎/✆ *020 7253 0666*

🚌 *Old Street LU/Rail*

🕐 *Mon-Fri 9am-7pm*

Formerly located in Camden Lock (hence the name), this small shop has relocated to Old Street Station. There is a general stock, both full price and discount, but with specialisms in photography, fashion and African-Caribbean writers. Combine this with a trip to the arty Hoxton/Shoreditch area.

John Carpenter Bookshop

⌨ *City of London School, Queen Victoria Street, EC4V 3AL*

☎ *020 7332 0223*

✆ *020 7329 6887*

🚌 *Blackfriars LU/Rail, St Paul's LU*

🕐 *Ring to arrange to visit*

A shop in a boys secondary school selling everything that the pupils may need by way of books; science fiction, fantasy, reference, revision and study guides for exams – plus other things vital to teenage existence such as phone top-ups. Owing to security issues in the school, members of the public need to telephone in advance to arrange access.

The Catholic Truth Society

⌨ *25 Ashley Place, SW1P 1LT*

☎ *020 7834 1363*

✆ *020 7821 7398*

✎ *www.cts-online.org.uk*

🚌 *Victoria LU?Rail*

🕐 *Mon-Tues & Thurs-Fri 10am-6pm,*
   Wed 10.30am-6pm, Sat 10am-4pm

Handily placed for Westminster Cathedral this small shop offers a comprehensive range of books on all aspects of Catholic spiritual and family life, religious biographies, books on liturgy, Bibles, prayer books and children's books. There are also statues, crucifixes, icons and a few greetings cards.

Centerprise

⊞ *136-138 Kingsland High Street, E8 2NS*
☎ *020 7254 9632*
✉ *020 7923 1951*
🖝 *www.centerprisetrust.org.uk*
🚌 *Dalston Kingsland Rail*
🕐 *Mon-Sat 10am-6pm*

Centerprise is a community arts centre with a particular emphasis on literature, based just a couple of minutes walk north of Dalston Kingsland Station. The bookshop is a superb local resource, stocking books and magazines of interest to the community, and with large sections on Black fiction and non-fiction, women's and gay and lesbian issues, health, history, politics, travel, welfare rights and local interest. There is also a good children's section which includes many educational titles. Centreprise hold regular readings and events as well as creative writing courses. There is an excellent community café attached to the shop.

Chappell of Bond Street

⊞ *50 New Bond Street, W1S 1RD*
☎ *020 7491 2777*
✉ *020 7491 0133*
🖝 *www.chappellofbondstreet.co.uk*
🚌 *Bond Street LU*
🕐 *Mon-Fri 9.30am-6pm, Sat 9.30am-5pm*

The entrance may be unpromising, sandwiched between the frontages of Bond Street's swanky fashion houses, but in this basement shop, alongside a brilliant range of musical instruments you'll find a monster choice of scores for music classical and modern, by composers famous and obscure. Virtually every instrument, style of playing and level of competence is covered and there are instrumental tutors for aspiring musicians. Backing tracks, music for every combination of ensemble playing and books on music complete the wonderful stock of this wonderful shop.

Chapter Two
🖃 *199 Plumstead Common Road, SE18 2UJ*
☎ *020 8316 4972*
✎ *www.chaptertwobooks.org.uk*
🚌 *Woolwich Arsenal & Plumstead Common Rail*
🕐 *Mon-Fri 9.30am-1pm & 2.30pm-5.30pm, Sat 10am-1pm*

A specialist on the Plymouth Brethren and Dispensational Christianity, this shop stocks new and second-hand books and Christian literature including many foreign editions.

Chener Books
🖃 *14-16 Lordship Lane, SE22 8HN*
☎ */✆ 8299 0771*
🚌 *East Dulwich Rail*
🕐 *Mon-Sat 10am-6pm*

A small local bookshop with a good general selection of fiction and non-fiction and generously spaced displays to encourage browsing. Fiction, travel, biography and history, including local history, are especially well-represented. Thoughtfully provided low level display boxes make the children's books easily accessible to junior readers. The local notice board is a useful resource and there are plenty of eateries on Lordship Lane and Northcote Road.

Chess & Bridge
🖃 *369 Euston Road, NW1 3AR*
☎ *020 7388 2404*
✆ *020 7388 2407*
✎ *www.chess.co.uk and www.bridgemagazine.co.uk*
🚌 *Great Portland Street LU*
🕐 *Mon-Sat 10am-6pm*

Two minutes east of Great Portland Street tube station, this is a specialist shop with a huge range of books as well as other items focusing on chess, bridge and poker and to a lesser extent backgammon, Go, draughts and mah-jong. The books section is extensive and there are also magazines, videos, DVDs, chess and bridge computers and software. Their fine selection of chess sets includes the elegant and more playful – Harry Potter and Simpsons sets are on display. The shop publishes a yearly catalogue.

Children's Book Centre

237 Kensington High Street, W8 6SA
020 7937 7497
020 7938 4968
www.childrensbookcentre.co.uk
High Street Kensington LU
Mon-Sat 9.30am-6.30pm (Thurs-7pm), Sun 12noon-6pm

A two storey shop bursting at the seams with toys, stationery, accessories, multimedia software and a good range of children's books. Fiction for all ages is especially well-represented.

Children's Bookshop

29 Fortis Green Road, N10 3HP
020 8444 5500
020 8883 8632
Highgate LU
Mon-Sat 9.15am-5.45pm, Sun 11am-4pm

Situated just opposite the Muswell Hill Bookshop (see p.98), this specialist shop has a huge stock of books for youngsters from baby's first books through to teenagers. Young bookworms can keep themselves up to the minute with the shops informative newsletter, published quarterly and including their useful lists of books on various topics. The staff know their stuff and there's a notice board for items of local interest.

Christian Books and Music

Kensington Temple, Kensington Park Road, W11 3BY
020 7727 8684
Notting Hill Gate LU
Tues-Fri 10am-7pm, Sat 10am-6pm, Sun 1pm-5pm

A well-stocked bookshop in the basement of the church featuring contemporary Christian literature, music, cards, DVDs and magazines.

Christian Books Plus

386 Brixton Road, SW9 7AW
020 7737 1089
christianbooksplus@aol.com
Brixton LU/Rail
Mon-Sat 9.30am-6.30pm, Sun 9.30am-1pm

Christian bookshop selling a wide range of books on Christian religion and life plus devotional music.

Church House Bookshop

📖 *31 Great Smith Street, SW1P 3BN*

☎ *020 7898 1300*

✆ *020 7898 1305*

🖱 *www.chbookshop.co.uk*

🚌 *Westminster & St James's Park LU*

🕐 *Mon–Wed & Fri 9am–5pm, Thurs 9.30am–6pm*

The official bookshop of the Church of England, just around the corner from Westminster Abbey, sells a wide range of Christian material from Church House Publishing and other specialist publishing houses. The stock includes Bibles, study guides, devotional material, theological texts and books for children plus gifts, greetings cards and Anglican music on CD.

The Cinema Store

📖 *4b Orion House, Upper St Martin's Lane, WC2H 9NY*

☎ *020 7379 7838*

✆ *020 7240 7689*

🖱 *www.the-cinema-store.com*

🚌 *Leicester Square LU*

🕐 *Mon–Wed & Sat 10am–6.30pm, Thurs & Fri 10am–7pm,*
   Sun 11am–5pm

A shop selling a wide range of books, DVDs, photographs, posters, postcards, T-shirts and other paraphernalia associated with vintage and modern cinema. The book stock covers directors, screenplays, screenwriting, directing, biography, filmography as well as books on individual films and genres. The Cinema Store also has a branch in Nottingham.

Clapham Bookshop

📖 *120 Clapham High Street, SW4 7UH*

☎ *020 7627 2797*

✆ *020 7627 1800*

🖱 *shop@claphambookshop.co.uk*

🚌 *Clapham Common LU*

🕐 *Mon–Fri 9am–6pm, Sat 9.30am–6pm, Sun 12.30pm–5pm*

Just a short walk from the tube, this general, local bookshop sells an excellent selection of well-displayed books covering all subjects and genres in a lively shopping street. There's a welcoming atmosphere and plenty of coffee shops nearby to enjoy purchases.

The Classic Camera

- 2 Pied Bull Yard, off Bury Place, WC1A 2JR
- 020 7831 0777
- 020 7831 0404
- www.theclassiccamera.com
- Holborn LU
- Mon-Fri 9.30am-5.30pm, Sat 10am-4.30pm

This shop is dedicated to Leica cameras, which photographers will know are among the best in the world. The cameras may be outside the reach of most budgets but the small stock of photography books is more accessible. There are volumes on classic Leica cameras, antique camera collecting and photography technique, plus a selection of glossy monographs by the big-name photographers who use Leica's.

CLC Bookshop

- 26-30 Holborn Viaduct, EC1A 2AQ
- 020 7583 4835
- 020 7583 6059
- www.clc.org.uk
- Farringdon & Chancery Lane LU
- Mon-Wed & Fri 10am-5.30pm, Thurs 10am-7.30pm, Sat 10am-5.30pm

The only London branch of a worldwide chain. Christian Literature Crusade is a missionary society dedicated to using books, music and other resources to establish a Christian presence across the globe – they currently have 180 centres and 40 book vans in more than 50 countries. The shop is huge with large sections of books on every aspect of Christianity and Christian living including biography, children's books, Bibles, commentaries, prayer books and books on theology, evangelism, preaching, and prophecy.

College of North West London Bookshop

- Dudden Hill Lane, Willesden, NW10 2XD
- 020 8208 5055
- 020 8208 5151
- Dollis Hill LU
- Mon-Thurs 9.30am-2.30pm & 5pm-7pm, Fri 9.30am-2.30pm

This is a specialist in academic books relating to the courses run by the college, which are mostly vocational. The stock covers plumbing, electrical installation, welding, IT, construction, refrigeration, air-conditioning, gas installation, brickwork, carpentry and auto-engineering.

Comicana

- 237 Shaftesbury Avenue, WC2H 8EH
- ☎ 020 7836 5630
- ✆ 020 7836 5640
- ⌨ www.comicana.com
- 🚌 Tottenham Court Road LU
- 🕐 Mon-Wed 10.30am-6.30pm, Thurs-Sat 10am-7pm, Sun 10am-4pm

A small shop packed full of current and back copies of Marvel and DC, independents and British comics plus Manga books. About 50% of their stock is new and 50% second-hand. Everything is extremely well-organised and labelled and there's a selection of merchandise.

The Comic Shack

- 720 High Road, Leytonstone, E11 3AJ
- ☎ 020 8539 7260
- ⌨ www.comicshack.uk.co
- 🚌 Leytonstone LU
- 🕐 Mon, Tues & Thurs-Sat 9.30am-5.30pm,
  Wed 9.30am-4pm, Sun 11am-4pm

A mecca for comics fans, selling new imports and second-hand American comics. The stock is huge ranging from cheapo £1 titles up to very rare 'Fantastic Four' and 'Daredevil' comics selling at a couple of thousand pounds per issue.

Comic Showcase

- 63 Charing Cross Road, WC2H 0NE
- ☎ 020 7434 4349
- 🚌 Leicester Square LU
- 🕐 Mon-Wed 10am-7pm, Thurs & Fri 10am-8pm,
  Sat 9.30am-7pm, Sun 10am-6pm

There's a huge range of English and American comics, Manga books in translation and books and merchandise associated with the most popular comic characters. There is also a branch in Oxford if you are out of town.

Cornerstone

- 45-51 Woodhouse Road, North Finchley, N12 9ET
- ☎ 020 8446 3056
- ✆ 020 8446 2227
- ✎ www.cornerstone.co.uk
- 🚌 Woodside Park or Finchley Central LU
- 🕐 Mon-Thurs & Sat 9.30am-5.30pm, Fri 9.30am-6.30pm

Ten to fifteen minutes walk from the Underground, this is a Christian bookshop covering all areas of Christian interest but with an evangelical leaning. Part of the shop is called Bedford Books and sells remaindered Christian titles. There is also a selection of Christian music, videos, software and gifts. They can supply academic theological books through their shop at Oak Hill Theological College.

Cornerstone

- 299-301 Lavender Hill, SW11 1LN
- ☎ 020 7924 2413
- 🚌 Clapham Junction Rail
- 🕐 Mon, Tues & Thurs 9.30am-5.30pm, Wed 9.30am-1pm,
  Fri 9.30am-7pm, Sat 9.30am-5pm

A large specialist shop selling Christian books on all aspects of Christianity including a children's section as well as music and greetings cards. A short walk from Clapham Junction station.

Courtauld Institute of Art Gallery Bookshop

- Somerset House, Strand, WC2R 0RN
- ☎ 020 7848 2579
- ✎ www.courtauld.ac.uk
- 🚌 Covent Garden, Holborn & Temple LU
- 🕐 Daily 10am-6pm

The Courtauld is one of the finest galleries in London with a world class collection of art (most notably Impressionist and Post-Impressionist works), extremely well displayed and on a much more manageable scale than many of the mega-galleries elsewhere in London. The shop has a selection of titles on art history as well as some architecture and fashion books and a good range of postcards, prints, stationery and assorted gifts and souvenirs featuring art from the gallery.

New Bookshops

Crafts Council Shop
- 44a Pentonville Road, N1 9BY
- 020 7278 7700/Shop 020 7806 2559
- 020 7837 6891
- www.craftscouncil.org.uk
- Angel LU
- Tues-Sat 11am-5.45pm, Sun 2pm-5.45pm

Specialist shop stocking books and magazines on all types of craft from blacksmithing to wood carving via ceramics, glass and textiles. A tempting selection of crafts by leading British makers are also on sale and there is also a reference library on the premises (see p.253).

D

Daisy and Tom
- 181 King's Road, SW3 5EB
- 020 7352 5000
- 020 7349 5818
- www.daisyandtom.com
- Sloane Square LU
- Mon-Wed & Fri 9.30am-6pm,
  Thurs & Sat 10am-7pm, Sun 11am-5pm

An amazing kid's emporium that sells a vast and imaginative array of children's goods, everything from clothing to must-have toys. Their book department is equally vast and delectable and is at the rear of the store, reached via a child sized roundabout. There are plenty of child-sized chairs, the stock covers fiction and non-fiction for all ages and there's a good selection of adult books on parenting as well.

Dar Al Dawa
- 97 Westbourne Grove, W2 4UW
- / 020 7221 6256
- Bayswater LU
- Daily 9am-10pm

Arabic books and books in English on all aspects of Islam and the Middle East. The stock also includes language learning materials, dictionaries and books for children.

Dar Al-Hikma

- 88 Chalton St, NW1 1HJ
- 020 7383 4037
- 020 7383 0116
- www.hikma.co.uk
- King's Cross, St Pancras LU/Rail
- Mon-Sat 10am-6pm

Publisher and seller of books in Arabic covering all subjects and all aspects of the Arab world including a selection of books for children. There is a range of books in English on these subjects and Arabic-English dictionaries as well.

Dar Al-Taqwa

- 7A Melcombe Street, NW1 6AE
- 020 7935 6385
- 020 7224 3894
- www.daraltaqwa.com
- Baker Street LU
- Mon-Sat 9am-6pm

Islamic bookshop with a huge stock of books in English and Arabic on religion, philosophy, politics, history, art, society and culture, economics, language and travel. There are also magazines and newspapers as well as gift items.

Darussalam

- www.dar-us-salam.co.uk

These two shops are the London outlets for the eponymous international publishing house which produces books about Islam. The greatest part of its stock is in English but there are also Arabic, Urdu, Spanish, French, Bengali, Hindi, Albanian and Chinese volumes.

- 226 High Street, Walthamstow, E17 7JH
- 020 8520 2666
- 020 8521 7645
- Walthamstow LU
- Mon-Sat 10am-6pm & Sun 11am-5pm

and

- Regent's Park Mosque, 146 Park Road, NW8 7RG
- 020 7725 2246
- 020 8539 4889
- Baker Street & St John's Wood LU
- Daily 10am-10.30pm

Daunt Books

Having made their reputation as sellers of travel-related books in Marylebone High Street Daunt are now general booksellers and enjoying considerable success. All subjects are well-selected and displayed especially the travel sections which are arranged by country and include guides, travel accounts, history, sociology, art, craft and literature (ancient and modern). They are also strong on fiction, biography, cookery, design and children's titles. Branches at:

- 83/84 Marylebone High Street, W1U 4QW
- 020 7224 2295   020 7224 6893
- orders@dauntbooks.co.uk
- Baker Street, Bond Street & Regent's Park LU
- Mon-Sat 9am-7.30pm, Sun 11am-6pm

Behind the dark green facade of Daunt's flagship store is a large and beautifully designed interior which boasts a balconied rear room and a stunning basement, lined floor to ceiling with books. The back of the shop remains the location of the enormous stock of travel titles, arranged by country. Marylebone High Street is packed with coffee shops and restaurants, the most original is Le Pain Quotidien at No 72-75 – just a little further along.

And at
- 193 Haverstock Hill, NW3 4QL
- 020 7794 4006   020 7431 2732
- Belsize Park LU
- Mon-Sat 10am-9pm, Sun 11am-7pm

With all the strengths of Daunt this is an appealing neighbourhood shop, set in the heart of Belsize Park's bustling shopping street.

And at
- 51 South End Road, NW3 2QB
- 020 7794 8206
- Hampstead Heath Rail
- Mon-Sat 9am-6pm, Sun 11am-6pm

This branch carries a good-quality, general stock along the lines of the other stores but with particular emphasis on children's books. The shop is just around the corner from Keat's House and, for those who like to combine literary pursuits with fresh air, Hampstead Heath is a short walk away. There are coffee shops a-plenty too.

AMERICA   AFRICA
ASIA   AUSTRALASIA

Daunt Books

Davenports

- ⌨ *5, 6 & 7 Charing Cross Underground Arcade, Strand, WC2N 4HZ*
- ☎ *020 7836 0408*
- ✎ *020 7379 8828*
- ⌕ *www.davenportsmagic.co.uk*
- 🚌 *Charing Cross LU/Rail*
- 🕑 *Mon-Fri 9.30am-5.30pm, Sat 10.15am-4.30pm*

Davenports has produced conjuring equipment and published books on magic since 1898 so it's perhaps no surprise that over one hundred years later it's still a prime destination for magicians. The huge stock of magic equipment and props caters to beginners and experts alike (the 'Demon Arm-Chopper', anybody?) and the shop carries an equally extensive choice of DVDs and magic books, including many foreign titles. Davenports is located in the underground shopping arcade attached to Charing Cross tube station. The London Society of Magicians meet here every fortnight on Friday evenings.

Design Museum Bookshop

- ⌨ *28 Shad Thames, SE1 2YD*
- ☎ *020 7940 8753*
- ✎ *0870 909 1909*
- ⌕ *www.designmuseum.org*
- 🚌 *London Bridge LU/Rail, Tower Hill LU*
- 🕑 *Daily 10am-5.45pm (longer opening hours on Fridays in the summer – ring for details)*

Located on the ground floor of this museum devoted entirely to design. The shop, although not enormous, sells a range of books on design including fashion, architecture, graphic design, multi-media and typography. There are always volumes related to current exhibitions as well as a brilliant selection of gifts.

Divine Bookshop

- ⌨ *185 Old Kent Road, SE1 5UT*
- ☎ *020 7207 0476*
- ✎ *020 7207 0983*
- ⌕ *www.divinebookshop.com*
- 🚌 *Elephant & Castle LU/Rail*
- 🕑 *Mon-Sat 10am-8pm*

There's a huge selection of books in this Christian bookshop about Christian living, from personal growth to business and finance.

Dominion Centre Bookshop

⌨ *9 The Broadway, Wood Green High Road, N22 6DS*
☎ *020 8829 0080*
🚌 *Wood Green LU*
🕐 *Mon-Sat 9am-7pm, Sun 1pm-4pm*

A Christian bookshop selling books on religion, the Christian life, prayer and worship and also a range of music.

The Dover Bookshop

⌨ *18 Earlham Street, WC2H 9LG*
☎ *020 7836 2111*
📠 *020 7836 1603*
🖱 *www.doverbooks.co.uk*
🚌 *Leicester Square LU*
🕐 *Mon-Wed 10am-6pm, Thurs-Sat 10am-7pm, Sunday 1pm-5pm*

Selling a vast selection of copyright-free images and pictorial reference material as well as design books, the stock includes postcard and stencil books, punch-out masks and model and paper doll books (whose subjects include George Bush and the Pope). They also publish a lot of material on CD-ROM. A mail order catalogue is available.

Dress Circle

⌨ *57/59 Monmouth Street, WC2H 9DG*
☎ *020 7240 2227*
📠 *020 7379 8540*
🖱 *www.dresscircle.co.uk*
🚌 *Leicester Square, Covent Garden & Tottenham Court Road LU*
🕐 *Mon-Sat 10am-6.30pm*

Billing itself as 'The Greatest Showbiz Shop in the World' this store is run by real enthusiasts who know and adore their subject. The shop carries a large stock of musical scores, original cast recordings and CD's of Broadway and London shows as well as scripts, DVDs, videos, magazines, posters and merchandise associated with current West End shows. A small selection of new books about musical theatre and the stars of stage and screen past and present completes the billing. A brilliant place for browsing if glamour is your bag and close to both Covent Garden and Theatreland.

Dulwich Books

6 Croxted Road, SE21 8SW

☎ 020 8670 1920

✆ 020 8670 9842

✉ dulwichbooks@yahoo.co.uk

🚌 West Dulwich Rail

🕐 Mon-Sat 9.30am-5.30pm

This is an excellent local bookstore, with a stock that is well displayed and organised. The shop offers all the general subject areas you'd expect but is especially strong in art and travel as well as having an extensive children's section complete with a suitably lilliputian table and chairs. There's also a great selection of greetings cards plus audiobooks. Join the e-mail list to receive a regular bulletin and special offers. Reading groups receives 10% off and there are often events at the shop. Café Rouge is a short walk away for a post-browse coffee, there's a toy shop next door and the heartily recommended Dulwich Music Shop on a nearby corner.

Dulwich Picture Gallery

College Road, SE21 7AD

☎ 020 8693 5254

✆ 020 8299 8700

✉ www.dulwichpicturegallery.org.uk

🚌 West Dulwich & North Dulwich Rail

🕐 Tues-Fri 10am-5pm, Sat-Sun & Bank Hols 11am-5pm

The book and gift shop is in the entrance hall of this historic South London gallery in the heart of Dulwich Village. The book stock is quite small but reflects the museum holdings so the history of art, Old Masters and monographs on artists such as Rembrandt, Rubens and Van Dyck are very much a feature. There is a selection of children's books about art plus a choice of general guides about London. The gift items here are lovely and the attached café/restaurant a complete delight.

E

Eastside Bookshop
- 166 Brick Lane, E1 6RU
- ☎ 020 7247 0216
- ✆ 020 7377 6120
- ⌨ www.eastsidebooks.co.uk
- 🚌 Liverpool St LU/Rail, Shoreditch LU (part-time opening), Whitechapel LU
- 🕐 Mon-Sat 11am-6pm, Sun 10am-5pm

This attractive shop specialises in local history but also has a general stock including an excellent range of multi-cultural fiction and children's books. The children's stock includes dual language books, including titles in Arabic, Bengali, Chinese, Somali, Russian and Tamil. There's a lovely selection of cards, a writer's group meets here regularly and the choice of nearby restaurants and cafés is downright bewildering.

East London Book Shop
- 96 Whitechapel Road, E1 1JQ
- ☎ 020 7247 4665
- 🚌 Aldgate East LU
- 🕐 Daily 10.30am-8pm (open late in summer and with different hours in Ramadan – ring for details)

Right next to the East London Mosque this is a well-stocked shop with a range of religious books plus titles on all aspects of Islam and Islamic life. There are books in both Arabic and English and a few in Bengali. There's also a stock of Islamic music on CD and tape.

The Estorick Collection Bookshop
- 39a Canonbury Square, N1 2AN
- ☎ 020 7226 3043
- ⌨ www.estorickcollection.com
- 🚌 Highbury & Islington LU/Rail
- 🕐 Wed-Sat 11am-6pm, Sun 12noon-5pm

The Estorick Collection displays modern Italian art. The small bookshop compliments this with titles about Italian art, culture, history and lifestyle plus some attractive gifts from Italy. There's a nice little café here if you need a rest from Highbury and Islington book shopping.

European Bookshop

- 5 Warwick Street, W1B 5LU
- ☎ 020 7734 5259
- ✆ 020 7287 1720
- 🖰 www.europeanbookshop.com
- 🚌 Piccadilly Circus LU
- 🕐 Mon-Sat 9.30am-6pm

This is a gem of a bookshop featuring materials in French, German, Spanish, Russian and Portuguese. They stock fiction and non-fiction books for students of every level as well as language courses, self-study texts, dictionaries, audio materials and DVDs. In addition there are materials to learn a wide range of other European languages from English. The Italian Bookshop (see p.78) and the Young Europeans Bookstore (see p.163) are their specialist offshoots in Cecil Court.

F

Falkiner Fine Papers

- 76 Southampton Row, WC1B 4AR
- ☎ 020 7831 1151
- ✆ 020 7430 1248
- 🖰 falkiner@ic24.net
- 🚌 Holborn LU
- 🕐 Mon-Fri 9.30am-5.30pm, Sat 10.30am-5.30pm

Primarily a seller of exquisite hand-crafted papers from around the world, this shop also stocks a fine assortment of books and journals on calligraphy, typography, bookbinding, papermaking, the history of print and anything associated with paper, its production and use. Should the creative urge overtake you, equipment for calligraphy, bookbinding, conservation and papermaking are in store. There are plenty of leaflets advertising courses, exhibitions, lectures and events for those with an interest in this area.

Fantasy Centre - see p.179

Farhangsara

- *Ashbourne Parade, 1261 Finchley Road,*
  Temple Fortune, NW11 0AD
- *020 8455 8184*
- *Golders Green LU*
- *Daily 10am-9pm*

Specialist Iranian book and music shop with a selection of music tapes, CDs, videos, DVDs and books in Farsi, including dictionaries.

Fielders

- *54 Wimbledon Hill Road, SW19 7PA*
- *020 8946 5044*
- *020 8944 1320*
- *www.fielders.co.uk*
- *Wimbledon LU/Rail*
- *Mon-Fri 9am-6pm, Sat 9.30am-5.30pm*

Booksellers in Wimbledon for over seventy years, Fielders has something of a split personality. The downstairs of the shop is a brilliantly-stocked stationery and art store whilst the upstairs book department specialises in art, architecture and design titles. They can order books on any subject and get those at a discount for customers where possible. They have a sister art shop in Kingston.

Forbidden Planet

Financial World Bookshop

⌑   *90 Bishopsgate, EC2N 4DQ*

☎   *020 7929 7794*

✆   *020 7626 8138*

✍   *www.thefinancialbookshop.com*

🚇   *Liverpool Street LU/Rail*

🕐   *Mon-Fri 9am-6pm*

At the corner of Bishopsgate and Camomile Street, this specialist bookshop sells books covering all aspects of banking and finance.

The Finchley Bookshop

⌑   *98 Ballards Lane, N3 2DN*

☎   *020 8346 7761*

✆   *020 8343 3659*

✍   *facultybooks@onetel.com*

🚇   *Finchley Central LU*

🕐   *Mon-Sat 9.30-5.30pm (ring for details of Sunday opening times)*

This is a friendly and attractively laid out local bookshop with soothing music in the background and a justifiably loyal local following.
There's a particularly large children's section offering picture books
right through to a young adult range with plenty of non-fiction as
well as fiction. Adults are also well catered for with a comprehensive
selection across all subject areas, but with especially good sections on
travel, quality modern fiction and reference. The shop also stocks a
selection of audiobooks and cards plus a range of remaindered books
at bargain prices.

Forbidden Planet – the Cult Entertainment Megastore

- 🖃 *179 Shaftesbury Avenue, WC2H 8JR*
- ☎ *020 7420 3666*
- ✆ *020 7420 3687*
- ✍ *www.forbiddenplanet.com*
- 🚌 *Tottenham Court Road or Leicester Square LU*
- ⏱ *Mon-Sat 10am-7pm, Thurs until 8pm, Sun 12noon-6pm*

One of a nationwide chain, this is a huge and comprehensively stocked shop specialising in science fiction, fantasy and cult material. The book department is downstairs and has mind-boggling selections in all these areas plus politics, counterculture, UFOlogy, alternate history and books based on role play games. There is also a vast range of comics, graphic novels, DVDs and videos. Plenty of the material is imported from overseas. There's a gargantuan stock of merchandise on the ground floor.

Fountain of Life

- 🖃 *69 Baring Road, SE12*
- ☎ *020 8851 7423*
- ✆ *020 8851 4682*
- 🚌 *Lee Rail*
- ⏱ *Mon-Fri 8.45am-5.45pm, Sat 10am-5.30pm*

Christian bookshop in a small shopping area.

Four Provinces

- 🖃 *244 Gray's Inn Road, WC1X 8JR*
- ☎ *020 7833 3022*
- ✍ *www.irishdemocrat.co.uk*
- ✍ *whippetdog@btinternet.com*
- 🚌 *Chancery Lane LU, King's Cross LU/Rail*
- ⏱ *Wed-Sat 11am-5.30pm (ring to check if you wish to visit outside these times because they are considering extending their hours)*

A specialist bookshop with books on all things Irish including history and politics, biography, literature and music. As well as material in English, they stock a range of Irish language books covering all subject areas and literature both classical and contemporary. They also sell courses for learning Irish and language aids. Plenty of leaflets advertise events with an Irish flavour and Irish music on CD can also be picked up here. They issue a catalogue which is updated regularly.

Foyles

- 📺 *113-119 Charing Cross Road, WC2H 0EB*
- ☎ *020 7437 5660*
- ✆ *020 7434 1574*
- 🖎 *www.foyles.co.uk*
- 🚇 *Tottenham Court Road LU*
- 🕐 *Mon-Sat 9.30am-9pm, Sun 12noon-6pm*

Foyles is the largest independent bookshop in London with a massive stock covering all subject areas laid out over five floors. Its prime Charing Cross premises are a bright and airy browser's delight, the stock is well displayed but still amazingly extensive and there's a buzzy but bookish feel about the place. Author signings and events are a feature and Ray's Jazz Shop (Tel 020 7440 3205, Mon-Sat 9.30am-8pm, Sun 12noon-6pm) and the Café (Mon-Sat 9am-8pm, Sun 10am-6pm) on the first floor both add to the atmosphere. The Silver Moon Bookshop on the third floor (Tel 020 7440 1562, fax 020 7434 1574, *www.silver-moonbookshop.co.uk*, Mon-Sat 9.30am-8pm, Sun 12noon-6pm) has always been a destination for books of interest to women but has now expanded and also sells books, films, and gifts of interest to the wider gay and lesbian community.

Also at:
- 📺 *Riverside, Level1*
  Royal Festival Hall, Southbank Centre, SE1 8XX
- 🚇 *Waterloo LU/Rail*
- 🕐 *Mon-Sat 10am-10pm*

R D Franks

- 📺 *Kent House, Market Place, W1W 8HY*
- ☎ *020 7636 1244*
- ✆ *020 7436 4904*
- 🖎 *www.rdfranks.co.uk*
- 🚇 *Oxford Circus LU*
- 🕐 *Mon-Fri 9am-6pm*

Hidden away behind Oxford Circus, this shop is stocked with a fabulous range of books on every aspect of fashion including design, textiles, cutting and pattern-making. They also have an exhaustive range of fashion magazines from across the globe. A catalogue and mail order service are available and staff will try to get special orders.

Freedom Press Bookshop

- *Angel Alley, 84b Whitechapel High Street, E1 7QX*
- *020 7247 9249*
- *020 7247 9249*
- *www.freedompress.org.uk*
- *Aldgate East LU*
- *Mon-Sat 12noon-6pm (ring for Sunday opening times)*

This anarchist publisher's bookshop is located two doors down from the Whitechapel Art Gallery and is reached via a pedestrian alleyway off the main road. It has a huge stock of books (mostly new but with a few second-hand), journals and magazines, both their own and other's publications, about every aspect of anarchism including anarchist history, sociology, politics and ecology, with many titles that you won't find elsewhere. They stock their own fortnightly newspaper *Freedom* and there's free internet access available in the Media Hacklab in the building. Anarchists that like to keep in touch by more traditional means can refer to the excellent selection of postcards on offer.

The French Bookshop

🖃 *28 Bute Street, SW7 3EX*
☎ *020 7584 2840*
✎ *020 7823 9259*
✍ *www.frenchbookshop.com*
🚇 *South Kensington LU*
🕐 *Mon-Fri 8.30am-6pm, Sat 10am-5pm*

Close to the Institut Français this is a good place for books in French on almost every subject, including dictionaries, language courses and children's books. There are also extensive selections of French newspapers (supplied on the day of publication), magazines, videos, DVDs, stationery and even French versions of Monopoly and Trivial Pursuit. Bute Street is awash with lovely little patisseries and coffee shops so you won't go hungry or thirsty and Librairie La Page (see p.85) is just around the corner in Harrington Road.

French's Theatre Bookshop

🖃 *52 Fitzroy Street, W1T 5JR*
☎ *020 7255 4300*
✎ *020 7387 2161*
✍ *www.samuelfrench-london.co.uk*
🚇 *Warren Street LU*
🕐 *Mon-Fri 9.30am-5.30pm, Sat 11am-5pm*

This large, well laid out and welcoming shop stocks scripts (including musicals) and books on every nuance of theatre and performance art. The selection encompasses everything from writing through to auditions and improvisation to performance itself, including guides to acting, lighting, make-up, costume and stage management as well as books on the great figures of the theatre. There's a folder of audition suggestions for aspiring actors and there are free booklists on all aspects of the stock which are also available on the website. If you buy 'The Guide to Selecting Plays', which lists over two thousand plays for amateur production, you'll receive the regular Supplement providing updates.

G

Gay's the Word

🏠 *66 Marchmont Street, WC1N 1AB*
☎ *020 7278 7654*
✏ *www.gaystheword.co.uk*
🚌 *Russell Square LU*
🕐 *Mon-Sat 10am-6.30pm, Sun 2pm-6pm*

As befits the only specialist gay and lesbian bookshop in the country, Gay's The Word stocks an enormous range of fiction and non-fiction books of gay and lesbian interest. History, biography, religion, parenting, psychology, travel and poetry are just some of the sections and although most books are new there is a limited stock of second-hand. Cards, videos and DVDs are also on sale. The shop issues a regular Book Review of new titles that can be sent by e-mail and there's a busy programme of events.

Geffrye Museum

- 136 Kingsland Road, E2 8EA
- 020 7739 9893
- 020 7729 5647
- www.geffrye-museum.org.uk
- Liverpool St or Old St LU/Rail
- Tues-Sat 10am-5pm, Sun & Bank Hols 12noon-5pm

The shop attached to this ever-popular museum of historic English interiors specialises in books relating to the museum's areas of interest. It has a selection of volumes on furniture, architecure, gardening, herbs, crafts, London and social history.

Stanley Gibbons

- 399 Strand, WC2R 0LX
- 020 7836 8444
- 020 7836 7342
- www.stanleygibbons.com
- Charing Cross LU/Rail
- Mon-Fri 9am-5.30pm, Sat 9.30am-5.30pm

This famous stamp dealer is the biggest stamp shop in the world with a stock of over 3 million stamps. They also have a large book section devoted to stamp catalogues and new and rare books on philately. The rare books are housed securely in the basement and can be viewed on request.

The Golden Treasury

- 29 Replingham Road, SW18 5LT
- 020 8333 0167
- www.thegoldentreasury.co.uk
- Southfields LU
- Mon-Fri 9.30am-6pm, Sat 9.30am-5.30pm

A welcoming, specialist shop with a large stock of new books for children of all ages. Fiction and non-fiction are well-represented and are complemented by an interesting range of audiobooks, games, puzzles and videos. There are a few general titles for adults plus a selection of books on pregnancy and childcare. There are several cafés nearby – the French pattisserie around the corner is divine.

Goldsboro Books - see p.184

Gays the Word

Good News Christian

⌨ *50 Churchfield Road, W3 6DL*

☎ *020 8992 7123*

✐ *www.getchristianbooks.com*

🚌 *Acton Town LU*

🕐 *Mon-Sat 9am-5.30pm, Thurs 9am-7pm*

Christian bookshop covering all aspects of the faith including children's books plus a small selection of Christian music.

Good News Shop

⌨ *654 High Road Leyton, E10 6RN*

☎ *020 8539 2906*

🚌 *Leyton Midland Road Rail*

🕐 *Mon-Sat 9am-6.30pm*

A shop specialising in Christian literature including children's books plus Christian music and greetings cards.

Gosh Comics

⬛ *39 Great Russell Street, WC1B 3NZ*

☎ *020 7636 1011*

✆ *020 7436 5053*

✉ *info@goshlondon.com*

🚌 *Tottenham Court Road & Holborn LU*

🕐 *Daily 10am-6pm (Thurs & Fri until 7pm)*

There is a huge range of old and new comics on offer here and all well-organised. There's also a good selection of comic books and graphic novels including Manga. A weekly information sheet of new and expected arrivals and details of upcoming events keeps fans up to speed.

Grant and Cutler

⬛ *55-57 Great Marlborough Street, W1F 7AY*

☎ *020 7734 2012*

✆ *020 7734 9272*

✉ *www.grantandcutler.com*

🚌 *Oxford Circus LU*

🕐 *Mon-Fri 9am-6pm (Thurs-7pm), Sat 9am-6pm, Sun 12noon-6pm*

This is the UK's largest foreign-language bookseller with more than 80,000 items in stock. Fancy something in Albanian, Hebrew, Tibetan, Mongolian or Xhosa? – they'll have it. With over one hundred and fifty languages covered, from every corner of the globe, you'll have to come up with something pretty obscure to confound them. Language courses, dictionaries, foreign language books, audio materials, games and DVDs of foreign-language films together make up an impressive stock. A variety of catalogues are available free on request and on the shop's website they have a worldwide mail order service. The shop is conveniently located just opposite the back door of Marks and Spencer's Oxford Street store.

Greenwich Book Time

⬛ *277 Greenwich High Road, SE10 8NB*

☎ *020 8293 0096*

🕐 *Daily 10am-8pm*

and

⬛ *44 Greenwich Church Street, SE10 9BL*

☎ *020 8293 3902*

🕐 *Daily 11am-7pm*

and

⌨ *22 Nelson Road, SE10 9JB*
☎ *020 8269 1149*
🕐 *Daily 11am-7pm*
🚌 *Cutty Sark DLR, Greenwich Rail*

These shops, all in the centre of Greenwich, sell a broad and ever changing range of discounted new books including fiction, art, cookery, history, biography and children's titles. The shops sell every title at the same price – currently £2 and some of the bargains are startling. Visit at the weekends to include a visit to the market or at any time to take in the other Greenwich sights.

Guanghwa

⌨ *7 Newport Place, WC2H 7JR*
☎ *020 7437 3737*
✎ *020 7831 0137*
🚌 *Leicester Square LU*
🕐 *Mon-Sat 10.30am-6.30pm, Sun 11am-6.30pm*

Located in London's bustling Chinatown district, this bookshop offers an extensive collection of books in Chinese plus dictionaries and some books in English on popular oriental subjects such as Tai Chi and Feng Shui. Downstairs is a specialist art department with books on Chinese arts and crafts as well as all the papers, brushes and inks necessary for Chinese painting and calligraphy.

Guildhall Library Bookshop

⌨ *Aldermanbury, EC2P 2EJ*
☎ *020 7332 1858*
✎ *020 7600 3384*
✐ *www.cityoflondon.gov.uk/corporation*
🚌 *Moorgate, St Paul's, Bank & Barbican LU*
🕐 *Mon-Fri 9.30am-4.45pm*

A must for anyone with an interest in London, The Guildhall Library Bookshop specialises in publications about the capital including fiction based in the city and biographies of famous Londoners. There's a large selection of gifts with a London theme.

H

Hammicks Legal Bookshop

- 191-192 Fleet Street, EC4A 2NJ
- 020 7405 5711
- 020 7831 9849
- www.hammickslegal.co.uk
- Temple LU
- Mon, Wed & Fri 9am-6pm, Tues 9.30am-6pm, Thurs 9am-7pm
  Sat 10am-5pm

Very close to the Royal Courts of Justice and near the Inns of Court, this specialist bookshop boasts lots of wood panelling and oozes a learned and opulent atmosphere. Its stock covers every aspect of the law and jurisprudence and also features a good section on computing. In addition, the shop offers a range of journals, stationery, cards, prints and gifts suitable for those in the legal profession.

Harrods Children's Book Department

- 87 Brompton Road, SW1X 7XL
- 020 7730 1234
- 020 7581 0470
- www.harrods.com
- Knightsbridge LU
- Mon-Sat 10am-7pm

Located on the fourth floor (the main bookshop, Waterstones, is on the second floor – see p.154), the stock here is vast with all ages catered for from first books up to teenage. They also sell tapes, DVDs and videos. However, this is clearly a bookshop in which adults buy books for children many of the shelves are very high, there are no toys, no small tables or chairs (or big ones for that matter) and generally very little to induce browsing or to entice junior readers to come in or stay. Sadly, the message seems to be leave the kids at home.

Hatchards - see Waterstones p.157

Hayward Gallery Bookshop
⌨ *South Bank, Belvedere Road, SE1 8XZ*
☎ *020 7960 5211*
✎ *www.hayward.org.uk*
🚌 *Waterloo LU/Rail*
🕐 *Mon, Thurs, Sat-Sun 10am-6pm, Tues-Wed 10am-8pm, Fri 10am-9pm (Note: opening times are different and variable during the periods when the Gallery is dismantling one show and erecting the next, this can take several weeks. It's therefore best to call before making a special journey)*

A delectable display of modern art, design, architecture and photography books including general titles and monographs. The stock includes plenty of South bank publications and well-chosen children's titles on art. There are also some lovely gifts, posters, cards and stationery in addition to the large choice of merchandise that accompanies each show.

Headstart Books & Crafts
⌨ *25 West Green Road, N15 5BX*
☎ *020 8802 2838*
🚌 *Seven Sisters LU*
🕐 *Mon-Sat 9.30am-6.30pm*

Specialists in African and Caribbean material, mostly in English but with a few books in African languages. There's an extensive selection packed into a tiny space including fiction, poetry, biography, spirituality and children's books. They also sell a range of magazines and African crafts.

Hebrew Book and Gift Centre
⌨ *24 Amhurst Parade, Amhurst Park, N16 5AA*
☎/✎ *020 8802 0609*
🚌 *Stamford Hill Rail*
🕐 *Mon-Thurs 9.30am-7.30pm, Fri & Sun 9.30am-2.30pm*

Specialist Jewish bookseller with a large stock of Jewish religious books plus books in English and Hebrew on all aspects of Jewish life, religion and culture. There are plenty of children's books and games as well as books on learning Hebrew.

Helios Homeopathic Pharmacy

⌨ *8 New Row, Covent Garden, WC2N 4LJ*
☎ *020 7379 7434*
🚆 *Leicester Square & Covent Garden LU*
🕐 *Mon-Fri 9.30am-5.30pm, Sat 10am-5.30pm*

This homeopathic pharmacy sells homeopathic remedies plus a selection of books about homeopathy, complementary therapies and health – there's a great range of toiletries as well.

The Hellenic Bookservice

⌨ *91 Fortess Road, NW5 1AG*
☎ *020 7267 9499*
✆ *020 7267 9498*
✏ *www.hellenicbookservice.com*
🚆 *Tufnell Park LU*
🕐 *Mon-Fri 9.30am-6pm, Sat 10am-5pm*

Specialists in books on anything to do with Greece and Ancient Rome from prehistoric, through classical to modern times including titles on art, literature, language, theology, mythology, religion and travel. They have a children's books section, a large second-hand department and sell books and audio courses for learning Latin as well as Ancient and Modern Greek. They also stock cards and Greek videos and DVDs but, if it's all still Greek to you there's a noticeboard advertising language teachers.

Thomas Heneage Art Books

⌨ *42 Duke Street St James's, SW1Y 6DJ*
☎ *020 7930 9223*
✆ *020 7839 9223*
✏ *www.heneage.com*
🚆 *Green Park LU*
🕐 *Mon-Fri 9.30am-6pm (or by appointment)*

An extensive range of new and out-of-print books on all aspects of art including monographs on individual artists and fine and applied arts worldwide. The stock is colossal, with many items that are unavailable elsewhere. Thomas Heneage publish 'The Art Book Survey' three times each year which details new and forthcoming art books and they also issue occasional catalogues. The shop is a short walk from the Royal Academy and just across the road from Sims Reed, another specialist art bookseller (see p.127)

G Heywood Hill

- *10 Curzon Street, W1J 5HH*
- *020 7629 0647*
- *020 7408 0286*
- *www.gheywoodhill.com*
- *Green Park LU*
- *Mon-Fri 9am-5.30pm, Sat 9am-12.30pm*

Located just at the rear of Shepherd Market off Piccadilly, this is a new, second-hand and antiquarian bookshop combined. The books are stacked on tables, reach from floor to ceiling and spill over every surface. There's a general stock but the best coverage is in literature, history, biography, travel and children's books (the latter form a large department in the basement). The shop was established in 1936 and retains an old-fashioned, refined air that makes a visit feel like a step back in time. Staff are justifiably proud of their ability to provide recommendations for customers based on their own extensive reading. A blue plaque on the front wall testifies to the fact that Nancy Mitford worked here from 1942-1945. Just across the road a covered passageway leads into Shepherd Market where the Chocolate Society Café is a required stop for all chocoholics.

The Highgate Bookshop

- *9 Highgate High Street, N6 5JR*
- *020 8348 8202*
- *020 8348 5989*
- *Archway LU*
- *Mon-Sat 10am-6pm, Sun 12noon-5pm*

On the corner of Bisham Gardens, a lovely, light, airy local shop serving a literary part of London. The stock is general but extensive and well laid out with plenty of shelf space devoted to the latest titles to keep readers up to date. The children's section at the back is welcoming and staff are friendly and helpful. Waterlow Park is nearby for a pleasant summer walk and Highgate Cemetery (see p.311) is easily reached from here. The charity shops on the High Street are definitely worth a browse if you are in the area (see p.232).

High Stakes

- 21 Great Ormond Street, WC1N 3JB
- 020 7430 1021
- 020 7430 0021
- www.highstakes.co.uk
- Russell Square & Holborn LU
- Mon-Fri 12noon-6pm

A fascinating shop specialising in books about gambling and covering all aspects of the subject from poker and horse racing through to the dogs, football and all other betting on sport. DVDs and software are also on offer as are poker chips, cards and card shufflers. Owned by publisher Ion Mills, the shop also stocks many of his publications, including titles from the No Exit Press crime imprint and Pocket Essentials series.

Hobgoblin

- 24 Rathbone Place, W1T 1JA
- 020 7323 9040
- 020 7323 1606
- www.hobgoblin.com
- Tottenham Court Road LU
- Mon-Sat 10am-6pm

Specialist folk music shop with instruments, tapes, CDs, DVDs and a big range of printed music and magazines covering folk. The emphasis is on the traditions of the British Isles but also includes some world music. The shop carries a vast number of adverts of interest for folk lovers including tuition and events and there's an instrument repairer in the basement.

Holland and Holland

- 31-33 Bruton Street, W1J 6HH
- 020 7499 4411
- 020 7499 4544
- www.hollandandholland.com
- Green Park LU
- Mon-Fri 9am-6pm, Sat 10am-5pm

An extremely exclusive specialist gunsmith and supplier of shooting accessories and country clothing. Alongside the huntin' and shootin' clobber are books about, well, huntin' and shootin'! The stock includes guides, sumptuous picture books on Africa and a smattering of game conservancy publications.

Holloway Stationers and Booksellers

⌨ *357 Holloway Road, N7 0RN*

☎/✆ *020 7607 3972*

🚌 *Holloway Road LU*

🕐 *Mon-Fri 9am-6pm, Sat 9.30am-6pm*

In the main Holloway Road shopping area, this is a stationers who also stock a good selection of popular fiction and non-fiction including reference and cookery titles. The children's section is large with plenty of educational titles.

Housmans

⌨ *5 Caledonian Road, N1 9DX*

☎ *020 7837 4473*

✆ *020 7278 0444*

🖱 *www.housemans.com*

🚌 *King's Cross LU/Rail*

🕐 *Mon-Fri 10am-6.30pm, Sat 10am-6pm*

Located in the heart of the reconstructions of the Kings Cross area, Housmans had its roots in the upsurge of the British pacifist movement in the 1930s. It first opened its doors in Shaftesbury Avenue in 1945. The Shop offers books on politics, current affairs, gay issues, ecology, pacifism, anarchism and socialism as well as more general stock, cards and stationery. Downstairs, Woburn/Porcupine sells second-hand books, (see p.214).

Hughes and Hughes

⌨ *London City Airport, King George V Dock, Silvertown, E16 2PX*

☎ *020 7646 0631*

✆ *020 7646 0630*

🖱 *www.hughesbooks.com*

🚌 *Silvertown & City Airport DLR*

🕐 *Mon-Fri 6am-9pm, Sat 6am-12noon, Sun 11am-9.15pm*

Located in the Departure Lounge of City Airport, this airport bookshop puts its emphasis on business and finance plus a few general titles, fiction and non-fiction, to while away the journey.

I

The Imperial War Museum Shop

⌖ *Lambeth Road, SE1 6HZ*
☎ *020 7416 5000*
✎ *020 7416 5374*
✐ *www.iwm.org.uk*
🚌 *Lambeth North LU*
🕐 *Daily 10am-6pm*

General interest books and specialist texts (some of them Imperial War Museum publications) covering both World Wars, more recent major conflicts, warfare on land, sea and air, as well as poetry, autobiography and fiction relating to war. The museum is especially engaging in its exploration of the way war impinges on the lives of ordinary people and the shop reflects this theme, stocking books on wartime life, fashion and food in Britain. There are also smaller shops in the museum's London outposts; The Churchill Museum and Cabinet War Rooms, Clive Steps, King Charles Street, SW1A 2AQ (strong on Churchill) and HMS Belfast, Morgan's Lane, Tooley Street, SE1 2JH (strong on naval material).

Index Bookcentre

⌖ *16 Electric Avenue, SW9 8JX*
☎ *020 7274 8342*
✎ *020 7274 8351*
✐ *www.indexbooks.co.uk/brixton.html*
🚌 *Brixton LU/Rail*
🕐 *Mon-Sat 10am-6pm*

A fabulous local bookshop in one of the main market streets of Brixton, just a short walk from the tube. It stocks an exceptional range of books on all subject areas, well-selected and attractively displayed. They have notable sections on Black history and fiction with many books difficult to find elsewhere. They also have wide selections on politics, current affairs and environmental issues as well as an excellent children's section. For those in search of lighter reading material they stock a good selection of magazines. Combine this place with a visit to Bookmongers (see p.170).

Indian Bookshelf

- 📖 *55 Warren Street, W1T 5NW*
- ☎ *020 7380 0622*
- ✆ *020 7419 9169*
- ✉ *indbooks@spduk.fsnet.co.uk*
- 🚇 *Warren Street LU*
- 🕐 *Mon-Fri 10am-6pm*

Distributor for Star Publishers from India and specialist in books from and about India and Pakistan (although there are a few on other parts of South Asia) in Hindi, Urdu, Bengali, Punjabi, Tamil, Marati and Gujerati. There is also a gigantic selection of books in English on all aspects of the subcontinent including religion, philosophy, history, medicine and politics and a range of language courses and dictionaries.

Inner Space

- 📖 *36 Shorts Gardens, WC2H 9AB*
- ☎ *020 7836 6688*
- ✉ *www.innerspace.org.uk*
- 🚇 *Covent Garden LU*
- 🕐 *Mon-Sat 10.30am-6pm (Fridays until 5pm)*

Based in the heart of bustling, commercial Covent Garden, Inner Space offers books on relaxation, meditation and spiritual growth. The Brahma Kumaris Information Service provides information about lectures and courses on yoga, meditation, empowerment, stress management and positive thinking. All courses and facilities are free as is the use of the meditation room.

Institute of Contemporary Arts Bookshop

- 📖 *Nash House, The Mall, SW1Y 5AH*
- ☎ *020 7766 1452*
- ✆ *020 7873 0051*
- ✉ *www.ica.org.uk/bookshop*
- 🚇 *Piccadilly Circus LU*
- 🕐 *Daily 12noon-9pm*

Founded in 1947 the ICA, is at the cutting edge of contemporary arts in London. The bookshop has an extensive stock of art, cultural theory, philosophy and media books as well as magazines, journals, cards and DVDs.

Institute of Education Bookshop

⌨ *20 Bedford Way, WC1H 0AL*
☎ *020 7612 6050*
✆ *020 7612 6407*
✍ *www.johnsmith.co.uk*
🚌 *Russell Square LU*
🕐 *Mon-Fri 9.30am-6pm, Sat 10am-4pm*

A diminutive but well-stocked shop on the ground floor of the main Institute of Education building. Its carefully selected range of titles covers everything to do with education both theoretical and practical and includes course books for the Institute as well as the Institute's own publications. There's also a small range of children's books. Given the size of the subject, it is no surprise that staff here operate an efficient ordering service for books that are not in stock.

International Islamic Dawah Centre

⌨ *57 Park Road, NW1 6XU*
☎ *020 7724 8099*
✆ *020 7724 8056*
✍ *www.idc.co.uk*
🚌 *Baker Street LU*
🕐 *Daily 9am-8pm*

Just a short walk away from the London Central Mosque, the Centre holds a huge stock of books about Islam in both Arabic and English. They also carry versions of the Koran in many languages and books on learning Arabic for speakers of other languages. There are also plenty of DVDs, CDs, tapes, clothing and religious and gift items.

Italian Bookshop

⌨ *7 Cecil Court, WC2N 4EZ*
☎ *020 7240 1634*
✆ *020 7240 1635*
✍ *www.ItalianBookshop.co.uk*
🚌 *Leicester Square LU*
🕐 *Mon-Sat 10.30am-6.30pm*

An outpost of the language specialist European Bookshop (see p.58) featuring a superb stock of books in Italian. Students of Italian are well served here with a wide choice of learning materials, a selection of Italian DVDs, videos and some books in English about Italy. The Young Europeans Bookstore is just next door (see p.163)

J

Jamyang Buddhist Centre
- The Old Courthouse, 43 Renfrew Road, SE11 4NA
- ☎ 020 7820 8787
- 020 7820 8605
- www.jamyang.co.uk
- Kennington, Elephant & Castle LU
- Mon-Fri 6pm-closing, 2pm-6pm by appointment

Books on all aspects of Buddhism including Buddhist thought and philosophy, biography, art and Tibetan language materials. There are also beautiful cards, gifts, statues, posters and religious hangings. The Courtyard Café at the Centre serves delicious meals and snacks.

Japan Centre Bookshop
- 212 Piccadilly, W1J 9HG
- ☎ 020 7439 8035
- 020 7255 8289
- www.japancentre.com
- Piccadilly Circus LU
- Mon-Fri 10am-7pm, Sat 10.30am-8pm, Sun 11am-7pm

Up on the first floor, this shop has an excellent stock of books, magazines and newspapers in Japanese and also a wide selection of books in English about Japan covering martial arts, history, Japanese society, business, religion, travel, art and design, as well as Japanese literature in translation. There is a useful section devoted to Japanese language courses, textbooks and dictionaries as well Japanese CD's and DVDs. There is a Japanese restaurant on the ground floor and a supermarket in the basement and, if you get the yen to travel, there's a travel centre here as well.

Jerusalem the Golden
- 146-148 Golders Green Road, NW11 8HE
- ☎ 020 8455 4960
- 020 8458 3953
- Golders Green LU

Specialist bookseller of Jewish books in English and Hebrew on all aspects of life and religion, gifts, silverware and religious items.

Joseph's Bookstore

⌨ *2 Ashbourne Parade, 1257 Finchley Road,*
Temple Fortune, NW11 0AD
☎ *020 8731 7575*
✆ *020 8731 6699*
✍ *www.josephsbookstore.com*
🚌 *Golders Green LU*
🕐 *Mon-Fri 9.30am-6.30pm, Sat & Sun 10am-5pm*

As well as being a publisher, Joseph's is also a lovely local bookshop with a pleasant atmosphere and the en-suite Café ideal for pre- or post-purchase refreshment. Joseph's features a good general stock alongside a broad choice of Jewish interest titles, many with discounts. Magazines and a fair-sized selection of original art are also on sale here. Events are organised in the bookshop and there's a noticeboard with details of other goings-on in the area. Readers can join an e-mail list to receive a monthly mailing about upcoming events.

Jubilee Books

⌨ *Eltham Green School Campus, Middle Park Avenue, SE9 5EQ*
☎ *020 8850 7676*
✆ *020 8294 0345*
✍ *www.jubileebooks.co.uk*
🚌 *Eltham Rail*
🕐 *Mon-Fri 9.30am-5.30pm*

Specialist school and children's book showroom warehouse.

Judd Books – see p.188

K

Karnac Books

📖 *118 Finchley Road, NW3 5HT*
☎ *Shop 020 7431 1075   Mail Order 020 8969 4454*
🖥 *www.karnacbooks.com*
🚌 *Finchley Road LU*
🕐 *Mon-Sat 9am-6pm*

A huge, largely academic stock concentrating on psychology, psychotherapy, psychoanalysis and related fields. The company also publishes books and translations in these fields, for which it has an international reputation.

And at:

📖 *Tavistock Clinic, 120 Belsize Lane, NW3 5BA*
☎ *020 7447 3757*
🚌 *Swiss Cottage LU*
🕐 *Mon-Fri 10am-6pm*

The Clinic is located at the corner of Belsize Lane and Fitzjohn's Avenue. This branch specialises in the areas that are of most relevance to the Clinic; organisations and family, child and adolescent studies.

Kensington Chimes Music

🖳 *9 Harrington Road, SW7 3ES*
☎ *020 7589 9054*
✆ *020 7225 2662*
🖉 *www.chimesmusic.com*
🚌 *South Kensington LU*
🕒 *Mon-Fri 9am-5.30pm, Sat 9am-4pm*

The sister-shop of Barbican Chimes (see p.14) is small but jammed full of classical and modern music scores for every instrument at every stage of proficiency with a plethora of tutors for those still learning. The shop also stocks books on all aspects of music and offers a selection of gift items.

KICC Bookshop

🖳 *57 Waterden Road, E15 2EE*
☎ *020 8525 0000*
✆ *020 8525 0002*
🚌 *Hackney Wick Rail*
🕒 *Mon 12pm-6.30pm, Tues-Fri 9.30am-6.30pm*

Christian bookshops selling music, videos and books plus gift items.

Kilburn Bookshop

🖳 *8 Kilburn Bridge, Kilburn High Road, NW6 6HT*
☎ *020 7328 7071*
✆ *020 7372 6474*
🚌 *Kilburn Park LU*
🕒 *Mon-Sat 10am-6pm*

An excellent local bookshop making good use of its limited space. Its attractive displays are home to particularly strong selections of Irish and Black studies as well as travel guides, fiction, general interest books and a few literary magazines and cards. Their sister shop is in Willesden (see p.161).

Kirkdale Bookshop

🖳 *272 Kirkdale, SE26 4RS*
☎ *020 8778 4701*
✆ *020 8776 6293*
🖉 *kirkdalebookshop@hotmail.com*
🚌 *Sydenham Rail*
🕒 *Mon-Sat 9am-5.30pm (Thurs-7pm)*

A glorious local bookshop and art gallery that has been on this site since

1966, where visitors can read the paper and have a cup of tea or coffee. The book stock is pretty evenly split between new, second-hand and out of print books and the basement is a treasure trove for browsers. Second-hand prices are keen, and there is a large bargain selection outside. Naxos classical CDs, cards and gifts join the book stock. Reading groups meet here, there's a Loyalty Card scheme and the shop hosts exhibitions by local artists.

Kiwi Fruits

  7 Royal Opera Arcade, Pall Mall, SW1Y 4UY
  020 7930 4587
  020 7839 0592
  www.kiwifruitsnzshop.com
  Piccadilly Circus LU
  Mon-Fri 9am-5.30pm, Sat 10am-4pm

A small shop that is full of Kiwi food, clothing, gifts and souvenirs but which also sells an excellent range of books from and about New Zealand. New Zealand literature, glossy picture books, guidebooks, books on sport, history, cooking, art and architecture all feature strongly here and there's a fascinating section devoted to Maori history, myth, culture and language. They also stock lots of children's titles and a few New Zealand magazines.

Walther Koenig at the Serpentine Gallery

  Kensington Gardens, W2 3XA
  020 7706 4907
  020 7706 4911
  www.koenigbooks.co.uk
  South Kensington & Lancaster Gate LU
  Daily 10am-6pm

The Serpentine Gallery is located in the heart of Kensington Gardens and specialises in modern and contemporary art. The bookshop reflects this with its covetable stock of books about modern and contemporary art including art theory, photography, architecture, design, criticism, catalogues and monographs, and a selection of artists' books. There are also remaindered books and a selection of magazines on art, design and fashion.

Krypton Komics

- 252 High Road, Tottenham, N15 4AJ
- 020 8801 5378
- www.keycomics.com or www.kryptonkomics.com
- Seven Sisters Road LU
- Tues 12noon-5.30pm, Wed 11am-6pm, Thurs 10.30am-6.30pm,
  Fri & Sat 10.30am-6pm

Situated almost next to Tesco's, a specialist comic shop with a colossal range of American comics from 1940 to date and over 300 current titles. More than a quarter of a million comics are listed on the website priced from 10 pence upwards.

L

The Lamb Bookshop

- 40 Lamb's Conduit Street, WC1N 3HQ
- 020 7405 6536
- 020 7405 6577
- www.lambbookshop.com
- Holborn, Chancery Lane & Russell Square LU
- Mon-Fri 10.30am-6pm, Sat 11am-5pm

An excellent discount bookshop with mostly half-price books sold in a welcoming atmosphere. They cover all subject areas but are especially good in fiction, history, cookery and gardening. There's a table and chairs for browsing and the stock is completed by cards and gifts. There are several other bookshops nearby, see Persephone (p.112), High Stakes (p.74) and Griffith and Partner (p.184).

LCL International Booksellers

- 104-106 Judd Street, WC1H 9PU
- 020 7837 0486
- 020 7833 9452
- www.lclib.com
- King's Cross LU/Rail, Russell Square LU
- Mon-Fri 9.30am-5.30pm, Sat 9.30am-2pm

A specialist language shop with books, dictionaries, language courses, tapes, videos, CD-ROMs and literature in over a hundred languages.

Librairie La Page – French Bookseller

⌨ *7 Harrington Road, SW7 3ES*
☎ *020 7589 5991*
✆ *020 7589 4429§§*
✎ *www.librairielapage.com*
🚇 *South Kensington LU*
🕐 *Mon-Fri 8.15am-6.15pm, Sat 10am-5pm*
   (shorter times during the French Lycée holidays – ring to check)

Selling a fine assortment of new and second-hand French books, this small but well-stocked shop is especially strong on literature and the social sciences. There's a good selection of children's books, cards, CDs and DVDs plus a basement packed with Clairefontaine stationery. Situated very close to the Institut Français and the enclave of delectable French patisseries on Bute Street.

The Library

⌨ *268 Brompton Road, SW3 2AS*
☎ *020 7589 6569*
🚇 *South Kensington LU*
🕐 *Mon-Sat 10am-6.30pm (Wed until 7pm), Sun 12.30pm-5.30pm*

You'll rarely have seen books for sale in surroundings like this before! This is a designer clothes shop, mostly men's but with some women's items, where the concept of the display is books in a library. The stock includes new and second-hand books on design, fashion, art, architecture, interior design and related topics.

London Buddhist Centre (Jambala Bookshop)

⌨ *51 Roman Road, E2 0HU*
☎ *0845 458 4716*
✆ *0871 433 5995*
✎ *www.lbc.org.uk*
🚇 *Bethnal Green LU*
🕐 *Mon-Fri 10am-5pm*

A specialist Buddhist bookshop with an extensive selection of books on Buddhism from most traditions. There are also meditation stools and cushions, statues, malas and cards. The Centre runs a range of courses and classes – contact them for information.

London City Mission Bookshop

🖭 *175 Tower Bridge Road, SE1 2AH*
☎ *020 7234 3580*
✎ *020 7403 6711*
🖉 *www.lcm.org.uk*
🚌 *London Bridge LU/Rail, Tower Hill LU*
🕐 *Mon-Fri 9am-4pm*

Small selection of books on Christianity and theology in the reception area of the Mission.

London Metropolitan University Bookshop

🖭 *The Basement, Calcutta House, Old Castle Street, E1 7NT*
☎ *020 7426 0442*
🖉 *www.johnsmith.co.uk*
🚌 *Aldgate East LU*
🕐 *Mon-Fri 9am-5.30pm*

Academic store stocking books related to the specialisms of the University – education, social work, counselling and speech therapy.

London Review Bookshop

London Review Bookshop

⌧ *14 Bury Place, WC1A 2JL*

☎ *020 7269 9030*

✆ *020 7269 9033*

✎ *www.lrb.co.uk/lrbshop*

🚌 *Tottenham Court Road or Holborn LU*

🕐 *Mon-Sat 10am-6.30pm, Sun 12noon-6pm*

A serious but not academic bookshop with a light and spacious atmosphere and chairs for comfortable browsing. The shop covers all areas but is particularly well-represented in literature, critical theory, literary studies, poetry (especially well covered), philosophy, history, politics and current affairs. There are journals on associated subjects, a regular catalogue and plenty of events are organised.

London Transport Museum Shop

⌧ *Covent Garden Piazza, WC2E 7BB*

☎ *020 7379 6344*

✎ *www.ltmuseum.co.uk*

🚌 *Covent Garden LU*

🕐 *Mon-Thurs, Sat & Sun 10am-6pm, Fri 11am-6pm*

Reflecting the content of the museum, the shop sells books, DVDs and videos covering most aspects of transport in trainspotterish detail. The emphasis is British but there is also some overseas material. Many titles are from specialist publishers such as British Bus Publishing, Capital Transport, Oxford Publishing Company, Ian Allan and Middleton Press. For those less interested in the Routemaster there are London guides and a huge selection of posters, cards and souvenirs – London Underground map boxer shorts anyone?

Lovejoys

⌧ *99A Charing Cross Road, WC2H 0DP*

☎ *020 7734 8175*

🚌 *Leicester Square & Tottenham Court Road LU*

🕐 *Mon-Sat 10am-10.30pm, Sun 12noon-8pm*

The ground floor features a range of new full price and discounted books in many subjects areas including film, music and military books. There's also a good selection of historical DVDs and a range of DVDs of films from 1920s to 1960s especially war and Western films. Lovejoy's stock of adult videos and books is kept well out of general view in the basement.

New Bookshops

M

Maghreb Bookshop

⌨ *45 Burton Street, WC1H 9AL*

☎/✎ *020 7388 1840*

✎ *www.maghrebreview.com*

🚇 *Euston & King's Cross LU/Rail, Russell Square LU*

🕐 *Opening hours vary, ring before visiting*

A tiny shop specialising in new, rare and out of print books on the Maghreb countries of North Africa (Tunisia, Algeria, Libya, Morocco and Mauritania), the Arab World and Islam. Many of the books are unavailable elsewhere (the shop claims 'here you can find the unfindable'), and they offer a worldwide mail order service.

Magma

✎ *www.magmabooks.com*

These compact spaces stock a top-notch range of cutting edge art (including street art), graphics, animation, media, design, architecture and photography books, magazines, DVDs, stationary, T-shirts and multi-media materials. There's also a branch in Manchester.

Clerkenwell

⌨ *117-119 Clerkenwell Road, EC1R 5BY*

☎ *020 7242 9503*

✎ *020 7242 9504*

🚇 *Farringdon LU/Rail, Chancery Lane LU*

🕐 *Mon-Sat 10am-7pm*

Covent Garden

⌨ *8 Earlham Street, WC2H 9RY*

☎ *020 7240 8498*

🚇 *Leicester Square LU*

🕐 *Mon-Sat 10am-7pm, Sun 1pm-7pm*

Magma

Manor House Books

🏠 *The Sternberg Centre, 80 East End Road, Finchley, N3 2SY*

☎ *020 8349 9484*

✆ *020 8346 7430*

🖰 *www.bibliophile.net/John-Trotter-Books.htm*

🚌 *Finchley Central LU*

🕐 *Mon-Thurs 9am-5pm, Fri & Sun 9am-1pm*

A small but extremely well-stocked specialist shop selling academic books on religion, theology and Judaism including some discounted titles. About 95% of the stock is from American and difficult to find elsewhere. There are also a lot of children's books and glossy gift volumes. See p.207 for John Trotter Books which shares the premises.

Manna Christian Centre

🏠 *147-149 Streatham High Road, SW16 6EG*

☎ *020 8769 8588*

✆ *020 8677 0893*

🚌 *Streatham Rail*

🕐 *Mon-Sat 9.30am-5.30pm, opens at 10am on Thurs,*
closes at 6pm on Friday

Christian material including books on theology, prayer, scripture and the Christian way of life as well as a children's department. There is also a small café attached to the shop.

Maritime Books

- 66 Royal Hill, SE10 8RT
- 020 8853 1727
- 020 8853 1727
- anthony@anthonysimmonds.demon.co.uk
- Greenwich Rail/DLR
- Ring for opening hours.

A specialist shop carrying 12,000–15,000 books including full-price, remaindered, second-hand, and antiquarian books on all things maritime. This is the only shop with this specialism in London. It's a short walk from the town centre in Greenwich but definitely worth the trip if this is your thing.

Marylebone Books

- University of Westminster, 35 Marylebone Road, NW1 5LS
- 020 7911 5049
- 020 7911 5046
- bookshop@westminster.ac.uk
- Baker Street LU
- Mon-Thurs 9.30-6.30pm, Fri 9.30am-5.30pm

Note: For 4 weeks from mid-Sept and 2 weeks from the second week in Feb (i.e. at the start of semesters) they are open Mon-Thurs 9.30am-8.30pm, Fri as usual plus Sat 9.30am-5.30pm. From the beginning of June until the start of the new semester in Sept they close at 5.30pm every evening

Located in the courtyard of the main University of Westminster campus the shop only stocks academic books relevant to the university's courses. Non University of Westminster customers need to report to Reception from where they will be collected or escorted to the shop.

Medical Books Plus

- ICSM, Reynolds Building, St Dunstan's Road, W6 8RP
- 020 7594 0767
- 020 7594 0767
- medicalbooksplus@hotmail.com
- Baron's Court LU
- Mon-Fri 11am-4.30pm

Specialist medical bookshop stocking the material needed by the undergraduate medical students in the college. The bookshop is inside the college buildings and security issues mean that visitors from outside should telephone first to say they are coming.

Mega-City Comics

- 18 Inverness Street, NW1 7HJ
- ☎ 020 7485 9320
- ✆ 020 7428 0700
- ✎ www.megacitycomics.co.uk
- 🚌 Camden Town LU
- 🕐 Mon-Wed & Sat-Sun 10am-6pm, Thurs & Fri 10am-7pm

Situated in the Inverness Street Market just north of Camden Town tube station, this store features comics and a range of graphic novels, with a considerable selection of imported titles and back issues. The website contains a vast listing of material that simply won't fit into the shop.

Menorah Book Centre

- 16 Russell Parade, Golders Green Road, NW11 9NN
- ☎ 020 8458 8289
- ✆ 020 8731 8403
- 🚌 Brent Cross LU
- 🕐 Sun-Thurs 9.30am-6pm, Fri 9.30am-1.30pm (12.30pm in winter)

Specialist Jewish bookseller with a good stock of Hebrew and English books on all aspects of Jewish religion, history, culture and life.

Mesoirah Bookshop

- 61 Oldhill Street, N16 6LU
- ☎ 020 8809 4310
- 🚌 Stoke Newington Rail
- 🕐 Sun-Thurs 9am-9pm, Fri 9am-4pm (1pm in winter)

Specialist Jewish bookseller whose stock includes books in Hebrew and English and a wide range of religious goods.

Metal Bulletin Books

- 16 Lower Marsh, SE1 7RJ
- ☎ 020 7827 9977
- ✆ 020 7928 6539
- 🚌 Waterloo LU/Rail
- 🕐 Mon-Fri 9am-4.30pm

Extremely specialist bookseller and publisher of material about the technical aspects of metal. The items for sale include magazines and a large number of directories and technical publications.

Metanoia Book Service

⊡ *14 Shepherds Hill, N6 5AQ*

☎ *020 8340 8775*

✆ *020 8341 6807*

✐ *www.menno.org*

🚌 *Highgate LU*

🕐 *Mon-Fri 9am-5pm*

A specialist shop stocking a range of titles exploring Christian perspectives on justice and peace drawing on an Anabaptist theological perspective and including many North American publications. They have strong sections on conflict and mediation and regard themselves as selling titles more radical than those likely to be found in more traditional Christian bookshops.

Metropolitan Tabernacle Bookshop

⊡ *Pastor Street, Elephant and Castle, SE1 6SD*

☎ *020 7735 7076*

✆ *020 7735 7989*

✐ *www.tabernaclebookshop.org*

🚌 *Elephant & Castle LU*

🕐 *Mon-Fri 9am-5.30pm, Sat 10am-1pm*

The Metropolitan Tabernacle is just opposite the huge shopping centre at the Elephant and Castle. This is a specialist Christian bookshop which also sells videos, DVDs, tapes and CDs of religious teachings alongside the books.

mph Bookshop

⊡ *25 Marylebone Road, NW1 5JR*

☎ *020 7467 5106*

✆ *020 7467 5229*

✐ *www.mph.org*

🚌 *Baker Street LU*

🕐 *Mon-Fri 9am-5pm*

A Christian bookshop located on the ground floor of Methodist Church House in central London, almost opposite Madam Tussaud's. It stocks books on all aspects of religion and theology including mph publications and children's books, as well as music, stationery and greetings cards.

Good as
its words.

FREE

JULIET GARDINER
WARTIME
BRITAIN 1939–1945

headline

Metropolitan Books

Metropolitan Books

🖃 *49 Exmouth Market, EC1R 4QL*

☎ *020 7278 6900*

✆ *020 7278 3433*

🖉 *www.metropolitanbooks.co.uk*

🚌 *Farringdon LU/Rail*

🕐 *Mon-Fri 10.30am-6.30pm, Sat 10.30am-6pm*

A lovely little bookshop selling new books on just about every subject but especially strong in fiction, children's titles, politics and history. The stock is well organised and the helpful staff run an efficient ordering system if they don't have what you want. A wonderful bookshop.

Midheaven

🖃 *396 Caledonian Road, N1 1DN*

☎ *020 7607 4133*

✆ *020 7700 6717*

🖉 *www.midheavenbooks.com*

🚌 *Caledonian Road LU, Caledonian Road & Barnsbury Rail*

🕐 *Mon-Sat 10.30am-5.30pm (closes 2.30pm on Thursdays)*

Specialist shop selling mostly new but also a few second-hand books on astrology (mostly Western astrology but with a few Vedic titles) as well as computer software. They are also agents for Astro★Intelligence (the world's most advanced astrological computer reports).

T Miles and Company Ltd

🖃 *66 King Henry's Walk, Islington, N1 4NJ*

☎ *020 7241 4466*

✆ *020 7241 6224*

🖉 *tmilesandco@hotmail.com*

🚌 *Highbury and Islington LU/Rail*

🕐 *Mon-Fri 9am-5pm*

A small shop mainly selling children's books and educational resources, but there is also a reasonable choice of local history titles, and other general books can be ordered.

Motor Books

🖥 *33 St Martin's Court, WC2N 4AN*

☎ *020 7836 5376/6728/3800*

📠 *020 7497 2539*

🖱 *www.motorbooks.co.uk*

🚇 *Leicester Square LU*

🕐 *Mon-Fri 9.30am-6pm (Thurs-7pm), Sat 10.30am-5.30pm*

The world's oldest motoring bookshop that has been on its present site, just off Charing Cross Road, since 1957. The shop (actually there are two here, just a few yards apart) is overflowing with books, magazines and DVDs on motoring, railways, canals, aviation and naval and military subjects. They estimate they stock around 35,000 books and DVDs.

95

Murder One

Murder One and Heartlines

- 76-78 Charing Cross Road, WC2H 0AA
- 020 7734 3483
- 020 7734 3429
- www.murderone.co.uk
- Leicester Square LU
- Mon-Wed 10am-7pm, Thurs-Sat 10am-8pm

Specialists in new and second-hand paperback and hardback crime and new romantic fiction. Crime lover's should ignore the rather pastel shades of the ground floor near the door and head further into the shop for the huge range of crime books.

Museum in Docklands Shop

- No 1 Warehouse, West India Quay,
  Hertsmere Road, E14 4AL
- 0870 444 3857
- West India Quay DLR
- Daily 10am-6pm

The emphasis in this bookshop is the same as that of the museum, namely the story of London's river, port and people from pre-Roman times through to the recent regeneration of the Docklands area. The book stock includes both adult and children's titles and takes in the Thames, local history, shipping, pirates, slavery, engineering and trade.

The Museum of Garden History Shop

- Lambeth Palace Road, SE1 7LB
- 020 7401 8865
- 020 7401 8869
- www.museumgardenhistory.org
- Lambeth North, Westminster & Vauxhall LU; Waterloo LU/Rail
- Daily 10.30am-5pm (closed for a short period at the end of
  December/beginning of Jan – contact Museum for details)

The gift shop attached to this charming specialist museum features a small but fascinating range of horticultural titles concentrating on the history of gardens worldwide and includes many that you won't find elsewhere. There are also some general books on London. They also sell attractive cards and gifts related to the museum.

The Museum of London Shop

⌨ *London Wall, EC2Y 5HN*

☎ *0870 444 3852*

✆ *020 7600 1058*

✍ *www.museumoflondon.org.uk*

🚌 *St Paul's or Barbican LU*

🕐 *Mon-Sat 10am-5.50pm, Sun 12noon-5.50pm*

London's history is of course the raison d'etre of this enjoyable museum. The shop unsurprisingly carries an extensive choice of books for adults and children (they estimate more than 1500 titles) concentrating on the city's history from Celtic, Roman and Viking times up to the present day including social history, art and architecture, food, fashion and transport. London-based fiction also features, as do specialist titles published by the Museum of London and the Museum of London Archaeology Service. It's all topped off with no end of gift and souvenir ideas for museum visitors.

Music Room

⌨ *19 Denmark St, WC2H 8NE*

☎ *020 7240 7777*

✍ *www.musicroom.com*

🚌 *Tottenham Court Road LU*

🕐 *Mon-Sat 10am-8pm, Sun 11am-5pm*

A bright, airy shop selling a wide selection of popular and classical sheet music, tutors and song books for all instruments. There are reference books and biographies on sale as well as DVDs and musical instruments. In the same small road as Argents (see p.10) and Rose-Morris (see p.120).

Muswell Hill Bookshop

⌨ *72 Fortis Green Road, N10 3HN*

☎ *020 8444 7588*

✆ *020 8442 0693*

✍ *www.muswellhillbooks.com*

🚌 *Highgate LU*

🕐 *Mon-Sat 9.30am-6pm, Sun 12noon-5pm*

In the main Muswell Hill shopping drag and opposite the Children's Bookshop (see p.45), this double-fronted general bookshop is extremely well-stocked with a very wide selection of fiction and non-fiction all stocked in considerable depth, including many subject areas rarely found in local shops, such as philosophy, politics, literary criticism and psychology. There are also cards, gift stationery and a community notice board. Café on the Hill is almost next door and is a great spot for some refreshment.

My Back Pages – see p.193

Mysteries

- 9-11 Monmouth Street, WC2H 9DA
- ☎ 020 7240 3688
- 🖝 www.mysteries.co.uk
- 🚌 Leicester Square LU
- 🕐 Mon-Fri 10am-7pm, Sat 10am-6pm, Sun 12noon-6pm

A shop specialising in anything associated with what could loosely be called 'New Age' subjects. The excellent range of books covers spirituality, yoga, health, self-development, numerology, palmistry, Tarot, channelling, Tibetan and Western Buddhism, astrology, mythology, shamanism and magic. There are also CDs and audio tapes for hypnosis, meditation and yoga plus huge numbers of accessories and gift items. Psychic readings of tarot, crystals and palms are available.

N

The National Army Museum Bookshop

- Royal Hospital Road, SW3 4HT
- ☎ 020 7730 0717
- ✆ 020 7823 6573
- 🖝 www.national-army-museum.ac.uk
- 🚌 Sloane Square LU
- 🕐 Daily 10am-5.30pm

The museum covers the history of the British army and the life of the soldier from the English Civil War through to the present day. Its bookshop stocks volumes dealing with topics across the same spectrum, as well as gift items. There are lots of books by specialist publishers such as Osprey, Leo Cooper, Pen and Sword and Wordsworth Military Library but also plenty of interest to general readers.

The National Gallery

Trafalgar Square, WC2N 5DN

☎ *General 020 7747 2885, Main shop 020 7747 2461*

www.nationalgallery.org.uk

Charing Cross LU/Rail

Daily 10am-5.45pm (Wednesday until 8.45pm)

There are three shops in the gallery; the small Room Three Shop in the older part of the building, another small outlet in the East Wing and the main shop in the Sainsbury Wing, with an extensive selective selection of art books. A lot of space is taken up with an array of postcards, greetings cards, stationery (this is the place to get your 'The Sunflowers' notebook, ruler or fridge magnet) and gifts. However, the range of books is excellent, including guides to the collection, exhibition catalogues and gift books, with sections on individual artists, art history, conservation, art theory, museum studies, architecture and sculpture. The Thames and Hudson World of Art series is prominently displayed, as are books from Phaidon and Taschen. There are also magazines, videos and DVDs of interest. Children's art books and London guides form part of the selection. The best place for refreshment is the National Gallery Café accessed from the Gallery and from St Martin's Place.

The National Gallery

National Map Centre

🖳 *22-24 Caxton Street, SW1H 0QU*
☎ *020 7222 2466*
✆ *020 7222 2619*
🖎 *www.mapstore.co.uk*
🚌 *St James's Park LU*
🕐 *Mon-Fri 9am-5pm*

Specialising in the full range of Ordnance Survey maps there is also a huge stock of guidebooks, travelogues, glossy picturebooks, street atlases and worldwide maps arranged over two floors.

The National Portrait Gallery Bookshop

🖳 *St Martin's Place, WC2H 0HE*
☎ *020 7306 0055*
✆ *020 7306 0056*
🖎 *www.npg.org.uk*
🚌 *Charing Cross LU/Rail, Leicester Square LU*
🕐 *Mon-Wed & Sat-Sun 10am-6pm, Thurs & Fri 10am-9pm*

If you are looking for books, ignore the more prominent gift shop on the ground floor and head down to the bookshop in the basement where there is an extensive selection of art, history, costume, biography and photography books and magazines. There's also a good choice of children's books. The café next door to the shop is an ideal place to rest weary feet.

National Theatre Bookshop

🖳 *South Bank, SE1 9PX*
☎ *020 7452 3456*
✆ *020 7452 3457*
🖎 *www.nationaltheatre.org.uk/bookshop*
🚌 *Waterloo LU/Rail*
🕐 *Mon-Sat 10am-10.45pm (check times on Bank Holidays)*
Note: Bookstalls in the foyers of Olivier and Cottesloe theatres are open before and after performances and during intervals.

At ground floor level in the Royal National Theatre complex this excellent shop has a stock of more than 6,000 items on all aspects of the theatre from ancient to modern times with books, magazines and playtexts supplemented by recordings on audiotape, CD, video and DVD. It is a brilliant shop for professionals involved in the theatre or for anyone interested in the subject. There's an excellent range of merchandise as well.

The Natural History Museum Shop

📠 *Cromwell Road, SW7 5BD*
☎ *020 7942 5310*
🖋 *www.nhm.ac.uk*
🚌 *South Kensington LU*
🕐 *Mon-Sat 10am-5.50pm, Sun 11am-5.50pm*

Alongside all the usual museum gifts there is a selection of books on all subjects relevant to the museum including evolution, dinosaurs, gardening, geology and the whole of the plant and animal kingdoms. As would be expected, they sell the full range of Natural History Museum publications (both academic and popular). There are also a few relevant books in the Earth Store in the Earth Galleries and the Dino Store close to the dinosaur exhibits.

New Beacon Books

📠 *76 Stroud Green Road, N4 3EN*
☎ *020 7272 4889*
🖋 *020 7281 4662*
🖋 *newbeaconbooks@btconnect.com*
🚌 *Finsbury Park LU*
🕐 *Mon-Sat 10.30am-6pm*

Long-established and highly experienced specialist sellers of new books on Black Britain and Europe, Africa, the Caribbean and African America plus plenty of titles on Asia, the Middle East and South America and well-stocked sections on cultural and women's studies. Fiction and non-fiction titles are also sold here and there is a great children's section. The staff are knowledgeable, can produce specialist book lists to cater for individual interests and offer a worldwide mail order service. Greetings cards and magazines are also available and there's plenty of information on events of interest.

New Covenant Christian Bookshop

📠 *Elephant and Castle Shopping Centre, SE1 6TE*
☎ *020 7703 9363*
🚌 *Elephant and Castle LU/Rail*
🕐 *Mon-Fri 10am-6.30pm, Sat 10am-6pm*

In the rather cheerless surroundings of the upper floor of the Elephant and Castle Shopping Centre this shop stocks adult and children's books on Christianity. There are Bibles in several languages and also Christian music CDs and Christian DVDs.

Newham Bookshop

- 745-747 Barking Road, E13 9ER
- ☎ 020 8552 9993
- ✆ 020 8471 2589
- ✉ info@newhambooks.fsnet.co.uk
- 🚌 Upton Park LU
- 🕐 Tues-Fri 9.30am-5pm, Sat 10am-5pm

Just around the corner from West Ham football ground this bookshop is a real treasure. Its general stock includes excellent fiction, poetry and drama sections and in non-fiction it is strong on history, local history (for which it is especially renowned), social work, counselling, sociology, sport (especially football), education, business, multi-ethnic issues, politics and a cracking range of magazines. The children's section takes up about half the shop covering babies to teens with loads of educational books and games as well as welcoming little chairs for small visitors. Newham books issues a twice-monthly newsletter (available on e-mail as well as in print), hosts events and signings both in the shop and elsewhere and there's also a regular reading group. The poet Benjamin Zephaniah lives locally and actively supports the shop.

Nomad Books

- 781 Fulham Road, SW6 5HA
- ☎ 020 7736 4000
- ✆ 020 7736 7081
- 🚌 Parson's Green LU
- 🕐 Mon-Fri 9am-8pm, Sat 10am-6pm, Sun 11am-5pm

A Fabulous, welcoming shop – there's even a café for book-buyers in need of sustenance serving drinks, cakes and sandwiches. The downstairs specialises in travel with an excellent selection of guidebooks, maps, travel literature and fiction associated with various destinations. Upstairs houses the café and the general stock and there's a big children's section at the rear. There is a regular reading group (phone for details) and a loyalty scheme.

Notting Hill Books - see p.194

Nutri Centre Bookshop

7 Park Crescent, W1B 1PF
020 7323 2382
www.nutricentre.com
Great Portland Street LU
Mon-Fri 9am-7pm, Sat 10am-5pm

Situated in the basement of the Hale Clinic, this bookshop carries an enormous selection of books on health and nutrition, alternative and complementary therapies, personal and spiritual development and oriental medical traditions. A great many of their titles are North American imports so hard to find elsewhere. The atmosphere is supremely relaxed, with no shortage of tables and chairs for leisurely browsing and the staff are approachable and highly knowledgeable.

O

OCS Bookshop

2 Grosvenor Parade, Uxbridge Road, W5 3NN
020 8992 6335
020 8993 0891
bookshop@ocsworldwide.co.uk
Ealing Common LU
Tues-Sat 10.30am-6pm, Sun 10.30am-5pm

A couple of minutes walk from the underground (turn right outside the station) specialising in books, magazines and newspapers in Japanese for adults and children. It also stocks courses and dictionaries for Japanese language learners and a selection of books in English about Japan including cookery, culture and art. Japanese stationery is on sale as is a range of Japanese foods.

Offstage

37 Chalk Farm Road, NW1 8AJ
020 7485 4996
offstagebookshop@aol.com
www.offstagebooks.com
Chalk Farm LU
Mon-Fri 10am-6pm, Sat 2pm-6pm

Half of this shop is a specialist film and theatre bookshop with a comprehensive selection of books including drama history and criticism, theory, writing, costume, design, scripts, physical theatre and dance, direction, animation and production. Magazines and DVDs complement the book stock and there's also a notice board advertising events, workshops and classes of interest. The other half of the shop houses a general second-hand stock specialising in fiction, art and photography; with a good range of quality books at reasonable prices.

Orbis Bookshop
- 206 Blythe Road, W14 0HH
- 020 7602 5541
- 020 8742 7686
- bookshop@orbis-books.co.uk
- Shepherd's Bush & Hammersmith LU
- Mon-Fri 10am-5pm

A shop specialising in Polish books, dictionaries, magazines and newspapers, the books cover history, literature, fiction, linguistics and memoirs – there are no technology or science books. They also have a good selection of books in Czech and Slovak.

Orvis
- 36A Dover Street, W1S 4NS
- 020 7499 7496
- 020 7491 8941
- www.orvis.co.uk
- Green Park LU
- Mon-Fri 9.30am-6pm (Tues opens at 10am), Sat 10am-4pm

This is a specialist fishing and outdoor shop selling equipment and clothing. They also have a large stock of books on all kinds of angling from deep sea to fly.

Ottakar's

www.ottakars.co.uk

A successful nationwide chain which has expanded rapidly since the opening of its first store in 1987. It now has more than 130 branches from Aberystwyth to Yeovil and several in London and further stores are planned. Their hallmark is welcoming, attractive shops with easy chairs, good music, well-displayed stock and special offers. They were recognised as the Bookselling Company of the Year in 2003 and 2004 at the British Book Awards. Branches at:

Ottakar's - Putney

- 6-6a Exchange Centre, Putney, SW15 1TW
- 020 8780 2401
- 020 8780 0861
- Putney Bridge LU
- Mon, Wed, Fri & Sat 9am-6pm; Tues 9.30am-6pm; Thurs 9am-7pm; Sun 11am-5pm

A large branch which positively invites browsing with comfy chairs, intelligently selected and displayed stock, a children's area and a fabulous coffee shop upstairs.

Ottakar's - Clapham Junction

- 70 St John's Road, SW11 1PT
- 020 7978 5844
- 020 7978 5855
- Clapham Junction Rail
- Mon, Wed, Thurs & Fri 9am-7pm; Tues 9.30am-7pm; Sat 9am-6pm; Sun 11am-5pm

This branch has an especially big children's section but also the usual solid range in all other areas.

Ottakar's - Greenwich

- 51 Greenwich Church St, SE10 9BL
- 020 8853 8530
- 020 8305 2841
- Cutty Sark DLR, Greenwich Rail/DLR
- Mon-Sat 9am-6pm (Tues from 9.30am), Sun 11am-5pm

Just a few yards from the riverside and the Cutty Sark in Greenwich, this two storey shop has a great atmosphere and a good coffee shop upstairs. There are also adult and teen reading groups that meet in the shop.

Ottakar's - Wood Green

⌨ *Unit 5-6 Shopping City, High Road, Wood Green, N22 6YDF*

☎ *020 8889 3777*

✆ *020 8889 9895*

🚌 *Wood Green LU*

🕐 *Mon, Wed, Thurs-Sat 9am-6.30pm;*
Tues 9.30am-6pm; Sun 11am-5pm

Ottakar's - Walthamstow

⌨ *Unit 30-31 Selborne Walk Shopping Centre,*
26 Selborne Walk, Walthamstow, E17 7JR

☎ *020 8521 3669*

✆ *020 8520 1221*

🚌 *Walthamstow LU*

🕐 *Mon-Sat 9am-6pm (Tues from 9.30am), Sun 11am-5pm*

Ottakar's at the Science Museum

⌨ *Exhibition Road, SW7 2DD*

☎ *020 7942 4481*

✆ *020 7942 4482*

🚌 *South Kensington LU*

🕐 *Daily 10am-6pm*

This shop sells a huge range of children's books on all subjects and adult books on areas covered by the museum. As you might expect there's a large choice of Science Museum publications as well as a big selection of videos and CD-ROMs. While you are in the Museum have a look in the gift shop, which offers further purchasing opportunities with a highly imaginative array of gifts and souvenirs for adults and children.

Oval Bookshop

⌨ *28B Clapham Road, SW9 0JQ*

☎ *0800 389 0463*

✎ *www.ovalbookshop.tbphost.co.uk*

🚌 *Oval LU*

🕐 *Mon-Fri 10am-7pm, Sat 9am-5pm, Sun 10am-5.30pm*

A cracking local bookshop just a few seconds walk from the Oval underground station. Despite the relatively small space the subject coverage is impressively broad and the shop feels light and airy – there are even chairs for browsing. The selection of children's books and arts titles is particularly strong and there are also plenty of attractive cards for sale.

The Owl and the Pussycat

106 Northfield Avenue, W13 9RT

020 8810 0880

020 8810 0880

www.pitshangerbooks.co.uk

Northfields LU

Mon-Fri 9.30am-5.30pm, Sat 9am-5.30pm

This welcome new addition to the West London book scene dedicates about 80% of its stock to books for and about children. There are sections on pregnancy through to the mid-teens (including the invaluable GCSE study guides). The adult stock includes bestsellers in fiction and non-fiction plus travel and gift books and a selection of gifts, games and jigsaw puzzles completes the stock. Their sister shop is the equally delightful Pitshanger Bookshop (see p.113).

Owl Bookshop

209 Kentish Town Road, NW5 2JU

020 7485 7793

020 7267 7765

owlbookshop1@btconnect.com

Camden Town & Kentish Town LU

Mon-Sat 9.30am-6pm, Sun 12noon-4.30pm

This is a rightly popular local shop that is well-stocked in all area with some tempting special offers. Children's books are a particular strength here and the shop is suitably child-friendly and welcoming. Regular book readings, poetry evenings and events are an extra attraction.

P

Padre Pio Bookshop

⌧ *264 Vauxhall Bridge Road, SW1V 1BB*

☎ *020 7834 5363*

🚇 *Victoria LU/Rail*

🕐 *Mon-Sat 10am-6pm (open Friday until 6.30pm and closed during daily prayers 3pm-4pm)*

Small Catholic bookshop selling Bibles and prayer books as well as theological books and videos, cards, rosaries, statues and religious gift items.

Pages of Fun

⌧ *16 Terminus Place, SW1V 1JR*

☎ *020 7834 7747*

🚇 *Victoria LU/Rail*

🕐 *Mon-Sat 9am-10pm, Sun 12noon-8pm*

This discount and full-price bookshop, opposite Victoria Train Station, specialises in crime and sci-fi paperbacks, plus military, film and cinema, cookery and glossy travel books. Its stock of sexually explicit adult material is tucked away at the back of the store.

Palmer's Green Bookshop

⌧ *379 Green Lanes, N13 4JG*

☎ *020 8882 2088*

✆ *020 8882 0660*

✉ *pgreenbooks@aol.com*

🚇 *Palmer's Green Rail*

🕐 *Mon-Sat 9.30am-6pm, Sun 12noon-5pm*

This is an attractive, general bookshop located in the heart of an extremely literary part of London. With many well known writers living in the area this shop has acquired a reputation as a venue for readings. As well as a good general stock they have a particularly fine children's section.

Pan Bookshop

📖 *158-162 Fulham Road, SW10 9PR*

☎ *020 7373 4997*

✆ *020 7244 7546*

✎ *panbookshop@btclick.com*

🚇 *South Kensington LU*

🕑 *Mon-Fri 9am-10pm, Sat 9.30am-10pm, Sun 10am-9pm*

Twice winner of The Independent Bookseller of the Year award at the National Book Awards, this shop combines a first-rate general stock with a fabulous atmosphere. The displays are enticing, staff are knowledgeable and enthusiastic and all major subject areas are extremely well covered. The art and design sections are particularly broad and signed first editions of new books are a speciality. The children's corner is full of things to lure junior browsers into reading. A fortnightly e-mail newsletter contains reviews of newly published books. This stretch of Fulham Road abounds in coffee shops where you can relax with your purchases. Well worth a trip across town, made easy by the long opening hours.

Parliamentary Bookshop

📖 *12 Bridge Street, Parliament Square, SW1A 2JX*

☎ *020 7219 3890*

✆ *020 7219 3866*

✎ *www.bookshop.parliament.uk*

🚇 *Westminster LU*

🕑 *Mon-Thurs 9.30am-5.30pm, Fri 9am-4pm*

Right opposite the Houses of Parliament this is the place to pick up official parliamentary publications including Hansard, Minutes, Select Committee Reports, Command Papers, Bills and Acts. The shop also stocks a range of material on parliamentary procedure, government and politics.

Pathfinder Bookshop

⌨ *120 Bethnal Green Road, E2 6DG*

☎/✉ *020 7613 3855*

✎ *www.pathfinderpress.com*

✎ *admin@pathfinderbooks.co.uk*

🚌 *Bethnal Green LU, Liverpool St LU/Rail, Shoreditch LU (part-time)*

🕓 *Mon-Fri 10am-7pm, Sat 10am-5pm, Sun 11am-3pm*

The struggles of working people throughout the world and black and women's studies are the focus of this radical bookshop at the northern end of Brick Lane – the entrance is actually on Brick Lane. Their extensive stock features numerous titles on 'liberation' movements and their leaders including Fidel Castro, Marx, Trotsky and Lenin. The shop also stocks current and back copies of New Internationalist – 'A Magazine of Marxist Politics and Theory'. If you join the Pathfinder's Readers Club (details from the shop) you get at least 15% discount on all Pathfinder titles. There's a weekly programme of events relevant to the subjects covered by the bookshop.

Pauline Books and Media

⌨ *199 Kensington High Street, W8 6BA*

☎ *020 7937 9591*

✉ *020 7937 9910*

✎ *www.pauline-uk.org*

🚌 *High Street Kensington LU*

🕓 *Mon-Sat 9.30am-5.30pm*

Christian bookshop with a huge range of books, CDs and DVDs and prayer posters. The books cover all areas of Christian theology, scripture, liturgy and prayer as well as everyday issues from a Christian perspective. There is a large children's selection and also books on world religions.

Persephone Books

- 59 Lamb's Conduit Street, WC1N 3NB
- 020 7242 9292
- 020 7242 9272
- www.persephonebooks.co.uk
- Holborn LU
- Mon-Fri 9am-6pm, Sat 12noon-5pm

One of a cluster of bookshops in the Lamb's Conduit/Great Ormond Street area. Perspehone is a small, independent publisher that republishes forgotten and neglected fiction and non-fiction in beautifully produced volumes with colourful endpapers and bookmarks. They issue two new books each quarter and their authors include Katherine Mansfield, Monica Dickens, and Marghanita Laski. Their catalogue and The Persephone Quarterly are both rewarding reads and enthusiasts can join the mailing list. Persephone lunches, books groups and even readers weekends are organised. A gift-wrapping service is available. Lamb's Conduit Street has several coffee bars – Sid's is next door.

Photo Books International

- 99 Judd Street, WC1H 9NE
- 020 7813 7363
- 020 7813 7363
- www.pbi-books.com
- King's Cross and St Pancras LU/Rail
- Wed-Sat 11am to 6pm (or by appointment)

A fabulous selection of new and used photography books from around the world are on display in this small and wonderfully atmospheric shop a few minutes walk from the British Library. The knowledge and enthusiasm of the owners is as encyclopedic as their stock and, for lovers of photography, this shop should be a place of regular pilgrimage.

Photographers' Gallery Bookshop

- 8 Great Newport Street, WC2H 7HY
- 020 7831 1772
- 020 7240 0591
- www.photonet.org.uk
- Leicester Square LU
- Mon-Sat 11am-6pm, Sun 12noon-6pm (most Thursdays until 8pm)

Well-known for its programme of innovative high quality photographic exhibitions, this gallery boasts a small specialist bookshop, tucked away at the rear of the gallery. The shop stocks an impressive range of photographic monographs and anthologies plus books on art theory and a few technical publications. In addition there are some collectable limited editions, a range of magazines, postcards and gifts. If you are in need of refreshment there's an excellent café at No 5.

The Pitshanger Bookshop

🖃 *141 Pitshanger Lane, W5 1RH*

☎ /✆ *020 8991 8131*

✑ *www.pitshangerbooks.co.uk*

🚌 *Ealing Broadway LU (then a bus)*

🕓 *Mon-Fri 9.30am-5.30pm, Sat 9am-5.30pm*

Located next to the public library this is an attractive and well laid out local bookshop offering a welcoming atmosphere for browsers. The stock is both well organised and comprehensive and they have an efficient ordering system if they do not have what you are looking for. There's also a selection of greetings cards, gift stationery, audiobooks and children's games. They have a sister shop in Teddington (Tel 020 8614 5777) and The Owl and the Pussycat (see p.108) is a branch specialising in children's books.

Playin' Games

🖃 *33 Museum Street, WC1A 1LH*

☎ *020 7323 3080*

🖉 *www.playingames.co.uk*

🚌 *Tottenham Court Road LU*

🕐 *Mon-Sat 10am-6pm (Thurs until 7pm), Sun 12noon-6pm*

Shop selling all the equipment for a huge range of both popular and obscure board and indoor games, supported by an excellent selection of related books on games such as chess, Chinese chess, Go and Shogi.

PMS Bookshop

🖃 *240 King Street, W6 0RF*

☎/🖨 *020 8748 5522*

🚌 *Ravenscourt Park LU*

🕐 *Mon-Thurs, Sat 10am-6pm, Fri 10am-7pm*

Located in the Polish Centre, the shop specialises in Polish books including children's titles, music, DVDs, videos and magazines. There are also language courses and dictionaries for those who want to learn Polish and books in English about all aspects of Poland as well as translations of Polish authors. The shop also stocks a selection of Polish gifts and souvenir items.

Political Cartoon Gallery

🖃 *32 Store Street, WC1E 7BS*

☎ *020 7580 1114*

🖨 *020 7580 1822*

🖉 *www.politicalcartoon.co.uk*

🚌 *Goodge Street LU*

🕐 *Mon-Fri 9.30am-5.30pm, Sat 11.30am-5.30pm*

This gallery is devoted to the political cartoon and arranges regular exhibitions. In addition to the cartoons they have a stock of new and second-hand books about the art – some of which the publish themselves. The café in the basement has a mural including artwork by Steven Bell and Martin Ronson. If you are looking for a special gift, prices for the cartoons start at just over £100.

Pollock's Toy Museum

- 🏠 *1 Scala Street, W1T 2HL*
- ☎ *020 7636 3452*
- 🖉 *www.pollockstoymuseum.com*
- 🚌 *Goodge Street LU*
- 🕐 *Mon-Sat 10am-5pm*

The shop attached to this enchanting small museum has an old fashioned charm. As well as being a toy shop, stocking traditional toys and an extensive selection of the toy theatres it also sells a selection of books on the history of toys and toy collecting.

Primrose Hill Books

- 🏠 *134 Regent's Park Road, NW1 8XL*
- ☎ *020 7586 2022*
- ✆ *020 7722 9653*
- 🖉 *www.primrosehillbooks.co.uk*
- 🚌 *Chalk Farm LU*
- 🕐 *Mon-Fri 9.30am-6pm, Sat 10am-6pm, Sun 12noon-6pm*

A peach of a bookshop set on a quiet, somewhat recherché local shopping street. There's a huge general range of nicely displayed hardback and paperback stock; fiction, travel and biography are especially well represented. The area abounds with cafés if you haven't come prepared with a picnic for nearby Primrose Hill.

Arthur Probsthain

- 🏠 *41 Great Russell Street, WC1B 3PE*
- ☎ *020 7636 1096*
- ✆ *020 7636 1096*
- 🖉 *www.oriental-african-books.com*
- 🚌 *Tottenham Court Road LU*
- 🕐 *Mon-Fri 9.30am-5.30pm, Sat 11am-4pm*

A specialist in books on Oriental and African subjects including the regions languages. The stock combines new and second-hand books and features many titles that you are unlikely to find elsewhere. As well as being a useful source of difficult to find information, Probsthain's is also a kind of living museum with pictures of the founders of the company displayed on a back wall and a manual typewriter still clattering its way through the days correspondence. There are regular catalogues in every subject area. A great little shop.

Prospero's Books

- 📠 32 The Broadway, Crouch End, N8 9SU
- ☎ 020 8348 8900
- 📞 020 8348 3604
- ✉ prosperobks@aol.com
- 🚌 Crouch Hill Rail
- 🕐 Mon-Sat 9.30am-6pm, Sun 11.30am-5.30pm

A cosy, welcoming bookshop close to the clock tower in Crouch End's main shopping street. Despite not being very big, the shop manages to display a hefty selection of titles with particular strengths being art and design, travel, biography, history and fiction.

Protestant Truth Society Bookshop

- 📠 184 Fleet Street, EC4A 2HJ
- ☎/📞 020 7405 4960
- ✉ www.protestant-truth.org
- 🚌 Temple and Chancery Lane LU, Blackfriars LU/Rail
- 🕐 Mon-Fri 9.30am-5.30pm

Christian bookshop featuring a large selection of religious books including theology, the sermons of eminent preachers and inspirational works. Also children's books, greetings cards, music, DVDs and videos.

Q

The Quaker Bookshop

- 📠 Friends House, Euston Road, NW1 2BJ
- ☎ 020 7663 1030
- 📞 020 7663 1001
- ✉ www.quaker.org.uk/bookshop
- 🚌 Euston LU/Rail
- 🕐 Mon-Fri 9am-5pm (Mon until 7pm)

Bookshop operated by the Society of Friends (Quakers) specialising in Quaker books published in the UK and around the world. They carry a large stock on liberal Christianity, social responsibility, conflict resolution and peace work. There is also a selection of general fiction and children's titles.

Queen's Park Books

- 87 Salisbury Road, NW6 6NH
- 020 7625 1008
- 020 7625 1009
- Queens Park LU/Rail
- Mon-Sat 10am-7pm, Sun 12noon-5pm

General local bookshop, related to West End Lane Books (see p.160) and covering all general areas but with an emphasis on children's books. They organise book readings and launches, sell cards and stationery and have experience in ordering hard to find titles, especially from the United States.

R

RCOG

- 27 Sussex Place, NW1 4RG
- 020 7772 6275
- 020 7724 5991
- www.rcog.org.uk
- Baker Street LU
- Mon-Fri 9am-5pm

Specialist medical bookshop for the Royal College of Obstetricians and Gynaecologists, stocking what is probably the most extensive range of books on these subjects in the UK.

Reel Poster Gallery

- 72 Westbourne Grove, W2 5SH
- 020 7727 4488
- 020 7727 4499
- www.reelposter.com
- Bayswater LU
- Mon-Fri 11am-7pm, Sat 12noon-6pm

This light and airy gallery specialises in original film posters, but they also sell a selection of new and out-of-print books on the subject.

Regent Hall

- 275 Oxford Street, W1C 2DJ
- 020 7629 2766
- www.regenthall.co.uk
- Oxford Circus LU
- Mon-Sat 9.30am-4pm

A Christian bookshop, which also sells magazines, gifts and CDs, in the Salvation Army's Regent Hall, just a few yards away from Oxford Circus underground station. They also have an on site café.

RIBA Bookshop

- Rotal Institute of British Architects,
  66 Portland Place, W1B 1AD
- 020 7251 0791
- 020 7637 7185
- www.ribabookshops.com
- Regent's Park, Portland St, and Oxford Circus LU
- Mon-Fri 9.30am-5.30pm (Tues until 6.30pm), Sat 10am-5pm

Specialist architecture shop covering all aspects of the built environment including history, practice, law, design, green and sustainable architecture and management. There is an enormous selection of magazines, journals and monographs detailing the work of individual architects but also a great deal for the general reader who is interested in the urban environment. Gifts, posters and cards complete the stock. The RIBA Coffee Bar upstairs is one of the most restful eating spots in central London.

RICS Bookshop

⌗ *Lower Ground Floor, 12 Great George Street,*
Parliament Square, SW1P 3AD

☎ *020 7222 7000 (ask for London bookshop)*

✎ *020 7222 9430*

⌨ *www.ricsbooks.com*

🚌 *Westminster LU*

🕐 *Mon-Fri 9am-5.30pm (ring before making a special journey)*

Specialist shop selling books related to the theory and practice of chartered surveying including topics such as building, construction, architecture, business, management, engineering, surveying and law.

Riverside Bookshop

⌗ *18/19 Hay's Galleria, London Bridge, Tooley Street, SE1 2HD*

☎ *020 7378 1824*

✎ *020 7407 5315*

🚌 *London Bridge LU/Rail*

🕐 *Mon-Fri 9am-6pm, Sat 10am-6.30pm, Sun 11am-6.30pm*

Hay's Galleria is a large, airy shopping and restaurant complex on the South bank of the River Thames. This lovely small bookshop has a well-displayed, carefully chosen selection of books covering all general subjects and a friendly team of helpful staff.

The Rocks

⌨ *www.rockbookstores.com*

Both shops stock a large range of Christian books, audio material and greetings cards. Branches at:

⌗ *103 Tower Bridge Road, SE1 4TW*

☎ *020 7378 9076*

🚌 *Elephant & Castle LU/Rail (then bus)*

🕐 *Mon & Tues 10am-6pm, Wed & Thurs 10am-7pm,*
Fri & Sat 10am-8pm

and

⌗ *144 High Street, Harlesden, NW10 4SP*

☎ *020 8961 4522*

✎ *020 8961 4540*

🚌 *Willesden Junction LU/Rail*

🕐 *Mon & Tues 10am-6pm, Wed-Sat 10am-7pm*

Roundabout

370 Mare Street, E8 1HR

020 8985 8148

Hackney Central Rail

Mon-Fri 7am-6pm, Sat 7.30am-7.30pm

In the heart of Hackney's main shopping area, this newsagents and stationers also sells a selection of books. The range is wide with popular fiction, children's books and reference material to the fore and there are often discounts on titles.

Rose-Morris

11 Denmark St, WC2H 8TD

020 7836 4766

Tottenham Court Road LU

Mon-Sat 10am-6pm, Sun 11am-5pm

Sheet music, mostly modern, plus books on modern music including biographies and recording techniques.

The Royal Academy of Arts Shop

Burlington House, Piccadilly, W1J 0BD

020 7300 5757

www.royalacademy.org.uk

Piccadilly Circus & Green Park LU

Daily 10am-5.45pm (Fri until 9.45pm)

As befits this most august of art institutions, even the RA's shop occupies a commanding position at the top of the grand staircase of the entrance hall – there is no admission fee to this part of the building. The shop offers a selection of books for adults and children on the history of art, art techniques and the work of individual artists alongside exhibition catalogues and periodicals on art. Alongside the books there are excellent gifts suitable for all ages, attractive greetings cards and an extensive range of videos and DVDs about art.

Royal Court Theatre

⌑ *Sloane Square, SW1W 8AS*
☎ *020 7565 5024*
✎ *bookshop@royalcourttheatre.com*
🚇 *Sloane Square LU*
🕐 *Mon-Fri 3pm-10pm, Sat 2.30pm-10pm*

It's perhaps overstating the case to call this a bookshop but there's an area in the bar area downstairs that is dedicated to twentieth and twenty-first-century playtexts and books on the theory and practice of modern drama. Staff pride themselves on helping with the selection of audition pieces.

Ruposhi Bangla

⌑ *220 Tooting High Street, SW17 0SG*
☎ *020 8672 7843*
✆ *020 8767 9214*
✎ *www.ruposhibangla.co.uk*
🚇 *Tooting Broadway LU*
🕐 *Open by appointment*

This is a specialist shop selling a huge range Bengali books (including children's titles) from Bangladesh and India. The subject coverage is wide taking in all fiction and non-fiction areas. The stock also includes music, slides and maps as well as English translations of Bengali texts, Bengali language courses and books in Bengali about learning English.

S

St Christopher's Hospice Bookshop

⌑ *51-59 Lawrie Park Road, SE26 6DZ*
☎ *020 8768 4660*
✆ *020 8776 9345*
✎ *www.stchristophers.org.uk*
🚇 *Sydenham & Penge East Rail*
🕐 *Ring for opening times*

Specialist shop selling books on hospices, palliative care and bereavement including books for bereaved children (some of which the hospice publish).

St James's Art Books

⌨ *15 Piccadilly Arcade, SW1Y 6NH*

☎ *020 7495 6487*

✆ *020 7495 6490*

✉ *marco.angelini@virgin.net*

🚇 *Piccadilly Circus & Green Park LU*

🕐 *Mon-Sat 10am-6pm*

This shop specialises in books on Old Master painters, sculpture from the medieval age to the nineteenth-century and the decorative arts. There is also a fine selection of good-value modern prints, especially Matisse, Picasso and Chagall. Shelved floor to ceiling, the mix of new, second-hand and rare books is extensive. The entrance to Piccadilly Arcade is almost opposite the Royal Academy of Arts.

St Paul's

⌨ *Morpeth Terrace, SW1P 1EP*

☎ *020 7828 5582*

✆ *020 7828 3329*

✉ *www.stpauls.org.uk*

🚇 *Victoria LU/Rail*

🕐 *Mon-Sat 9.30am-6pm*

Next door to Westminster Cathedral, the stock in this shop is vast. In what must be one of the largest religious bookshops in London, every aspect of Christianity for both the lay reader and serious student is covered. They also stock a huge range of videos, tapes, CDs, DVDs, vestments, candles, greetings cards and gift items.

John Sandoe

⌨ *10 Blacklands Terrace, SW3 2SR*

☎ *020 7589 9473*

✆ *020 7581 2084*

✉ *www.johnsandoe.com*

🚇 *Sloane Square LU*

🕐 *Mon-Sat 9.30am-5.30pm (Wed until 7.30pm)*

Note: open Sundays in December 12noon-5pm and Mon, Tues, Thurs, Fri and Sat until 7pm

This diminuitive shop in a fabulous eighteenth-century building that used to be a poodle parlour, represents all that is good in bookselling and is justifiably one of the most renowned bookshops in London. Just fifty metres from the King's Road, the shop is packed to overflowing with an extensive and well chosen range of literature, arts, architecture, history, biography, reference, travel, drama and children's books with plenty of unusual editions and books you're unlikely to find elsewhere. The staff are incredibly enthusiastic, well-informed and welcoming, despite the danger of customers dislodging piles of books at every turn (have a look at the ingenious display system upstairs that makes the most of every inch). This place is well worth a visit. If you can't make it to the shop, the website is still an interesting experience and the shop issues four catalogues each year detailing forthcoming books and other favourites.

Sangeeta

- 📖 *22 Brick Lane, E1 6RF*
- ☎ *020 7247 5954*
- ✆ *020 7247 5941*
- ✍ *www.sangeetaltd.co.uk*
- 🚌 *Aldgate East LU*
- 🕐 *Daily 11am-9pm*

In the heart of the restaurant area of Brick Lane, this shop specialises in Bangladeshi books, newspapers, magazines and dictionaries including children's books plus British Asian lifestyle magazines. There's also a huge choice of music and films on tapes, CDs and DVDs

Sao Paulo Imports

- 📖 *Unit L1A, Queensway Market, 23-25 Queensway, WC2 4QJ*
- ☎ *020 7792 2931*
- ✆ *020 7243 0042*
- ✍ *www.spi-london.com*
- 🚌 *Bayswater & Queensway LU*
- 🕐 *Mon 1pm-7.30pm, Tues-Fri 10am-7.30pm,*
  Sat 10am-7pm, Sun 1pm-6pm

In Casa Brasil, the Brazilian Shop, they are a specialist importer of Brazilian books (fiction and non-fiction), magazines, DVDs and CDs.

Sathya Sai Book Centre

⌨ *19 Hay Lane, NW9 0NH*

☎ *020 8732 2886*

✆ *020 8732 2886*

🖃 *www.srisathyasaibooks.org.uk*

🚇 *Colindale LU*

🕐 *Mon-Fri 11am-5pm, Sat & Sun 11am-3pm*

Religious books about and by the Indian Guru Sri Sathya Sai Baba (in English, Chinese, Gujarati and Hindi) plus books on spirituality, yoga and health. There are videos and CDs as well and a selection of artifacts and gift items.

School of Oriental and African Studies Bookshop

⌨ *Brunei Gallery, Thornhaugh Street, WC1H 0XG*

☎ *020 7898 4470*

🖃 *bookshop@soas.ac.uk*

🚇 *Russell Square LU*

🕐 *Mon-Fri 9.30am-5.30pm, Sat 12noon-5pm (term times only Oct-Feb)*

Located in the foyer of the Brunei Gallery building just opposite the main SOAS entrance, this tiny shop is immensely well-stocked with books covering the school's areas of study. This includes Africa, South East Asia, China, Japan, the Middle East and Islam. Literature, history, economics, politics and culture are covered and for linguists there are dictionaries and language learning materials. Take a few minutes to check out the current exhibitions at the Brunei Gallery – they have some fascinating shows here. There is also a café and a Japanese-inspired roof garden accessed from the first floor of the gallery.

Schott Universal

⌨ *48 Great Marlborough Street, W1F 7BB*

☎ *020 7437 1246*

✆ *020 7437 6115*

🖃 *www.schott-music.com*

🚇 *Oxford Circus LU*

🕐 *Mon-Fri 9am-6pm, Sat 11am-5pm*

Music publisher with a huge range of classical sheet music for all instruments and standards. There is a huge range of miniature scores, tutors for all instruments and music education materials.

Shipley

Selfridges

⌨ *400 Oxford Street, W1A 1AB*
☎ *020 7318 3678*
✆ *020 7495 8321*
✑ *www.selfridges.com*
🚇 *Bond Street LU*
🕐 *Mon-Sat 10am-8pm (until 9pm on Thurs), Sun 11.30am-6pm*

The basement book department of this vast shopping emporium features an extensive, attractively displayed stock covering all areas, with fiction, travel and cookery being notably well-represented. The art, design, interiors, fashion and photography section is particularly browser friendly with plenty of comfortable seating. A modern and fashionable place to look for books.

Shipley

✑ *www.artbook.co.uk*
🚇 *Leicester Square LU*

A small, specialist chain of art booksellers within a few metres of each other on Charing Cross Road selling new and out-of-print volumes. Each shop specialises in a different area but staff are uniformly knowledgeable, enthusiastic and helpful. Branches at:

⌨ *70 Charing Cross Road, WC2H 0BQ*
☎ *020 7836 4872*
✆ *020 7212 9938*
🕐 *Mon-Sat 10am-6pm*

The stock here incudes fine art, history of art, aesthetics, architecture, interior design, planning, urban design and art theory. Books are piled floor to ceiling and they also sell magazines and exhibition catalogues. There's an open fire on cold winter days as an additional welcome.

And at
⌨ *72 Charing Cross Road, WC2H 0BE*
☎ *020 7240 1559*
✆ *020 7379 7678*
🕐 *Mon-Sat 10am-6.30pm*

Architecture, interior design, planning, urban design, advertising, fashion, photography, film, graphic design, furniture, typography and illustration.

Silverprint

⌨ *12 Valentine Place, SE1 8QH*

☎ *020 7620 0844*

✆ *020 7620 0129*

✎ *www.silverprint.co.uk*

🚌 *Waterloo Rail/LU*

🕐 *Mon-Fri 9.30am-5.30pm*

A specialist photographic supply shop par excellence. Photographers make pilgrimage here from near and far. The stock of books is quite small but highly selective and specialised, covering darkroom, studio and photographic techniques, experimental processes and digital photography. The staff are knowledgeable and helpful and the store has all the equipment and materials you'll need to apply the techniques refered to in the books

Sims Reed

⌨ *43a Duke Street, St James's, SW1Y 6DD*

☎ *020 7493 5660*

✆ *020 7493 8468*

✎ *www.simsreed.com*

🚌 *Green Park LU*

🕐 *Mon-Fri 10am-6pm*

A specialist art bookseller at the very top of the quality and price range. The stock is a heady mixture of new, second-hand, rare and antiquarian volumes and covers all areas with avant-garde art being particularly well-served. The shop is located just across the road from the other major art bookseller in the area, Thomas Heneage (see p.72), and is a few minutes walk from the Royal Academy of Art. There are about four thousand books detailed on their website and occasional catalogues are produced.

W H SMITH

www.whsmith.co.uk

It's very easy to be snooty about the populist book stock of this general stationery, newspaper, magazine, music and DVD store but in many neighbourhoods of London it is the only bookshop on offer. Despite facing increase competition from chains such as Waterstones and Borders, WH Smith still maintains well over 500 stores selling more than 40million books annually. The stores offer huge discounts on many titles and the W H Smith Clubcard is a way of collecting points on purchases which can then be exchanged for goods. The chain has over fifty outlets in London from small railway shops selling a few best sellers to vast outlets such as the one at Brent Cross.

Branches at:

Baker Street
116 Baker Street, W1M 1LB
Tel: 020 7935 2493
Fax: 020 7935 3962
Transport: Baker Street LU
Open: Mon-Fri 8am-7pm,
Sat 9.30am-6.30pm

Balham
176 High Road, SW12 9BW
Tel: 020 8675 4907
Fax: 020 8772 1368
Transport: Balham LU
Open: Mon-Sat 9am-6pm,
Sun 10.30am-4.30pm

BBC Television Centre
Wood Lane, W12 7RJ
Tel: 020 8743 9435
Transport: Wood Lane LU
Open: Mon-Fri 7am-6pm, Sat 8am-1pm

Beckton
Unit 7, Gallions Reach Retail Park,
E6 7FB
Tel: 020 7474 9684
Fax: 020 7474 9630
Transport: Gallions Reach DLR or
Beckton DLR and bus
Open: Mon-Sat 10am-8pm,
Sun 11am-5pm

Brent Cross
Brent Cross Shopping Centre,
Hendon, NW4 3FB
Tel: 020 8202 4226
Fax: 020 8202 8369
Transport: Brent Cross &
Hendon Central LU
Open: Mon-Fri 10am-8pm, Sat 9am-7pm, Sun 11am-5pm
The major bookselling branch of Smith's in London.

Brixton

427 Brixton Road, SW9 8HE
Tel: 020 7274 5813
Fax: 020 7326 0453
Transport: Brixton LU
Open: Mon-Fri 7am-4pm

Catford

23 Winslade Way, SE6 4JU
Tel: 020 8690 1972
Transport: Catford & Catford Bridge Rail
Open: Mon-Sat 9am-5.30pm

Chiswick

370-372 High Road, W4 5TA
Tel: 020 8995 9427
Transport: Turnham Green LU
Open: Mon-Sat 9am-6pm,
Sun 10.30am-4.30pm

Ealing Broadway

21-23 The Broadway, W5 2NH
Tel: 020 8567 1471
Fax: 020 8579 2768
Transport: Ealing Broadway LU
Open: Mon-Fri 8.30am-6pm (Thurs-
6.30pm), Sat 9am-6pm, Sun 11am-5pm

East Ham

125 High Street North, E6 1HZ
Tel: 020 8552 4875
Transport: East Ham LU
Open: Mon-Sat 9am-6pm,
Sun 10am-4pm

Elephant & Castle

Elephant & Castle Shopping Centre,
SE1 6SZ
Tel: 020 7703 8525
Fax: 020 7703 4029
Transport: Elephant & Castle LU
Open: Mon-Sat 8.30am-6pm,
Sun 10am-4pm
On the ground floor of the shopping
centre – cheerier inside than it
appears from the street – this branch
offers a small general book selection.

Eltham

92-94 High Street, SE9 1BW
Tel: 020 8859 3019
Fax: 020 8859 0215
Transport: Eltham Rail
Open: Mon-Sat 9am-5.30pm,
Sun 10am-4pm
Small two storey branch in the centre
of the main Eltham shopping area.

Fleet Street

71 Fleet Street, EC4Y 1EU
Tel: 020 7583 4165
Transport: Blackfriars LU
Open: Mon-Fri 8.30am-6pm

Forest Hill

Devonshire Road, SE23 3HD
Tel: 020 8699 2789
Transport: Forest Hill Rail
Open: Mon-Fri 7am-4pm

Fulham

320 North End Road, SW6 1NG
Tel: 020 7385 9585
Transport: Fulham Broadway LU
Open: Mon-Fri 9am-5.30pm,
Sat 9am-6pm

Hammersmith

16 King's Mall,
King Street Northside, W6 0PZ
Tel: 020 8748 2218
Fax: 020 8846 9702
Transport: Hammersmith LU
Open: Mon-Fri 8.30am-6pm, Sat -6pm,
Sun 10.30am-4.30pm
This shop is big and spacious with a
very good general book selection,
plenty of children's books and lots of
special offers – definitely one of the
better London branches.

Holborn Circus

124 Holborn, EC1N 2QX
Tel: 020 7242 0535
Transport: Holborn & Chancery Lane LU
Open: Mon-Fri 8.30am-6pm

Kensington

Hornton Court, 132-136 Kensington
High Street, W8 7RP
Tel: 020 7937 0236
Fax: 020 7376 2434
Transport: High Street Kensington LU
Open: Mon-Sat 8.30am-7pm,
Sun 11am-5pm
The book department here is one of
the better Smith's bookhops in
London.

Kilburn

113 Kilburn High Road, NW6 6JH
Tel: 020 7328 3111
Fax: 020 7624 2357
Transport: Kilburn LU
Open: Mon-Sat 9am-5.30pm,
Sun 11am-5pm
A small, high street branch with the
emphasis on other goods but a basic,
general selection of popular books.

Kingsway

7-11 Kingsway, WC2B 6YA
Tel: 020 7836 5951
Fax: 020 7836 9118
Transport: Holborn & Temple LU
Open: Mon-Fri 8.30am-5.30pm
There is more of an emphasis here on
magazines, videos, music and
stationery, but the shop does have a
small general book stock, with a
reasonable paperback fiction section.

Leadenhall

15 Lime Street,
Leadenhall Market, EC3M 7AA
Tel: 020 7283 4135
Fax: 020 7283 4165
Open: Mon-Fri 8am-6pm
Catering mainly for office workers in
search of diversions, there are magazines, video and audio titles aplenty
in this branch but also travel, fiction
and cookery books – with some on
special offer. Leadenhall Market has
been beautifully refurbished and is
full of places to eat, drink, relax and
enjoy your book purchases.

Lewisham

59 Riverdale,
The Lewisham Centre, SE13 7EP
Tel: 020 8318 1316
Fax: 020 8318 7478
Transport: Lewisham Rail
Open: Mon-Fri 9am-6pm,
Sat 8.30am-6pm, Sun 11am-5pm
Large convenient branch in the main
Lewisham shopping centre with a
good-sized book selection occupying
a large part of the store.

Mill Hill

29 The Broadway, NW7 3DA
Tel: 020 8959 1316
Transport: Mill Hill Broadway Rail
Open: Mon-Sat 9am-5.30pm

Muswell Hill

117 Muswell Hill Broadway, N10 3RS
Tel: 020 8883 1706
Transport: Highgate LU (then bus)
Open: Mon-Fri 9am-5.30pm,
Sat 9am-6pm, Sun 10am-5pm

North Finchley

766 High Road, N12 9QH
Tel: 020 8445 2785
Fax: 020 8446 4453
Transport: Woodside Park LU
Open: Mon-Fri 9am-5.30pm,
Sat 9am-6pm, Sun 10.30am-4.30pm

Notting Hill Gate

92 Notting Hill Gate, W11 3QB
Tel: 020 7727 9261
Transport: Notting Hill Gate LU
Open: Mon-Fri 8.30am-7pm,
Sat 9am-6pm, Sun 11am-5pm

Oxford Street

The Plaza,
120 Oxford Street, W1N 1LT
Tel:020 7436 6282
Fax: 020 7637 0918
Transport: Tottenham Court Road &
Oxford Circus LU
Open: Mon-Sat 10am-7pm (Thurs-
8pm), Sun 11am-6pm
Located at the far end of the ground
floor of the off-street shopping
centre, this is a huge branch with an
extensive book range. There are lots
of special deals on popular titles.

Palmer's Green

5 Alderman's Hill, N13 4YD
Tel: 020 8886 4743
Transport: Palmer's Green Rail
Open: Mon-Fri 8.30am-5.30pm,
Sat 9am-6pm

Peckham

Unit 10, The Aylesham Centre,
Rye Lane, SE15 5EW
Tel: 020 7358 9601
Transport: Peckham Rye Rail
Open: Mon-Fri 9am-5.30pm,
Sat 9am-6pm, Sun 11am-4pm
Small shop in the main shopping
street, with around half the space
taken up with books. It has the usual
prominent display of popular fiction
with some good-priced special offers,
and a satisfactory general stock.

Putney

111-115 High Street, SW15 1SS
Tel: 020 8788 2573
Fax: 020 8246 5760
Transport: Putney Bridge LU
Open: Mon-Fri 9am-6pm,
Sun 10.30am-4.30pm

St Thomas's Hospital

Lambeth Palace Road, SE1 7EH
Tel: 020 7928 0793
Transport: Waterloo & Westminster LU
Open: Mon-Fri 7.30am-7pm,
Sat & Sun 9am-5pm

Selfridges

400 Oxford Street, W1A 1AB
Tel: 020 7318 3679
Transport: Bond Street LU
Open: Mon-Fri 10am-8pm,
Sat 9.30am-8pm, Sun 12noon-6pm
Located inside the famous Oxford
Street department store.

South Hampstead

9-10 Harben Parade,
Finchley Road, NW3 6JS
Tel: 020 7722 4441
Transport: Swiss Cottage LU
Open: Mon-Sat 9am-5.30pm,
Sun 11am-5pm
Above average selection of general,
popular books on the ground floor of
this high street branch.

Stratford East

41-42 The Mall, E15 1XE
Tel: 020 8534 5955
Fax: 020 8221 2795
Transport: Stratford LU
Open: Mon-Fri 9am-6.30pm,
Sat 9am-6pm, Sun 11am-5pm

Streatham

180-182 High Street, SW16 1BH
Tel: 020 8677 3031
Fax: 020 8769 0820
Transport: Streatham Rail
Open: Mon-Fri 9am-5.30pm,
Sat 9am-6pm, Sun 11am-5pm

Surrey Quays

Shopping Centre,
Redriff Road, SE16 1LL
Tel: 020 7237 5235
Fax: 020 7567 9551
Transport: Surrey Quays LU
Open: Mon-Sat 9am-6pm (Fri until
8pm), Sun 11am-5pm

Temple Fortune

22 Temple Fortune Parade,
Finchley Road, NW11 0QS
Tel: 020 8455 2273
Fax: 020 8455 9434
Transport: Golders Green LU (then bus)
Open: Mon-Sat 9am-6pm,
Sun 10.30am-4.30pm

Wandsworth

69 Centre Mall, SW18 4TG
Tel: 020 8877 1979
Transport: Wandsworth Town Rail
Open: Mon-Sat 9am-5.30pm
Located within the revamped local
shopping centre that is now a bright,
airy place to visit.

Wimbledon

16 Wimbledon Bridge, SW19 7NW
Tel: 020 8543 1055
Fax: 020 8542 8594
Transport: Wimbledon LU
Open: Mon-Fri 9am-6.30pm,
Sat 8.30am-6pm, Sun 11am-5pm
The book section here doesn't offer
much competition to the neighbour-
ing Waterstones but can be useful for
special offers on popular titles.

Wood Green

110 High Road, N22 6HE
Tel: 020 8889 0221
Fax: 020 8889 9159
Transport: Wood Green LU
Open: Mon-Sat 9am-7pm,
Sun 11am-5pm

Woolwich

68-72 Powis Street, SE18 6LQ
Tel: 020 8854 7108
Fax: 020 8316 6542
Transport: Woolwich Arsenal Rail
Open: Mon-Sat 8.30am-5.30pm,
Sun 9am-3pm

STATION branches inevitably lack
the large book choice of the High
Street branches but in the mainline
stations, the choice is surprsingly
wide and most readers will be able to
find something to while away their
journey, often available on special
offer.
Here is a list of station branches that
sell books:

Baker Street

Metropolitan Booking Hall,
NW1A 5LA
Tel: 020 7486 9591
Mon-Fri 7am-9.30pm,
Sat 9am-9.30pm, Sun 10am-7pm

Blackfriars Station

Queen Victoria Street, EC4V 4DY
Tel: 020 7236 6394
Open: Mon-Fri 7am-6.45pm

Cannon Street Station

Cannon Street, EC4N 6AP
Tel: 020 7623 5643
Open: Mon-Fri 6am-7.30pm

Charing Cross Station

Charing Cross, WC2N 5HS
Tel: 020 7839 4200
Open: Mon-Fri 6.30am-11pm,
Sat 6.30am-9pm, Sun 8am-8pm
The shop at the front exit of the
station has more books but shorter
opening hours.

Clapham Junction
Unit 7A Shopstop, SW11 1RU
Tel: 020 7223 6807
Open: Mon-Fri 7am-7.30pm,
Sat 8am-6pm, Sun 10am-4pm

Ealing Broadway Station
W5 2NU
Tel: 020 8579 6403
Open: Mon-Fri 7am-8pm,
Sat 9am-6pm, Sun 9am-5pm

Euston Station
Euston, NW1 2DU
Tel: 020 7387 4640
Open: Mon-Fr 6am-10pm,
Sat 6am-7pm, Sun 7am-6pm

Fenchurch Street Station
Fenchurch Street, EC3M 4AJ
Tel: 020 7480 7295
Open: Mon-Fri 6.30am-8pm,
Sat 9am-5pm

Hammersmith
34b Broadway Shopping Centre,
W6 9YD
Tel: 020 8563 7155
Open: Mon-Fri 7.30am-8pm,
Sat 8am-7pm

King's Cross Station
King's Cross, N1 9AP
Tel: 020 7837 5580
Open: Mon-Sat 6am-10pm,
Sun 7am-10pm
Large branch with a good book
selection for travellers.

Liverpool Street Station
Western Mall, EC2M 7QA
Tel: 020 7247 7606
Open: Mon-Fri 6.30am-10pm,
Sat 7am-8pm, Sun 8am-8pm
The larger of the two branches on
this station, there's a smaller branch at
Retail Units 8-10, Station
Concourse, EC2M 7QH, Tel: 020
7628 1617

London Bridge Station
London Bridge, SE1 9SP
Tel: 020 7403 3288
Open: Mon-Fri 6.30am-8.30pm,
Sat 8.30am-5.30pm, Sun 10am-4pm

Marylebone Station
Marylebone, NW1 6JJ
Tel: 020 7723 7377
Open: Mon-Fri 7am-11pm,
Sat 8am-8pm, Sun 10am-6pm

North Greenwich
Blackwall Road, SE10 0AY
Tel: 020 8858 8431
Open: Mon-Fri 7am-8pm,
Sat 9am-6pm, Sun 9am-5pm

Paddington Station
Paddington, W2 1HB
Tel: 020 7723 3153
Open: Mon-Fri 6.30am-10pm,
Sat 7am-10pm, Sun 7.30am-10pm

St Pancras Station
St Pancras Road, NW1 2QL
Tel: 020 7833 5811
Open: Mon-Sat 7am-10pm,
Sun 9.30am-10pm

Stratford

East Side Unit, E15 1DE
Tel: 020 8534 1179
Open: Mon-Sat 6am-8pm,
Sun 8am-6pm

Victoria Station

Victoria Station, SW1V 1JT
Tel: 020 7630 9677
Open: Mon-Fri 6am-10.45pm,
Sat & Sun 7am-9.45pm
Two storey glass centrepiece to the
station; with the books and magazines
on the ground floor. The book stock
is extensive, but concentrates on best-
sellers from the big publishing houses.
There's also a smaller branch at
Victoria Station (East), SW1V 1JT, Tel:
020 7630 9677

Waterloo Station

Waterloo, SE1 7NQ
Tel: 020 7261 1616
Open: Mon-Fri 5am-midnight,
Sat 7am-10pm, Sun 8am-10pm
Located in a central island in the
middle of the station with a fair
selection of books. There's a smaller
branch near the Ticket Office with a
more restricted book selection (Tel:
020 7633 9259).

Wimbledon Station

Station Approach, SW19 7NL
Tel: 020 8946 6143
Open: Mon-Fri 6am-8pm,
Sat 8am-7pm, Sun 9am-5pm

Society of Genealogists

14 Charterhouse Buildings, Goswell Road, EC1M 7BA
020 7251 8799
020 7250 1800
www.sog.org.uk
Barbican LU
Tues-Sat 10am-6pm (Thurs until 8pm)

The bookshop here supplements the work of the library (see p.274),
which enables people to trace their family history. The shop sells books
published by the Society on all aspects of genealogy, with information
about how to embark on the whole process plus books on local and
social history.

SoHo Original Bookshop

Having started life as single shop in the heart of the Soho sex trade, this discount book chain has now expanded while retaining its essential character. All the stores offer a good value selection of general books in a modern and bright environment with adult, more sexually explicit titles tucked away downstairs for those who are interested. The shops are strong in art, photography, interior design and glossy gift books. There's also a discount video shop next door to their Brewer Street store.

Branches at:

11 & 13 Brewer Street, W1R 3SN
Tel: 020 7287 3844
Transport: Piccadilly Circus LU
Open: Mon-Sat 10am-1am,
Sun 11am-11pm

12 Brewer St, W1
Tel: 020 7494 1615
Transport: Piccadilly Circus LU
Open: Mon-Sat 10am-1am,
Sun 11am-11pm

121-125 Charing Cross Road,
WC2H 0EA
Tel: 020 7734 4121
Transport: Tottenham Court Rd LU
Open: Mon-Sat 10am-1am,
Sun 11am-11pm

63 Cowcross Street, EC1M 6BP
Tel: 020 7251 8020
Transport: Farringdon LU/Rail
Open: Mon-Fri 11am-7.45pm

23/25 Leather Lane, EC1N 7TE
Tel: 020 7404 3594
Transport: Chancery Lane LU
Open: Mon-Fri 10am-7pm

124 Middlesex Street, E1 7HY
Tel: 020 7377 5309
Transport: Liverpool Street LU/Rail
Open: Mon-Wed 10am-8pm,
Thurs-Fri 10am-9pm, Sat closed,
Sun 10am-4pm

231 Kilburn High Rd, NW6 7JN
Tel: 020 7328 9026
Transport: Kilburn or
Kilburn Park LU
Open: Mon-Sat 11am-8pm,
Sun 12noon-6pm

Soma
- 38 Kennington Lane, SE11 4LS
- ☎ 020 7735 2101
- ✆ 020 7735 3076
- Indian bookswww.somabooks.co.uk
- Children's bookswww.childrens-books.uk.com
- Kennington LU
- Mon-Fri 10am-5.30pm

Soma's enormous selection of children's books is staggeringly international in scope – about thirty different languages are represented including Albanian, Polish and Serbo-Croat and many other European, Asian
and African languages and they sell a vast array of dual language books.
They also stock adult books of Asian interest and titles about race and
education worldwide. As importers and distributors of books from
India, they are agents for Penguin India and other publishers, and are a
great source of foreign titles that you're unlikely to find elsewhere.

Souvenir Press
- 43 Great Russell St, WC1B 3PD
- ☎ 020 7580 9307
- ✆ 020 7580 5064
- Tottenham Court Road LU
- Mon-Fri 9.30am-5.15pm (closed 12.30pm-2.30pm for lunch)

A general non-fiction publisher with a huge selection of titles both
serious and comic. History, science, health, philosophy, education and
art are all covered.

SPCK
- Faith House, 7 Tufton Street, SW1P 3QN
- ☎ 020 7799 5083
- ✆ 020 7233 4297
- www.spck.org.uk
- St James's Park & Westminster LU
- Mon-Fri 9.30am-5.30pm

Located a very short walk away from Westminster Abbey, this shop offers
books on all aspects of Christian theology and life. There is a huge
selection of titles including children's books, some remaindered titles
and rare and antiquarian volumes. Greetings cards, CDs and gifts
complete the stock.

Spink

🖵 *69 Southampton Row, WC1B 4ET*
☎ *020 7563 4000*
✆ *020 7563 4066*
🖉 *www.spink.com*
🚇 *Holborn & Russell Square LU*
🕐 *Mon-Fri 9.30am-5.30pm*

This specialist coin and medal dealer has a bookshop with a large specialist new and second-hand stock of titles covering all aspects of numismatics.

Sportspages

🖵 *Caxton Walk, 94-96 Charing Cross Road, WC2H 0JW*
☎ *020 7240 9604*
✆ *020 7836 0104*
🖉 *www.sportsbooksdirect.co.uk*
🚇 *Leicester Square LU*
🕐 *Mon-Sat 9.30am-7pm, Sun 12noon-5pm*

There is something here for everyone interested in sport whether they are an armchair enthusiasts or active, lycra clad, participant. There are books, DVDs, videos and magazines on every sport imaginable from fishing and American football to greyhound and pigeon racing via the martial arts, with large sections on sports psychology, medicine, training and exercise. The atmosphere is relaxed and there is often a television showing a recent sporting event. The shop is a favourite venue for sports book signings and Mohammed Ali is among the stars who have visited the store.

Spurgeon's Book Room

🖵 *Spurgeon's College, 189 South Norwood Hill, SE25 6DJ*
☎ *020 8653 3640*
🖉 *www.tcbconline.co.uk*
🚇 *Crystal Palace or Norwood Junction Rail*
🕐 *Ring for opening hours*

In the grounds of the theological college which specialises in the training of Baptist ministers, this shop sells Christian and theological books. It also stocks a range of cards, small gift items, posters, tapes and CD's.

Sportspages

Stanfords

🖼 *12-14 Long Acre, WC2E 9LP*

☎ *020 7836 2260*

✆ *020 7836 0189*

✐ *www.stanfords.co.uk*

🚌 *Leicester Square LU*

🕐 *Mon, Wed & Fri 9am-7.30pm; Tues 9.30am-7.30pm;*
Thurs 9am-8pm; Sat 10am-7pm; Sun 12noon-6pm

Stanfords is probably the best-stocked guidebook and travel bookshop in London and is fast becoming a one-stop travel shop. Its displays of atlases, globes, books and magazines on walking, climbing, boats and seamanship are equally extensive. Ranging over three floors, the stock spans the globe and includes a vast selection of worldwide maps, nautical charts and OS maps. There are maps on CD-ROM and OS Select allows the printing of unique maps with whatever the customer wants placed at the centre. Reproduction antique maps, jigsaws of maps, travel games, compasses, gifts, Global Positioning Sytems, travel equipment and a travel agent upstairs make it possible to buy everything you'll need for your trip under one roof.

Steimatzky Hasifira

⌂ *46 Golders Green Road, NW11 8LL*

☎ *020 8458 9774*

✆ *020 8458 3449*

🚌 *Golders Green LU*

🕐 *Mon-Thurs 10am-7pm (Fri until 2pm), Sun 10.30am-8pm*

Jewish bookseller with a large selection of books in English and Hebrew on all aspects of Jewish religion, life and experience. The stock includes publications for English speakers wanting to learn Hebrew as well as Jewish and Israeli music and videos plus a selection of guidebooks to Israel.

Rudolf Steiner Bookshop

⌂ *Rudolf Steiner House, 35 Park Road, NW1 6XT*

☎ *020 7724 7699*

✆ *020 7724 7699*

🖉 *www.anth.org.uk*

🚌 *Baker Street LU*

🕐 *Mon & Tues 10.30am-1pm and 2pm-6pm, Wed-Fri 10.30am-6pm,*
   Sat 10.30am-2pm & 3pm-5pm

This bookshop specialises in texts by Rudolf Steiner and associated authors which develop the ideas of Steiner and the Anthroposophical movement. Subjects covered include; education, child development, parenting, medicine and health, plus a general section of children's books.

Stepping Stones

⌂ *97 Trafalgar Road, SE10 9TS*

☎ *020 8853 2733*

🖉 *www.steppingstonesgreenwich.co.uk*

🚌 *Maze Hill Rail*

🕐 *Daily 10am-6pm*

This little shop is located about fifteen minutes walk (it's worth the effort) from the centre of Greenwich, beyond the Maritime Museum. It's an inspirational New Age shop selling gifts, cards and a range of books on complementary and alternative medicine, self-development and improvement, religion and philosophy. There's a Mind, Body and Soul Centre attached where clients can choose from a menu of therapies including massage, reiki, tarot reading and reflexology.

Stoke Newington Bookshop

⌨ *159 Stoke Newington High Street, N16 0NY*
☎ *020 7249 2808*
✎ *020 7249 7845*
🚌 *Stoke Newington Rail*
🕐 *Mon-Sat 9.30am-6pm, Sun 11am-5pm*

Soothing music, well-displayed stock and tempting special offers greet visitors to this spacious local bookshop. Their fiction and children's sections are particularly impressive but non-fiction and newly published books also have a strong presence. A fabulous selection of cards top off the stock. The regular author readings here are very popular. They are linked with Books Ink (see p.28) a few doors away.

Henry Stokes and Co

⌨ *58 Elizabeth Street, SW1W 9PB*
☎ *020 7730 7073*
✎ *www.henrystokes.co.uk*
🚌 *Victoria LU/Rail or Sloane Square LU*
🕐 *Mon-Fri 9am-6pm, Sat 9am-4pm*

A local shop displaying a judicious selection of novels in hardback and paperback, non-fiction books in all subject areas, especially travel, and a good range of children's books. They offer an efficient ordering service to supplement the relatively small stock and also sell greetings cards, gifts and stationery. Book lovers who are also foodies should be aware that Elizabeth Street is also the location of two fabulous bakeries Poilâne and Baker and Spice.

Swedenborg Society Bookshop

⌨ *20-21 Bloomsbury Way, WC1A 2TH*
☎ *020 7405 7986*
✎ *020 7831 5848*
✎ *www.swedenborg.org.uk*
🚌 *Tottenham Court Road or Holborn LU*
🕐 *Mon-Fri 9.30am-5pm*

Specialists in the philosophical writings of Emanuel Swedenborg (in both English, the original Latin and a range of foreign languages) and books about his life and works. There are second-hand and antiquarian books as well as new ones.

T

Tales on Moon Lane

- 25 Half Moon Lane, SE24 9JU
- 020 7274 5759
- www.talesonmoonlane.co.uk
- Herne Hill Rail
- Mon-Sat 9.15am-5.30pm

This is a specialist children's bookshop with a fabulous range of books, highly knowledgeable staff and lots of sofas and chairs to make browsing a comfortable experience. The books themselves are arranged in helpful ways including sections on Dinosaurs and Dragons, Boy Interest, Newly Confident Readers and Fairies, Princesses and Ballerinas. There are also lots of gifts and toys from which to choose in addition to the book stock. The enthusiasm of the staff here is demonstrated by the wonderful window displays which are a feature of the store. Mimosa just opposite the shop is good for coffee and Brockwell Park is just around the corner.

Talking Bookshop

- 11 Wigmore Street, W1U 1PE
- 020 7491 4117
- 020 7629 1966
- www.talkingbooks.co.uk
- Bond Street & Oxford Circus LU
- Mon-Fri 9.30am-5.30pm, Sat 10am-5pm

This shop is just a short walk from Oxford Street and stocks purely spoken word CDs and tapes. The range is catholic to say the least and includes bestsellers, classics, drama and poetry, radio comedy and children's stories as well as some non-fiction, stress reduction, self-improvement and language courses. There's also a large stock of normally hard to find unabridged books – much more satisfying in the opinion of many listeners. Staff are friendly and extremely knowledgeable; they produce their own catalogue annually with quarterly updates and if you visit the showroom there are plenty of other catalogues to consult as well. Prices here are very competitive and if you've a favourite book you want to find on CD or tape, this is the place to look.

Tate Britain Shop

⌨ *Tate Britain, Millbank, SW1P 4RG*

☎ *020 7887 8876*

✎ *www.tate.org.uk*

🚌 *Pimlico LU*

🕐 *Mon-Sat 10am-5.30pm, Sun 10am-5.30pm*

The main shop, although smaller than its sister in Tate Modern (see below) still stocks an impressive number of books on the Tate's collections. British art from 1500 to the present day is the emphasis here and the art essays and monographs are supplemented by art magazines and journals and books on recent exhibitions plus more general titles on art history and theory and British history and culture. It's a good place to look for unusual gifts and stationery items too and there's a huge array of postcards and posters of works in the collection. There is also a Gallery 61 shop (same opening times as the main shop) just off the main hallway, selling goods relating to the current show and an exhibition shop (daily 10.30am-5.50pm) near the Manton Street entrance selling items related to the exhibition there.

Tate Modern Shop

⌨ *Tate Modern, Bankside, SE1 9TG*

☎ *020 7401 5167*

✎ *www.tate.org.uk*

🚌 *Blackfriars LU/Rail*

🕐 *Sun-Thurs 10am-6pm, Fri & Sat 10am-10pm*

From power station to powerhouse art gallery, Tate Modern is London's Modern Art success story. It's also home to the most extensive art bookshop in London, situated just next to the towering main turbine hall, and boasting over 10,000 titles. The stock reflects the enormous scope of the Tate's art holdings and caters for all levels of knowledge and interest – art techniques, art history, cinema, live arts, photography, installation art and architecture are just some of the subjects covered. There are posters and postcards galore as well, and a natty range of designed gifts. Be sure to journey to the upper floors of the gallery for great views across the City of London.

Teerans Booksellers

- 🔲 *4A Castletown Road, W14 9HQ*
- ☎ *020 7385 0565*
- ✆ *020 7385 4185*
- 🚌 *West Kensington LU*
- 🕐 *Daily 10am-8pm*

This specialist deals in books about the Indian subcontinent in English as well as Indian languages. There's also a distinctly musical flavour to the stock with music CDs and music books, instruments and artifacts also for sale here. The shop is located in the Institute of Indian Culture, The Bhavan Centre, which also has a small reference library (see p.260).

The Theosophical Society in England

- 🔲 *50 Gloucester Place, W1U 8EA*
- ☎ *020 7935 9261*
- ✆ *020 7935 9543*
- ✉ *www.theosophical-society.org.uk*
- 🚌 *Baker Street LU*
- 🕐 *Tues-Fri 2pm-6.30pm (during lectures opening times can vary))*

This bookshop is based in the foyer of the British headquarters of the Theosophical Society which is a centre for lectures and meditation and has a library. The bookshop has mostly new, full price, books concerning Theosophy but also sells books about other religions, and has some discounted and second-hand titles.

Tibet Foundation Shop

- 1 St James's Market, SW1 4SB
- ☎ 020 7930 6005
- ✉ 020 7930 6002
- ✉ info@tibetshop.org.uk
- 🚌 Piccadilly Circus LU
- 🕐 Tues-Sat 11am-6.30pm

Accompanying a range of beautiful religious images and artifacts, there are some excellent books on Tibetan art, religion, culture and language, including materials for anyone wanting to learn Tibetan.

Titles of Penge

- 94 High Street, SE20 7EZ
- ☎/✉ 020 8676 0926
- 🚌 Penge East Rail
- 🕐 Mon-Fri 10am-6pm, Sat 9am-6pm, Sun 11am-3pm

A pleasant, general local bookshop with tables and chairs for comfortable browsing. They sell full-price and discounted new books in all subject areas but with particular strengths in children's, fiction, art, photography and music. They also sell sheet music and discounted CDs and audio books. Chas' Guitars have an extensive selection of guitars in a room at the back of the shop.

Torah Treasures

- 4 Sentinel Square, NW4 2EL
- ☎ 020 8202 3134
- 🚌 Hendon Central LU
- 🕐 Mon-Wed & Thurs 9.30am-6pm,
  Fri 9.30am-3.30pm (earlier in winter), Sun 9.30am-4pm

Specialist Jewish bookseller stocking religious texts and a large choice of fiction and non-fiction books in Hebrew plus a selection in English on Jewish thought and philosophy. There are plenty of books to interest and inspire children and young people plus CDs and games.

The Travel Bookshop

⌧ *13-15 Blenheim Crescent, W11 2EE*
☎ *020 7229 5260*
✆ *020 7243 1552*
✐ *www.thetravelbookshop.com*
🚌 *Ladbroke Grove & Notting Hill Gate LU*
🕒 *Mon-Sat 10am-6pm, Sun 12noon-5pm*

One of the few specialist travel bookshops in London, and the inspiration for the film 'Notting Hill' starring Hugh Grant and Julia Roberts, although it's a good deal more orderly and attractive than it appears in the film and the staff far less bumbling than Hugh Grant. The shop demonstrates a delightfully eclectic definition of what comprises 'travel' with guides, phrasebooks, history, travelogues and fiction all rubbing shoulders together. Although space is tight the shop aspires to hold as many titles as possible on every country in the world and new books and current book reviews are well-displayed. Amidst all the exotic locations, the UK is also very well accounted for on the shelves. It does get busy at the weekend – come during the week for a more relaxing browse. Readers can contact the shop to receive a reading list by e-mail of books relating to particular interests. One of a great trio of shops in Blenheim Crescent; Books For Cooks (see p.30) and Blenheim Books (see p.20) are nearby.

Triangle Bookshop

⌧ *The Architectural Association,*
  36 Bedford Square, WC1B 3JW
☎ *020 7631 1381*
✆ *020 7436 4373*
✐ *www.trianglebookshop.com*
🚌 *Goode Street LU*
🕒 *Mon-Fri 10am-6pm*

Specialist architectural bookseller situated in the basement of the Architectural Association. It's a great shop full of a cutting edge choice of books, magazines and journals on architecture, design, landscape and urban development – in fact, everything to do with buildings and their aesthetics both inside and out. There is plenty here to satisfy general as well as scholarly and technical interest.

TSO (The Stationery Office)

📖 *123 Kingsway, WC2B 6PQ*

☎ *020 7242 6393*

✎ *020 7242 6394*

🖉 *www.tso.co.uk*

🚎 *Holborn LU*

🕐 *Mon-Fri 9am-5.30pm (Tues opens 9.30am), Sat 10am-3pm*

A shop that sells all government publications including most white papers, legislation and publications from the British Standards Institute, the Health and Safety Executive, the CBI and The Stationery Office themselves. However, they also stock a wide range of business, economics, law, finance, management, health and education titles from many other publishers plus some maps.

U

Ukrainian Booksellers

📖 *49 Linden Gardens, W2 4HG*

🕐 *020 7229 0140*

🚎 *Notting Hill Gate LU*

🕐 *Telephone for opening times*

Books in Ukrainian and in English about the Ukraine.

Under Two Flags

📖 *4 St Christopher's Place, W1U 1LZ*

☎/✎ *020 7935 6934*

🖉 *www.undertwoflags.com*

🚎 *Bond St LU*

🕐 *Tues-Sat 10.30am-5pm*

A tiny shop selling toy and model soldiers plus a small selection of military books and magazines. There are some new and some second-hand volumes and many of the books are from the specialist publisher Osprey.

University of East London Bookshop

- 🖃 *Stratford Campus, The Green, Off Romford Road, E15 4LZ*
- ☎ *020 8522 0520*
- ✆ *020 8522 0520*
- ✐ *www.johnsmith.co.uk*
- 🚌 *Stratford LU*
- 🕐 *Mon-Fri 9am-5.30pm (term time), Mon-Fri 10am-4pm (vacations)*

Academic shop from the reliable John Smith stable catering for the students at UEL.

University of Greenwich Bookshop

- 🖃 *Dreadnought Library, Maritime Campus, Park Row,*
  Old Royal Naval College, SE10 9LS
- ☎ *020 8331 8186*
- ✆ *020 8331 7581*
- ✐ *www.johnsmith.co.uk*
- 🚌 *Cutty Sark DLR*
- 🕐 *Mon-Thurs 9am-5.30pm, Fri 9am-5pm*

And at:

- 🖃 *Avery Hill Campus, Mansion Site,*
  Bexley Road, Eltham, SE9 2PQ
- ☎ *020 8331 7584*
- ✆ *020 8331 7581*
- 🚌 *New Eltham Rail*
- 🕐 *Mon-Thurs 9am-5.30pm, Fri 9am-5pm*

Academic shops run by John Smith specialising in books to support the courses run by the University.

Unsworths Booksellers – see p.209

Urban Gospel UK

⌧ *76 Bolton Crescent, SE5 0SE*
☎ *020 7582 1299*
✆ *020 7820 1508*
✑ *dunamisbrixton@aol.com*
🚌 *Oval LU (then bus)*
🕐 *Tues, Wed & Fri 10am-6pm, Thurs 10am-7pm, Sat 11am-3pm*

Specialist Christian stockist including children's books and Bibles in several different languages. They also stock CDs and DVDs and a good selection of black gospel music.

URC Bookshop

⌧ *86 Tavistock Place, WC1H 9RT*
🕐 *020 7916 8629*
✆ *020 7916 2021*
✑ *www.urc.org.uk*
🚌 *King's Cross LU/Rail or Russell Square LU*
🕐 *Mon-Fri 9am-4.30pm*

On the corner of Tavistock Place and Wakefield Street, this independent shop sells a broad range of Christian books including theology, worship, children's books and literature on the United Reformed Church. There's also a range of gift items.

V

Victoria and Albert Museum Shop

⌧ *Cromwell Road, South Kensington, SW7 2RL*
🕐 *020 7942 2687*
✑ *www.vam.ac.uk*
🚌 *South Kensington LU*
🕐 *Daily 10am-5.40pm (Wed & the last Friday
of the month open until 9.50pm)*

One of the best museums shops in London with a scintillating range of gifts, cards and stationery as well as an extensive selection of books. They cover all areas featured in the museum, embracing every sphere of artistic endeavour including jewellery, textiles, woodwork, fashion, ceramics, glass and metalwork.

Village Games

⌨ *65 Camden Lock, NW1 8AF*
☎ *020 7485 0653*
✆ *020 7485 0653*
✍ *information@villagegames.com*
🚇 *Camden Town LU*
🕐 *Wed-Sun 10.30am-5.30pm*

Just at the back of the main Camden Lock market, this tiny shop specialises in games and puzzles of all sorts. Its book selection covers mainstream games like chess, Go and Mah Jong as well as more esoteric mathematical and geometric puzzles. They aim to stock every English-language Go book.

The Vine

⌨ *34 Neal Street, WC2H 9PS*
🕐 *020 7240 1599*
🚇 *Covent Garden LU*
🕐 *Mon-Sat 11am-5.30pm*

This is a Christian space in the heart of Covent Garden a few minutes walk from the tube. In true modern bookselling style, it combines a bookshop (which sells Christian literature for adults and children) with a coffee bar (located to the rear). Several London City Mission publications are available free of charge.

W

The Wallace Collection

⌨ *Hertford House, Manchester Square, W1U 3BN*
☎ *020 7563 9522*
✆ *020 7563 9566*
✍ *www.wallacecollection.org.uk*
🚇 *Bond Street & Baker Street LU*
🕐 *Mon-Sat 10am-5pm, Sun 12noon-5pm*

The Wallace Collection houses the extraordinary art collection amassed by the Hertford family and is especially renowned for its eighteenth-century French pictures, porcelain, furniture and armoury. The museum shop sells a classy range of gift items inspired by the collection as well as a carefully edited selection of art, fashion and design books including catalogues relating to the museums collection. They also stock a good selection of London guides.

Waterstones

WATERSTONES

✎ *www.waterstones.co.uk*

Waterstones are shops with a serious literary feel to them, an emphasis on the books rather than peripherals (there are coffee shops in very few branches, so far at any rate). There are also a good supply of chairs for comfortable browsing. The staff are generally pretty clued up about their subject and always willing to locate a book in another store if it isn't on their shelves. Their magazine *Books Quarterly* is a fabulous read full of interviews and reviews of all the latest publications.

Branches at:

Camden

128 Camden High St, NW1 0NB
Tel: 020 7284 4948
Fax: 020 7482 3457
Transport: Camden Town LU
Open: Mon-Fri 9am-7pm,
Sat 9.30am-6pm, Sun 12noon-6pm

A large, two-storey branch. Readers may enjoy their purchases at the natural café next door.

Chelsea

150-152 King's Road, SW3 3NR
Tel: 020 7351 2023
Fax: 020 7351 7709
Transport: Sloane Square LU
Open: Mon-Sat 9.30am-7.30pm,
Sun 12noon-6pm

There are two floors in this bustling and justifiably popular branch in the heart of the King's Road shopping area. The shop itself is spacious, well-stocked and attractively laid out.

Chiswick

220-226 Chiswick High Road, W4 1PD
Tel: 020 8995 3559
Fax: 020 8995 3550
Transport: Turnham Green LU
Open: Mon-Fri 9.30am-7pm,
Sat 9am-6.30pm, Sun 11am-5.30pm

City University

Northampton Square, EC1V 0LH
Tel: 020 7608 0706
Fax: 020 7251 2813
Transport: Angel LU or Farringdon LU/Rail
Open: Mon-Fri 9am-6pm (term time),
Mon-Fri 9am-5.30pm (vacations)

Academic as well as a general stock.

Covent Garden

9-13 Garrick Street, WC2E 9BA
Tel: 020 7836 6757
Fax: 020 7836 4458
Transport: Covent Garden LU
Open: Mon-Sat 10am-8pm,
Sun 12noon-6pm

Fiction, travel and art related titles are very prominent on the ground floor but there is the usual extensive Waterstones stock in the basement. If you fancy a coffee there are a host of cafés in the area.

Ealing

64 Ealing Broadway Centre, W5 5JY
Tel: 020 8840 5905
Fax: 020 8567 3246
Transport: Ealing Broadway LU
Open: Mon-Sat 9.30am-6pm,
Sun 11am-5pm

Finchley

782 High Street, N12 8JY
Tel: 020 8446 9669
Fax: 020 8446 3663
Transport: Woodside Park LU
Open: Mon & Wed-Fri 9.30am-6pm,
Tues 10am-6pm, Sat 9am-6pm,
Sun 11am-5pm

Goldsmiths' College

University of London,
New Cross, SE14 6NW
Tel: 020 8469 0262
Fax: 020 8694 2279
Transport: New Cross Gate LU
Open: Mon-Fri 9.30am-6pm,
Sat 11am-2pm
Located inside the college, the
academic books reflect the college
courses, with a limited general stock.

Gower Street

82 Gower Street, WC1E 6EQ
Tel: 020 7636 1577
Fax: 020 7580 7680
Transport: Goodge Street LU
Open: Mon, Wed-Fri 9.30am-8pm,
Tues 10am-8pm, Sat 9.30am-7pm,
Sun 12noon-6pm
The best academic bookstore in
London – just around the corner
from London University. Hundreds

of thousands of titles are ranged over
five floors. Thankfully the staff are
knowledgeable and can give advice
on titles in their specialist fields. The
second-hand section is also fairly
extensive (see p.212).

Hampstead

68-69 Hampstead High St, NW3 1QP
Tel: 020 7794 1098
Fax: 020 7794 7553
Transport: Hampstead LU
Open: Mon-Sat 9.30am-8pm
(Wed opens at 10am), Sun 12noon-6pm
A large, well-stocked and bustling
branch of this chain with two floors
packed with every subject under the
sun – but sadly lacking in enough
life-saving chairs and tables where
you can relax and browse. There are
often readings and signings.

Harrods

Waterstones at Harrods,
87 Brompton Road, SW1X 7XL
Tel: 020 7730 1234
Fax: 020 7225 5920
Transport: Knightsbridge LU
Open: Mon-Sat 10am-7pm
On the second floor of the world
famous store (best reached by the
hugely kitsch Egyptian Escalator), this
Waterstones branch is a terrific book
department in a stunning shop.
Visitors should note that Harrods has
a dress code in the store which does
not permit backpacks. The range of
books is extensive and, catering for
the well-heeled customers, there are
more hardback books here than you'll

find almost anywhere else in London. All subject areas (excluding children's books, which has its own department see p.70), are covered and there is a quietly bookish bustle here that is attractive. There is something wonderfully comforting about walking through archways into rooms lined with well stocked book shelves. The books are well-displayed and there's a good selection of magazines in English and European languages. To top it all, you'll get one of Harrods' distinctive green and gold bags if you buy a book here.

Imperial College

Imperial College Road, SW7 2AZ
Tel: 020 7589 3563
Fax: 020 7591 3810
Transport: South Kensington LU
Open: Mon-Fri 8.30am-8pm, Sat
10am-5pm (term time), call for information on vacation opening hours
Located in the Central Library Building of the College, the stock reflects their specialisms in science, technology and business.

Islington

11 Islington Green, N1 2XH
Tel: 020 7704 2280
Fax: 020 7704 2152
Transport: Angel LU
Open: Mon-Sat 9.30am-8pm (from 10am on Tues), Sun 12-6pm
This branch has a decidedly literary feel and plenty of signings. There's a big children's section upstairs. The shop overlooks Islington Green

which is a pleasant place to relax when the weather is fine.

Kensington

193 Kensington High St, W8 6SH
Tel: 020 7937 8432
Fax: 020 7938 4970
Transport: High Street Kensington LU
Open: Mon-Sat 9am-8pm,
Sun 12noon-6pm
A large branch with a wide selection of books over three floors, and a good deal of academic stock. There are plenty of tables displaying promoted books and an especially dynamic fiction section. This branch often hosts readings and signings by well-known authors.

Leadenhall

1-7 Whittington Avenue,
Leadenhall Market, EC3V 1PJ
Tel: 020 7220 7882
Fax: 020 7220 7870
Transport: Monument LU
Open: Mon-Fri 8am-6.30pm
The market itself is lovely – a tiny haven of character in the midst of the impersonal City. The Waterstones here is a two storey shop with a wide ranging stock including extensive fiction, cookery, cinema, history and sports sections and some magazines on the ground floor. The basement stocks mostly the more serious subjects of management, finance and law appropriate for a branch surrounded by City institutions.

London School of Economics

Clare Market,
Portugal Street, WC2A 2AB
Tel: 020 7405 5531
Fax: 020 7430 1584
Transport: Holborn LU
Open: Mon-Fri 9.30am-7pm,
(Tues open at 10am), Sat 9.30am-6pm
Located very close to the London
School of Economics, the stock
includes a wide range of academic
and professional titles as well as a
limited general stock.

Ludgate Circus

Procession House,
Ludgate Circus, EC4M 7LW
Tel: 020 7236 5858
Fax: 020 7236 5533
Transport: Blackfriars LU/Rail
Open: Mon-Fri 8.30am-7pm

Margaret Street

28 Margaret Street, W1N 7LB
Tel: 020 7580 2812
Fax: 020 7637 1790
Transport: Oxford Circus LU
Open: Mon-Fri 9am-7pm,
Sat 9.30am-6pm, Sun 12noon-5pm

Notting Hill

39-41 Notting Hill Gate, W11 3JQ
Tel: 020 7229 9444
Fax: 020 7229 3991
Transport: Notting Hill Gate LU
Open: Mon-Fri 9am-8pm,
Sat 9am-7pm, Sun 12noon-6pm

Old Brompton Road

99-101 Old Brompton Rd, SW7 3LE
Tel: 020 7581 8522
Fax: 020 7225 2920
Transport: South Kensington LU
Open: Mon-Sat 9.30am-7pm,
Sun 12noon-6pm
This three-storey branch is very
welcoming with plenty of chairs and
a display of the latest book review
pages from the newspapers.

Oxford Street

19-23 Oxford Street, W2D 2DL
Tel: 020 7434 9759
Fax: 020 7434 3154
Transport: Tottenham Court Road LU
Open: Mon-Sat 9am-9pm,
Sun 12noon-6pm
This branch is not as big or as well-
stocked as the Gower Street branch
(see p.154) but it is handy for Oxford
Street shoppers or those browsing in
nearby Charing Cross Road. It also
has in its favour a busy, bustling
atmosphere and good general stock.

Oxford Street

311 Oxford St, W1C 2HP
Tel: 020 7499 6100
Fax: 020 7408 4858
Transport: Oxford Circus LU
Open: Mon-Sat 9.30am-8pm
(Thurs until 9pm), Sun 11.30am-6pm
One of the newer stores in the chain
and certainly one of the best with
three vast floors and an impressive
range of stock.

Piccadilly

203-206 Piccadilly, W1V 9LE
Tel: 020 7851 2400
Fax: 020 7851 2401
Transport: Piccadilly Circus LU
Open: Mon-Sat 10am-10pm,
Sun 12noon-6pm

Flagship store based in the glorious art deco surroundings of what was once Simpsons – a few minutes walk from Piccadilly Circus. There are six floors each heaving with a capacious stock, and the shop also boasts several refreshment outlets and long opening hours. Sofas and chairs are scattered everywhere.

Piccadilly
Hatchards

187 Piccadilly, W1J 9LE
Tel: 020 7439 9921
Fax: 020 7494 1313
Website: www.hatchards.co.uk
Transport: Piccadilly Circus LU
Open: Mon-Sat 9.30am-7pm,
Sun 12noon-6pm

Now taken over by Waterstones, this shop, founded by John Hatchard in 1797 – his portrait is on the staircase – retains much of the old world charm and character. The shop is full of dark wood, plush carpets and comfortable chairs but is still enviably well-stocked, although the paperback fiction section is hidden away in the basement. Catalogues are produced twice each year. Next door is Fortnum and Mason, definitely worth a mouth-watering browse in its own right.

Queen Mary

329 Mile End Road, E1 4NT
Tel: 020 8980 2554
Fax: 020 8981 6774
Transport: Whitechapel LU
Open: Mon-Fri 9am-5.30pm
(Tues opens 9.30am)

Academic books relevant to the courses at the University including law, business and finance but with a general stock too including a substantial children's section.

Trafalgar Square

The Grand Building,
Trafalgar Square, WC2N 5EJ
Tel: 020 7839 4411
Fax: 020 7839 1797
Transport: Charing Cross LU/Rail
Open: Mon-Sat 9.30am-9pm,
Sun 12noon-6pm

This three storey branch has a massive basement and is extremely well-stocked with a particularly good children's section. There's also a coffee shop on the first floor.

Wimbledon

12 Wimbledon Bridge, SW19 7NW
Tel: 020 8543 9899
Transport: Wimbledon LU
Open: Mon-Fri 10am-7pm, Sat 9am-7pm, Sun 11am-5pm

Opposite the station in the main Wimbledon shopping area, the store is not one of the largest but carries an extensive range nonetheless.

Watkins

🖳 *19 Cecil Court, Charing Cross Road, WC2N 4EZ*

☎ *020 7836 2182*

✒ *020 7836 6700*

🖉 *www.watkinsbooks.com*

🚇 *Leicester Square LU*

🕐 *Mon-Sat 11am-7pm*

Established in 1894 Watkins claims to be the world's oldest esoteric bookshop. It carries a huge and varied stock of books, magazines, CD's, DVDs and videos on ancient and modern philosophy, astrology, spirituality, religion and alternative therapies. Staff are knowledgeable and helpful and a mail order service is also available. As well as new titles, magazines and journals they also stock a good selection of second-hand books. Just along the road at 13 Cecil Court, Watkins Esoteric Centre (Tel 020 7379 4554) has many expert readers offering Tarot, Palm and Card Readings as well as astrologers and also stocks religious artefacts and gift items. The Watkins Review is the in-house magazine featuring new and forthcoming books plus feature articles.

Wellspring Bookshop Rudolf Steiner Books

🖳 *5 New Oxford Street, WC1A 1BA*

🕘 *020 7405 6101*

✎ *www.rudolfsteinerbooks.co.uk*

🚌 *Holborn LU*

🕘 *Mon-Fri 10.30am-5.30pm, Sat 12noon-5.30pm*

Specialist in the texts of Rudolf Steiner and other philosophical writers and including sections on arts, sciences, Celtic studies, grail studies, Arthurian Christianity and biography. They also sell wooden children's toys and books. Most books are new but there is a small second-hand stock.

Wesley Owen Books & Music

✎ *www.wesleyowen.com*

A nationwide chain specialising in Christian books, music, DVDs, software, gifts and stationery. The book selection includes Bibles and prayer books, biblical reference titles, books about the Christian life, social issues, counselling and fiction as well as children's literature. Branches at:

🖳 *82 High Street, South Woodford, E18 2NA*

☎ *020 8530 4244*

✉ *020 8518 8924*

🚌 *South Woodford LU*

🕘 *Mon-Sat 9.30am-5.30pm*

And

🖳 *3-9 Wigmore Street, W1U 1AD*

☎ *020 7493 1851*

✉ *020 7493 4478*

🚌 *Oxford Circus LU*

🕘 *Mon-Fri 9.30am-6pm (Thurs until 7pm), Sat 10am-6pm*

West End Lane Books

- 277 West End Lane, NW6 1QS
- 020 7431 3770
- 020 7431 7655
- www.welbooks.co.uk
- West Hampstead LU
- Mon-Sat 10am-7pm, Sun 12noon-5pm

A lovely, general bookshop with an extensive, well-displayed stock, including quite a few American books, and mats for children to lounge on in a dedicated area – the parenting and cookery sections are thoughtfully located nearby. Fiction is strong and the poetry section benefits from an expert at the helm. However psychology, politics, culture, religion, food, travel and health are also first-rate. The shop hosts events and a book club. They are related to Queen's Park Books (see p.117).

Westminster Bookshop

- 8 Artillery Row, SW1P 1RZ
- 020 7802 0018
- 020 7828 1244
- www.westminsterbookshop.co.uk
- St James's Park LU or Victoria LU/Rail
- Mon-Fri 9.30am-6pm, Sat 11am-4pm

Located a shortish walk from the Houses of Parliament this shop specialises in British, European and World history and politics but with a good range of fiction, business and biography titles as well. There are some remaindered books, magazines, greetings cards, CDs and DVDs. The shop also hosts regular book events.

The Who Shop

- 4 Station Parade, High Street North, East Ham, E6 1JD
- 020 8471 2356
- 020 8471 2356
- www.thewhoshop.com
- East Ham LU
- Mon-Sat 9.30am-5.30pm

Just across the road from the tube station, this shop (you won't miss it, it has a life-size Dalek in the window) specialises in books, models and merchandise linked to 'Dr Who'. They stock DVDs and videos of episodes of the TV programme that you won't find elsewhere and also sell some 'Buffy' and other sci-fi material.

Wildy & Sons Ltd

www.wildy.com

This company was established in 1830 and has two specialist law book-shops in the centre of legal London. Branches at:

Lincoln's Inn Archway, Carey Street, WC2A 2JD

020 7242 5778

020 7430 0897

Chancery Lane LU

Mon-Fri 8.45am-5.15pm

This branch also sells second-hand and antiquarian law books.
and

16 Fleet Street, EC4Y 1AU

020 7353 3907

020 7353 4395

Chancery Lane LU

Mon-Fri 9am-6pm, Sat 10am-4pm

Willesden Bookshop

Willesden Green Library Centre, 95 High Road, NW10 2SF

020 8451 7000

020 8830 1233

www.willesdenbookshop.co.uk

Willesden Green LU

Mon-Fri 10am-6pm, Sat 9.30am-5.30pm

A short walk from the tube and next to the library, this well-established general bookshop specialises in multicultural children's books, from very simple picture books to young adult level including many dual language books.

Wimbledon Books and Music

40 The High Street, Wimbledon Village, SW19 5AU

020 8879 3101

www.wimbledonbooksandmusic.co.uk

Wimbledon LU

Tues-Sat 10am-6pm, Sun 11am-4pm

Located in the heart of Wimbledon Village, the Common is 50 metres away and coffee shops abound, this is a general local bookseller with an excellent children's section – their speciality. It is also the only special-ist classical CD shop for miles around so definitely worth a visit.

Witherby

✑ *www.witherbys.com*

Specialist insurance and marine publisher and bookseller. There are two shops, one specialising in the marine titles and the other in insurance. Branches at:

Insurance Bookshop

🏠 *Chartered Insurance Institute Building, 20 Aldermanbury, EC2V 7HY*

🕐 *020 7417 4431*

🚇 *Bank, Moorgate & St Paul's LU*

🕐 *Mon-Thurs 10am-5.30pm, Fri 10am-4pm*

and

Book Department, Second Floor,

🏠 *32-36 Aylesbury Street, EC1R OET*

🕐 *020 7251 5341*

✎ *020 7251 1296*

🚇 *Farringdon LU/Rail*

🕐 *Mon-Fri 9am-4.30pm*

Word Play

🏠 *1 Broadway Parade, Crouch End, N8 9TN*

☎ *020 8347 6700*

✎ *020 8347 6500*

🚇 *Crouch Hill Rail*

🕐 *Mon-Sat 9am-5.30pm, Sun 11am-5pm*

Opposite the Clock Tower, the shop is half toys and half books. The book stock is mostly fiction with a range from early picture books to those for young adults as well as some poetry, non-fiction titles and audiobooks. The toy stock is also fun – the kids have plenty to choose from, including some great pocket money items for as little as 25p.

Wordsworth Bookshop *(will soon be known as Camberwell Bookshop)*

🏠 *11 Butterfly Walk Shopping Centre, Camberwell Green, SE5 8RW*

☎ *020 7277 1377*

✎ *020 7277 1168*

✑ *wordswothbooks@hotmail.com*

🚇 *Denmark Hill Rail*

🕐 *Mon-Fri 9am-7.30pm, Sat 9am-6.30pm*

Located in the covered shopping mall this shop is an attractive, lively and welcoming venue selling a broad spectrum of titles for adults and children. The shop is spacious, there's seating to encourage browsing and there are plenty of events with local authors who include Jenny Eclair, Steven Appleby, Terry Jones and Jeremy Bowen. There's a mailing list to keep customers up to date with forthcoming events. Refreshment can be found at Seymour Bros on Grove Lane or Tadim Café on Camberwell Church Street.

The Works

⌨ *www.works.gb.com*

There are two London branches of this discount bookshop chain. They feature books in all subject areas but glossy cookery, gardening, interior design and art books seem to be something of a speciality. There are also plenty of children's books, attractively-priced stationery, DVDs, videos and art materials. Branches at:

🖳 *Unit 2, 191 Camden High Street, NW1 7BT*
☎ *020 7284 3033*
🚌 *Camden Town LU*
🕔 *Mon-Sat 9am-8pm, Sun 10am-8pm*
and
🖳 *Unit 24, Lewisham Centre, SE13 7HB*
☎ *020 8318 0519*
🚌 *Lewisham Rail*
🕔 *Mon-Sat 9am-5.30pm & Sun 11am-5pm*

Y

Young Europeans Bookstore

🖳 *5 Cecil Court, WC2N 4EZ*
☎ *020 7836 6667*
✎ *020 7240 1635*
⌨ *www.YoungLinguists.com*
🚌 *Leicester Square LU*
🕔 *Mon-Sat 10.30am-6.30pm*

Allied to the European Bookshop (see p.158) and next door to the Italian Bookshop (see p.78) this is a great little shop specialising in books for children (birth to GCSE level) in French, Spanish, German, Portuguese and Italian plus a few in Russian. Fiction and all non-fiction areas are covered with plenty of materials for language learners.

Z

Zainab
- 112 Tooting Bec Road, SW17 8BQ
- 020 8672 9001
- 020 8672 9001
- Tooting Bec LU
- Mon-Sat 9am-5.30pm *(Friday closed 1pm-3pm)*

Specialist Islamic bookseller dealing in books in Arabic and English for adults and children. There are also gift and religious items. Zainab has other shops around London including Croydon and Hounslow.

Zam Zam
- 61 Brick Lane, E1 1JQ
- Shoreditch LU
- Daily 10am-9.30pm

Specialist in books for adults and children in Arabic, English, Bengali and Urdu on all aspects of the Islamic faith and life. There are also a few titles in English about Islam and books on learning Arabic. Situated in the middle of the renowned restaurants of Brick Lane, there are plenty of places for refreshment nearby.

1,2,3...

30th Century Comics
- 18 Lower Richmond Road, SW15 1JP
- 020 8788 2052
- www.30thcenturycomics.co.uk
- Putney Bridge LU
- Mon-Wed 10.30am-6pm, Thurs & Fri 10.30am-7pm,
  Sat 10.30am-6pm, Sun 11am-5pm

Specialist in new and vintage UK and US comics and annuals including Superman, Spiderman, Batman and X-Men (from the US) and Beano, Dandy, Bunty, Rupert and Eagle (from the UK). Their vintage stock dates largely from the 1930's to 1970's with a few titles from even earlier. They also stock some related merchandise plus some second-hand books about the comic genre.

Second-Hand &
Antiquarian Bookshops

Any Amounts of Books

A

Abbey Books

⌨ 4 The Apprentice Shop,
Merton Abbey Mills, Merantum Way, SW19 2RD

🚉 Colliers Wood LU

🕐 Sat, Sun & Bank Holidays 9am-6pm

This weekends-only shop has a huge well-organised, browser-friendly stock of second-hand fiction and non-fiction, rare titles, and particularly worthwhile selections of art, psychology, media, history, alternative health and Irish interest material. When the weather is fine the huge tables outside the shop groan beneath the weight of even more books. Their antiquarian stock is developing, especially anything with fine bindings. The shop is popular with dealers – so follow the experts to sniff out the bargains.

Adanami Bookshop

⌨ 387 Edgeware Road, NW9 6NL

☎ 020 8201 3499

🚉 Colindale LU

🕐 Sat & Sun 12noon-7pm

A bookshop specialising in second-hand Japanese books. If you're on the hunt for cheap books in Japanese this is the place to visit with prices starting from £1.

and

⌨ 30 Brewer Street, W1F 9TT

☎ 020 7439 5238

🚉 Piccadilly Circus LU

🕐 Mon-Sat 12noon-9pm, Sun 12noon-8pm

A few minutes walk into Soho from Piccadilly Circus, this tiny shop is piled floor to ceiling with the second-hand Japanese language books that are its sole business.

Altea Gallery

35 St George St, W1S 2FN

020 7491 0010

020 7491 0015

www.alteamaps.com

Oxford Circus, Green Park and Bond Street LU

Mon-Fri 10am-6pm (appointment recommended)

Antique maps and atlases plus travel books and reference books on maps.

Amwell Book Company

53 Amwell Street, EC1R 1UR

/ *020 7837 4891*

sixrobins@aol.com

Angel LU

Mon-Fri 11am-6pm, Sat 1pm-5pm

Second-hand, rare and out-of-print specialist in fashion, photography, art, architecture, design, children's and illustrated books and modern first editions including detective fiction. The architecture and photography sections are especially strong, there's a great sofa for browsing and a wide range of quality paperback fiction as well.

Any Amount of Books

56 Charing Cross Road, WC2H OQA

020 7836 3697

020 7240 1769

www.anyamountofbooks.com

Leicester Square LU

Mon-Sat 10.30am-9.30pm, Sun 11.30am-8.30pm

Long-standing Charing Cross Road favourite with an excellent general stock of second-hand books and a high turnover. It's always busy and the basement houses a huge number of special bargains. There's a great deal of stock listed on the website that is housed in one of the warehouses so look there if you're searching for a particular book. An annual catalogue details the rare and antiquarian stock, mostly literature. There are plenty of other good shops a short walk away, on Charing Cross Road itself and also on Cecil Court, closer to Trafalgar Square.

Archive Books and Music

📖 *83 Bell Street, NW1 6TB*

☎ *020 7402 8212*

🚌 *Edgware Road & Marylebone LU*

🕐 *Mon-Sat 10.30am-6pm*

Probably one of the most disorganised, overwhelming bookshops in London – and an absolute delight. Books are stacked floor to ceiling and tottering piles occupy every surface. Step-ladders are provided for the exploration of the heights while venturing down to the music cellar is rather like an expedition to a virgin jungle peopled with the ghosts of composers past. With bargains galore spilling from boxes outside, also in total disarray, this shop carries a general stock but is especially strong on sheet music and books about music. They don't come much more eccentric than this. Stephen Foster's is just along the street (see p.181).

Atlantis - see p.13

Avalon Comics - see p.14

B

Biblion

- 🖼 *1-7 Davies Mews, W1K 5AB*
- ☎ *020 7629 1374*
- ✆ *020 7493 7158*
- ✍ *www.biblionmayfair.com*
- 🚌 *Bond Street LU*
- 🕐 *Mon-Sat 10am-6pm*

Tucked away behind Gray's Antique Market just off Oxford Street, this is a real gem for lovers of collectible books. Over a hundred top-quality dealers operate from here with well-displayed stock (around 20,000 volumes) in quiet surroundings and helpful yet unintrusive staff. Many of the dealers are based outside London or otherwise operate by post or on the internet, so this is a good opportunity to view their stock at first hand. The books on show cover the full range of collectible material from contemporary first editions to rare, antiquarian, leatherbound volumes. This is the perfect destination for those who want to learn a bit more about book collecting and see some examples of top quality antiquarian books. Moreover, as Biblion's wide ranging stock shows, its a hobby that needn't break the bank – there's plenty on sale for £20 with prices going up to as much as £50,000. Follow the link on their website to *www.biblion.com* and access more than 3 million books.

Black Gull

- 🖼 *70-71 The West Yard, Camden Lock Place, NW1 8AF*
- ☎ *020 7267 5005*
- 🚌 *Camden Town LU*
- 🕐 *Daily 10am-6pm*

Second-hand shop with a general stock but especially strong on quality fiction, philosophy, psychology, art, mind, body and spirit, film and counter culture.

Book and Comic Exchange

⌗ *14 Pembridge Road, W11 3HL*

☎ *020 7229 8420*

🚇 *Notting Hill Gate LU*

🕐 *Daily 10am-8pm*

This shop is always busy with a fast turnover of stock and has a huge choice of mostly paperback books and a wide range of comics and magazines. The emphasis is on fiction (both literary and popular), music, film, biography and art but all other subjects are covered. The longer a book stays on the shelf, the lower its price goes and there's a bargain basement with all books for 50p or less.

Bookmarks - see p.23

Bookmongers

⌗ *439 Coldharbour Lane, SW9 8LN*

☎ /✆ *020 7738 4225*

✎ *www.freespace.virgin.net/book.mongers*

✎ *bookmongers@virgin.net*

🚇 *Brixton LU/Rail*

🕐 *Mon-Sat 10.30am-6.30pm*

There's much for the bargain minded book lover to appreciate at this brilliant second-hand bookshop just around the corner from the Ritzy Cinema in Brixton. The stock is wide ranging, keenly priced and well organised with sections on professional subjects, books by Irish and Scottish writers and foreign language titles, as well as mainstream fiction and more academic books on history and science. Their website is also a useful resource which offers more books than can be held in the shop. This is definitely one of the best second-hand bookshops south of the river. Head up and into Market Row to Rosie's for excellent snacks.

Books and Lyrics

- 7 *The Apprentice Shop, Merton Abbey Mills,*
  Merantum Way, SW19 2RD
- ☎ *020 8543 0625*
- 🚇 *Colliers Wood LU*
- 🕐 *Tues-Fri 11am-5pm, Sat & Sun 10am-5pm*

This is a well-organised, tidy shop with a general stock and specialisms in classical and pop sheet music and arts and crafts books. It is a good idea to visit at the weekend when you can also enjoy Merton Abbey Mills Market.

The Bookshop on the Heath

- 74 *Tranquil Vale, Blackheath, SE3 0BU*
- ☎ *020 8852 4786*
- ✎ *020 8318 9875*
- 🚇 *Blackheath Rail*
- 🕐 *Mon-Sat 9am-4pm, Sun 12noon-6pm*

Located on the corner of Blackheath village near to the heath, this shop carries second-hand and out of print books in all subject areas, including local history and guidebooks, plus modern first editions. The range is wide, from the £1 paperback up to a First Edition of James Bond. There are lots of coffee shops and restaurants nearby for refreshment and a picnic on the heath is a fine weather option.

T. Alena Brett

- 24 *Cecil Court, WC2N 4HE*
- ☎ /✎ *020 7836 8222*
- 🚇 *Leicester Square LU*
- 🕐 *Mon-Sat 9am-6pm*

Seller of antiquarian books, maps, prints and documents, with a generalist approach but specialising in Vanity Fair material. The building has had a long history; it is said that Mozart had his hair cut here and when it was a tea room prior to the First World War Rupert Brooke was a regular customer.

Tim Bryars

- 📷 *8 Cecil Court, WC2N 4HE*
- ☎ *020 7836 1901*
- 📠 *020 7836 1910*
- 🖉 *www.timbryars.co.uk*
- 🚇 *Leicester Square LU*
- 🕐 *Mon-Fri 11am-6pm, Sat 12noon-5pm*

There are maps dating from the sixteenth-century upstairs (from £20 up to £10,000). Downstairs there is a small, specialist selection of antiquarian books including classical texts and translations.

Steve Burak Books

- 📷 *18 Leigh St, WC1H 9EW*
- ☎ *020 7388 1153*
- 🖉 *steveburaklondon@yahoo.com*
- 🚇 *Russell Square LU*
- 🕐 *Mon-Sat 11am-7pm and Book fair Sundays (ring to confirm opening hours before visiting)*

A general out-of-print and antiquarian bookseller with stock supplemented by surplus stock booksales. The shop also sells ephemera, manuscripts and pictorial art. Prices from £1 to £1000.

C

Marcus Campbell Art Books

- 📷 *43 Holland Street, Bankside, SE1 9JR*
- ☎ *020 7261 0111*
- 📠 *020 7261 0129*
- 🖉 *www.marcuscampbell.co.uk*
- 🚇 *Blackfriars LU/Rail*
- 🕐 *Mon-Sat 10.30am-6.30pm, Sun 12noon-6pm*

Handily located next to Tate Modern and close to the River Thames, this shop deals in out-of-print, rare and second-hand books on twentieth-century art (British and International). Stock includes books on important movements, artist's monographs, catalogues, artists' books, magazines and emphemera. There's also a selection of exhibition catalogues from £1 to £3000 and beyond.

Chapter Two - see p.44

Cecil Court

173

Church Street Bookshop

- 142 Stoke Newington Church Street, N16 0JU
- 020 7241 5411
- Stoke Newington Rail
- Mon-Fri 11.30am-6pm, Sat 11am-6pm, Sun 11.30am-6pm

This is one of two excellent second-hand shops (see Ocean Books p.194) located in the heart of a street renowned for its restaurants. Small but amply stocked, the shop has a good general stock with a particularly extensive range of children's books. They always have plenty of recently published review copies and well stocked bargain boxes with books for as little as 50p. You can survey their academic and antiquarian stock on *www.abebooks.com*.

Classic Bindings

- 61 Cambridge St, SW1V 4PS
- 020 7834 5554
- 020 7630 6632
- *www.classicbindings.net*
- Pimlico LU or Victoria LU/Rail
- Mon-Fri 10am-5.30pm

Specialists in English and French literature, history, bound sets, first editions, voyages, travel and illustrated books.

Collinge and Clark

- 13 Leigh Street, WC1H 9EW
- 020 7387 7105
- 020 7388 1315
- *collingeandclark@aol.com*
- Russell Square LU
- Mon-Fri 11am-6.30pm, Sat 11am-3.30pm

A small, high quality, second-hand, antiquarian and rare bookshop which specialises in volumes from private presses and books on history, arts and crafts, literature and typography. Much of the stock is leather-bound and in mint condition with price tags to match, but there are some leatherbound volumes for as little as £30. The shop's façade features as 'Black Books' in the TV series of the same name. Catalogues are issued once or twice a year on particular subjects.

Comicana - see p.48

The Comic Shack - see p.48

Copperfield's

📧 *37 Hartfield Road, SW19 3SG*

☎ *020 8542 0113*

🚇 *Wimbledon LU/Rail*

🕐 *Mon-Wed 10am-7pm, Thurs & Fri 10am-8pm,*
   Sat 10am-6pm, Sun 11am-5pm

Dazzling gem of a second-hand bookshop a few minutes walk from the main Wimbledon shopping centre. The shop is jam-packed with titles in all subject areas with an estimated 30,000 books in the shop plus another 20,000 in storage. It's hard to select any area in particular for mention but they are very strong on philosophy, psychology, poetry, anthropology, politics and history. The stock is not all heavy-weight academic books – with plenty of entertaining page-turners from which to guiltily choose. It's a hard-hearted book lover who leaves empty-handed.

D

Davenports - see p.54

David Drummond

- 🖼 *11 Cecil Court, WC2N 4EZ*
- ☎/✆ *020 7836 1142*
- ✍ *drummond@popt.fsnet.co.uk*
- 🚌 *Leicester Square LU*
- 🕐 *Mon-Fri 11am-2.30pm & 3.30pm-5.45pm, first Sat of the month*
  11am-2.30pm (extended hours are possible by arrangement)

Specialising in books and ephemera (including playbills) related to the performing arts, the Victorian era and social history. It is very strong on music hall, variety, circus and conjuring. There is also a selection of pre-World War II children's books and an enormous range of postcards.

E

Earlsfield Bookshop

- 🖼 *513 Garratt Lane, Wandsworth, SW18 4SW*
- ☎ *020 8946 3744*
- 🚌 *Earlsfield Rail*
- 🕐 *Mon-Thurs 4pm-6pm, Fri 11am-6pm, Sat 10am-5pm*

Right next door to Earlsfield Station, this is a small, general second-hand book dealer with extremely competitive prices and a 50p bargain table outside. There's a pleasant coffee shop next door if you need refreshment.

Francis Edwards

⊞ *13 Great Newport Street, WC2H 7JA*

☎ *020 7379 7669*

✆ *020 7836 5977*

✍ *www.francisedwards.co.uk*

🚇 *Leicester Square LU*

🕐 *Mon-Sat 10am-7pm*

Just around the corner from the tube station and the other bookshops on Charing Cross Road, this shop has a general antiquarian stock although it is especially strong on art, military history, first editions, natural history, typography, and travel. They have large weekly deliveries of books that replenish the shelves and make this store worth a regular visit. There are lots of catalogues on various subjects and a glance at these will reassure buyers that the stock here is of good quality and fairly priced with books starting at £25.

Francis Edwards is part of the Quinto group. See Quinto of Charing Cross Road (p.200) and Quinto of Great Russell Street (p.200).

Peter Ellis

⊞ *18 Cecil Court, WC2N 4HE*

☎ *020 7836 8880*

✍ *peter-ellis.co.uk*

🚇 *Leicester Square LU*

🕐 *Mon-Fri 10.30am-7pm, Sat 10.30am-5.30pm*

A small Cecil Court shop specialising in modern literature, modern first editions, history, illustrated books and books on London.

Eltham Books

⊞ *5 Chequers Parade, SE9 1DD*

☎ *020 8859 4479*

🚇 *Eltham Rail*

🕐 *Mon-Sat 9am-5.30pm*

Just off Eltham High Street in a short pedestrian walkway, this small shop is packed to bursting with second-hand books, the majority paperbacks and most at 99p. Cards, stationery and gifts make up the rest of the stock here.

F

Fantasy Centre

⌑ *157 Holloway Road, N7 8LX*

☎/✆ *020 7607 9433*

✍ *www.fantasycentre.biz*

🚌 *Holloway Road LU*

🕐 *Mon-Sat 10am-6pm*

This long-established specialist shop catering for readers and collectors of sci-fi, fantasy and horror with a huge second-hand, rare and out-of-print stock of paperback and hardback titles. They offer a wide range of collectable books as well as some newer titles from specialist publishers such as Ash Tree, Tartarus and Nesfa Press.

Keith Fawkes

⌑ *1-3 Flask Walk, NW3 1HJ*

☎ *020 7435 0614*

🚌 *Hampstead LU*

🕐 *Mon-Sat 10am-5.30pm, Sun 1pm-6pm*

Just around the corner from the underground station in a pedestrian alleyway, this is a quintessential second-hand bookshop, with a massive stock ranged high on shelves and in piles that would take days rather than hours to sift through. The stock covers all general subjects including musical scores and is especially strong on art, literature and first editions.

Simon Finch Rare Books

This high-profile bookseller of rare and antiquarian books paid a world record auction price of US$2.2million for a scientific manuscript in 1998. Times have changed and at the time of going to press the future of the company is uncertain. Prospective customers should phone before making a special trip to their London Store. At:

⌑ *53 Maddox Street, W1S 2PN*

☎ *020 7499 0974*

✆ *020 7499 0799*

✍ *www.simonfinch.com*

🚌 *Bond Street & Oxford Circus LU*

🕐 *Mon-Fri 10am-6pm*

Specialist in literature, social sciences, science, medicine, early printing art, architecture, design, photography and fine bindings, There are also plenty of modern first editions.

Fine Books Oriental

- 38 Museum Street, WC1A 1LP
- ☎ 020 7242 5288
- ✆ 020 7242 5344
- www.finebooks.demon.co.uk
- Holborn or Tottenham Court Road LU
- Mon-Fri 9.15am-5.30pm, Sat 11am-5.30pm

An extensive stock of antiquarian, rare and second-hand books on the Far and Middle East – just across the road from the British Museum.

Fisher & Sperr

- 46 Highgate High Street, N6 5JB
- ☎ 020 8340 7244
- ✆ 020 8348 4293
- Highgate LU
- Mon-Sat 10.30am-5pm

Labyrinthine in layout, the shop rambles over four storeys with books packed floor to ceiling on every floor. Virtually every subject of human enquiry is represented here although the specialities of the house are London, art, history, classical history and sets of books. Most of the stock is in hardback. It would take a lifetime to explore all the nooks and crannies of this place but book lovers will enjoy trying.

Sam Fogg

- 15D Clifford Street, W1S 4JZ
- ☎ 020 7534 2100
- ✆ 020 7534 2122
- www.samfogg.com
- Bond Street, Green Park or Oxford Circus LU
- Mon-Fri 9.30am-5.30pm

Specialists in gorgeous medieval and oriental manuscripts that are at the top of the quality and price-range. You ring the bell for entry but the staff here are approachable, so don't be put off. The exhibitions of art and manuscripts change every month or two and are accompanied by gorgeous catalogues that are works of art in their own right.

Foster's

⌨ *183 Chiswick High Road, W4 2DR*

☎ *020 8995 2768*

🚌 *Turnham Green LU*

🕐 *Thurs, Fri & Sat 10.30am-5pm*

A lovely little second-hand bookshop with an eclectic stock – anything that appeals to the owners finds space, anything that doesn't is rejected. This makes for a highly attractive and personal selection encompassing everything from bargains on the table outside to rarer, antiquarian, leatherbound and highly-collectible books. There are a few selected magazines such as Picture Post. There's a great sign in the window 'Children, Dogs and Mad Grannies welcome' – but we can state from experience that the welcome extends far beyond that.

Paul Foster's Bookshop

⌨ *119 Sheen Lane, East Sheen, SW14 8AE*

☎ *020 8876 7424*

📠 *020 8876 7424*

✉ *paulfosterbooks@btinternet.com*

🚌 *Mortlake Rail*

🕐 *Wed-Sat 10.30am-6pm*

A big stock of second-hand, rare and antiquarian books covering most subjects with an emphasis on art, ninteenth and twentieth-century first editions, children's and illustrated books and volumes with fine bindings.

Stephen Foster

⌨ *95 Bell Street, NW1 6TL*

☎ *020 7724 0876*

📠 *020 7724 0927*

✉ *www.sfbooks.co.uk*

🚌 *Edgware Road LU*

🕐 *Mon-Sat 10am-6pm*

A well-stocked, characterful, second-hand shop with a superb art section which fills more than half of the shop, covering all periods, nationalities and styles as well as applied arts. There are also comprehensive history, literature and travel sections as well as a range of rare and antiquarian books. Just down the road is Archive Books & Music (see p.168 for details).

Robert Frew Ltd

- 31 Maddox Street, W1S 2PB
- ☎ 020 7290 3800
- www.robertfrew.com
- Oxford Circus LU
- Mon-Fri 10am-6pm

This shop has relocated from Great Russell Street but its imposing stock of leatherbound antiquarian books (many in sets) displayed in glass cabinets remains unchanged and the business still caters for the serious and affluent collector. Specialisms are pre-nineteenth century leatherbound volumes of literature, travel or any illustrated subject. Staff are friendly and prices range from £20 to £80,000. The shop also sells a handsome selection of prints and maps.

G

Gay's the Word - see p.65

R A Gekoski

- Pied Bull Yard, 15A Bloomsbury Square, WC1A 2LP
- ☎ 020 7404 6676
- 020 7404 6595
- www.gekoski.com
- Holborn LU
- Mon-Fri 10am-5.30pm

Specialists in 20th-century literature and modern first editions at the very top end of the market. Gekoski also stock important letters and manuscripts from authors including Conrad, James, Joyce and Plath to name just a few. Prices start at £200 rising to £150,000 – although they sold an inscribed first edition of Ulysses in 2002 for US$460,000. The shop is conveniently located in the British Museum area with a host of other booksellers nearby. The eponymous Rick Gekoski is also an author and broadcaster.

Gibberd Secondhand Books

🖂 *20 Lower Marsh, SE1 7RJ*
☎ *020 7633 9562*
🚌 *Waterloo LU/Rail*
🕘 *Wed-Fri 11am-7pm*

A general second-hand shop in the heart of the lunchtime market area. They are strong in fiction, history, travel and geography and also have a few discounted classic DVDs.

Stanley Gibbons - see p.66

Martin Gladman

🖂 *235 Nether Street, Finchley, N3 1NT*
☎ *020 8343 3023*
🚌 *West Finchley LU*
🕘 *Tues-Fri 11am-8pm, Sat 10am-6pm*

This second-hand and out-of-print bookshop is located in a parade of shops right next to West Finchley underground. They specialise in mostly hardback scholarly and serious books (particularly history, the humanities, social sciences, psychology, military subjects and transport), but also have a large general stock which includes paperback fiction. The comfy armchair in the corner is ideal for browsers and for the last 28 years customers have been welcomed with mince pies during December.

Gloucester Road Bookshop

🖂 *123 Gloucester Road, SW7 4TE*
☎ *020 7370 3503*
📠 *020 7373 0610*
✉ *manager@gloucesterbooks.co.uk*
🚌 *Gloucester Road LU*
🕘 *Mon-Fri 9.30am-10.30pm, Sat-Sun & Bank Holidays*
   10.30am-6.30pm

One of the most welcoming second-hand bookshops in London with a good quality stock, rapid turnover and decent prices. There are some excellent books on the £1 shelves outside, while inside fiction, literary criticism, art, history and children's books are all well represented. A small stock of antiquarian and rare books as well as twice-yearly catalogues are also available. Highly recommended.

Gosh Comics - see p.68

Goldsboro Books

⌂ *1 Cecil Court, WC2N 4EZ*

☎ *020 7497 9228*

✎ *www.goldsborobooks.co.uk*

🚌 *Leicester Square LU*

🕐 *Mon-Sat 10am-7pm*

This store specialises in signed first editions, including newly published books. On some of the stock the ink is barely dry as the shop hosts regular book signings. Like many of the bookshops on Cecil Court there's an excellent choice of bargain books on display outside.

Griffith and Partners

⌂ *31-35 Great Ormond Street, WC1N 3HZ*

☎ *020 7430 1394*

🚌 *Russell Square LU*

🕐 *Mon-Fri 12noon-6pm*

A small shop selling a general stock of second-hand books, especially literature, biography, poetry, history, travel and the Arab World. Russian and classical literature also put in an appearance here and the bargain trays outside are well worth a rummage. The shop is opposite the Great Ormond Street Hospital for Children and around the corner from Lamb's Conduit Street in an area with a growing number of bookshops.

H

Halcyon Books

⌂ *1 Greenwich South Street, SE10 8NW*

☎ *020 8305 2675*

✎ *www.halcyonbooks.co.uk*

🚌 *Greenwich Rail/DLR*

🕐 *Daily 10am-6pm*

Great shop close to the main tourist sights in Greenwich offering a large selection of second-hand and out-of-print books in all subject areas. There's a particularly broad range of fiction, literary criticism, history and travel but keep an eye out too for books in foreign languages including French, Spanish and Japanese. There's a busy, literary atmosphere with restful music playing in the background.

185

Adrian Harrington

⌨ *64A Kensington Church Street, W8 4DB*
☎ *020 7937 1465*
✆ *020 7368 0912*
✍ *www.harringtonbooks.co.uk*
🚌 *High Street Kensington or Notting Hill Gate LU*
🕐 *Mon-Sat 10am-6pm*

Small but beautiful shop that is lined from floor to ceiling with shelves of superb quality antiquarian books – most of them gorgeously bound – covering subjects right across the board. They specialise in literature, voyages and travel, children's (including Harry Potter) and illustrated books and first editions – Ian Fleming, Winston Churchill and Graham Greene are especially well represented. Catalogues are published regularly.

Peter Harrington

⌨ *100 Fulham Road, SW3 6HS*
☎ *020 7591 0220*
✆ *020 7225 7054*
✍ *www.peter-harrington-books.com*
🚌 *South Kensington LU*
🕐 *Mon-Sat 10am-6pm*

A book lover's dream selling fabulous rare and antiquarian books. All subjects are covered but the specialisms are bound sets, English literature, children's, travel, voyages, fore-edge paintings and fine bindings. This is a shop dealing in quality books at the top end of the market. There are four or five catalogues a year, to coincide with prestigious book fairs and generally detailing more recently acquired volumes.

The Hellenic Bookservice - see p.72

Thomas Heneage Art Books - see p.72

G Heywood Hill - see p.73

P J Hilton

📠 *12 Cecil Court, WC2N 4HE*
☎ *020 7379 9825*
✎ *paul.hilton@rarebook.globalnet.co.uk*
🚌 *Leicester Square LU*
🕐 *Mon-Sat 10.30am-6pm*

Specialists in rare and antiquarian literature including Christianity, ecclesiastical history, Bibles and prayer books. There are plenty of sumptuous volumes to covet here, but luckily there's a bargain shelf outside to keep impecunious browsers happy.

Hoxton Book Depository

📠 *97 Hoxton Street, N1 6QL*
☎ *020 7613 4841*
🚌 *Old Street LU/Rail*
🕐 *Mon-Sat 11am-7pm*

A well stock second-hand bookshop in one of London's most fashionable districts. All kinds of books are to be found here, but popular fiction, art, media, film and biography are particularly well represented. As well as books there is a more limited range of vintage magazines, videos and vinyl. The opening times for this store are a little erratic and the service eccentric, but the shop is still worth a visit.

Hurlingham Books

📠 *91 Fulham High Street, SW6 3JS*
☎ *020 7736 4363*
🚌 *Putney Bridge LU*
🕐 *Ring for details of opening hours*

Rather hidden away on the north side of Putney Bridge but well worth searching out, this small second-hand shop is piled high with enticing bargains. Most general subjects are covered and there are some rare and antiquarian titles to view on request. The selection of modern fiction is especially broad with many in the £3-£5 range. The shop keeps wonderfully erratic opening hours so telephone before making a journey. Next door is The Eight Bells pub – good for a reviving drink and a pub lunch.

Second-Hand & Antiquarian Bookshops

J

Jarndyce

▭ 46 Great Russell Street, WC1B 3PA
☎ 020 7631 4220
✆ 020 7631 1882
✐ www.jarndyce.co.uk
🚇 Holborn and Tottenham Court Road LU
🕐 Mon-Fri 10.30am-5.30pm

Just across the road from the British Museum, housed in a building where nineteenth-century artist and illustrator Randolf Caldecott lived, Jarndyce specialises in nineteenth-century books covering literature and social history, but also has some eighteenth-century stock. There are many top quality antiquarian books and rare volumes on show, with fine bindings and prices to match, although the majority of their titles can be bought for a price below £50. The shop publishes regular catalogues on various themes, e.g women writers, Dickens and London, Plays and the Theatre. Among the attractions of the shop is a chair in the corner which W M Thackeray reputedly once occupied and in the winter they keep an open fire. Although you must ring for admission, this is only to allow staff to undertake other tasks. Upon entering you will find the staff both welcoming and helpful.

Judd Books

▭ 82 Marchmont Street, WC1N 1AG
☎ 020 7387 5333
✐ ad@juddbooks.demon.co.uk
🚇 Russell Square LU
🕐 Mon-Sat 11am-7pm, Sun 11am-6pm

There is so much stock in this two storey gem (about ten minutes from the British Library), that step ladders are provided so customers can reach the upper shelves. The shop is full of second-hand and discounted new books in all subject areas with particularly strong sections on African studies, economics, history, philosophy, Ireland, humanities, Eastern Europe, architecture, fiction, film, literary biography, photography and printing and publishing. The scope and number of volumes is vast and the prices are competitive, with bargain tables outside, plus a 10% student discount. One of the most enticing bookshops in London.

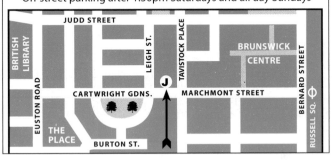

K

Kirkdale Bookshop – see p.82

Krypton Komics –see p.84

L

Judith Lassalle

🔲 *247A Liverpool Road, N1 1LX*

☎ *020 7354 9344 / 020 7607 7121*

🚌 *Angel LU*

🕘 *Wed 7.30am-4pm, Sat 9.30am-4p*m

Specialist dealer in rare Juvenilia. As well as some very fine books the stock includes children's games, toys, peepshows, optical toys, pop-up books and panoramas – all dating from pre-1914.

Librairie La Page – French Bookseller – see p.85

See The Library – p.85

M

Maggs Bros Ltd

- 🖃 *50 Berkeley Square, W1J 5BA*
- ☎ *020 7493 7160*
- ✆ *020 7499 2007*
- 🖉 *www.maggs.com*
- 🚌 *Green Park LU*
- 🕓 *Mon-Fri 9.30am-5pm*

Established in 1853, and with a royal warrant to boot, Maggs Bros is one of the premier rare and antiquarian booksellers in London with prices reflecting the superb quality of material. Operating out of a lovely town house overlooking Berkeley Square, each department is looked after by highly knowledgeable, often multilingual staff. A few of the specialisms are travel, natural history and early British books supplemented by an enormous range of autographed letters and manuscripts. Their beautifully produced catalogues are published frequently, each covering a specific subject area.

Maghreb Bookshop - see p.88

The Map House
- 54 Beauchamp Place, SW3 1NY
- 020 7589 4325
- 020 7589 1041
- www.themaphouse.com
- Knightsbridge LU
- Mon-Fri 10am-6pm, Sat 10.30am-5pm

Specialising in antique maps, atlases and globes, this shop is definitely worth a visit if you are interested in cartography as they have a good selection of books on the subject, both new and out-of-print.

Marcet Books
- 4A Nelson Road, SE10 9JB
- 020 8853 5408
- marcetbooks@btconnect.com
- Cutty Sark DLR or Greenwich Rail/DLR
- Daily 10am-5.30pm

Shortage of space is no obstacle at this small bookshop on one of the alleyways leading to Greenwich Market. The modest premises are packed full of second-hand books in a broad range of subjects including review copies of recent publications. It is particularly strong on fiction, poetry, history, and art. For those in search of a bargain there are discounted books of only £1. Easily combined with a visit to Greenwich Market (see p.241).

Marchpane
- 16 Cecil Court, WC2N 4HE
- 020 7836 8661
- 020 7497 0567
- www.marchpane.com
- Leicester Square LU
- Mon-Sat 10.30am-6.30pm

Lovely little two-storey shop selling antiquarian and second-hand children's and illustrated books, especially Lewis Carroll titles and other classics of the genre. Visitors of a certain age will enjoy the original BBC Dalek that is on display.

Maritime Books - see p.90

Marlborough Rare Books
- 📖 *144-146 New Bond Street, W1S 2TR*
- ☎ *020 7493 6993*
- ✉ *020 7499 2479*
- ✍ *sales@mrb-books.co.uk*
- 🚇 *Bond Street LU*
- 🕐 *Mon-Fri 9.30am-5.30pm*

On the fourth floor, high above the Bond Street fashion windows, this quiet shop has a small but quality stock specialising in art, architecture, illustrated books and any subject with fine bindings. Regular catalogues are published.

Mega-City Comics - see p.91

Midheaven - see p.94

Murder One, New Worlds and Heartlines - see p.97

My Back Pages
- 📖 *8-10 Balham Station Road, SW12 9SG*
- ☎ *020 8675 9346*
- ✍ *douglasjeffers@aol.com*
- 🚇 *Balham LU/Rail*
- 🕐 *Mon-Fri 10am-8pm, Sat 10am-7pm, Sun 11am-6pm*

This great little shop is just down the side of Balham Station (you can hear station announcements in the shop), and is required visiting for South London book enthusiasts. They stock second-hand books as well as full-price and discounted new books with a few rarer and antiquarian titles and cover most subject areas (both general and more academic). If you want to combine a trip here with other entertainment, The Banana Comedy club is just around the corner at The Bedford pub.

Second-Hand & Antiquarian Bookshops

N

Notting Hill Books

⬜ *132 Palace Gardens Terrace, W8 4RT*
☎ *020 7727 5988*
✆ *020 7625 1409*
🚌 *Notting Hill Gate LU*
🕐 *Mon-Sat 10.30am-6pm (Thurs until 1pm)*

A small shop, but packed full of discounted and second-hand books on a variety of serious subjects, with excellent coverage of art, literary criticism, architecture, design and history. A selection of serious fiction is offered at half the publisher's price and there are bargain books outside.

O

Ocean Books

⬜ *127 Stoke Newington Church Street, N16 0UH*
☎ *020 7502 6319*
✉ *oceanbooksn16@yahoo.co.uk*
🚌 *Stoke Newington Rail*
🕐 *Mon-Sat 11.30am-6pm, Sun 12noon-6pm*

This street is famed for its restaurants but Ocean Books (along with Church Street Bookshop, see p.174) make it equally a prime destination for book lovers. There is a good general second-hand stock at fair prices but fiction, art, photography and design are notable strengths. Some of the stock is listed on ABE.

Offstage - see p.104

Omega Bookshop (formerly Rees and O'Neill)

⬜ *27 Cecil Court, WC2N 4EZ*
☎ *020 7836 3336*
✆ *020 7836 0336*
✉ *www.omegabookshop.com*
🚌 *Leicester Square LU*
🕐 *Mon-Fri 10am-6pm, Sat 10am-5pm*

The name has changed but this shop still specialises in modern first editions with additional literature, art, design and illustrated books. There's a good display of £10 volumes inside and £1 and £2 bargains outside. There are regular catalogues detailing new acquisitions.

P

Pendleburys

- 🖃 *Church House, Portland Avenue, N16 6HJ*
- ☎ *020 8809 4922*
- ✍ *www.pendleburys.com*
- 🚌 *Stoke Newington Rail*
- 🕐 *Mon-Sat 10am-5pm (closed Wed)*

Created out of part of a church just behind Stamford Hill Library, Pendlebury's is one of the largest dealers in second-hand and out of print theology books in the country. There's a stock of 20,000 titles including large sections on philosophy, Christianity, Judaism, Islam and Eastern religions. Don't be deterred by having to ring for admittance – this is a welcoming place to browse.

Photo Books International – see p.112

Pickering & Chatto

- 36 St George Street, W1S 2FW
- ☎ 020 7491 2656
- ✆ 020 7491 9161
- *www.pickering-chatto.com*
- Oxford Circus LU
- 🕐 *Mon-Fri 9.30am-5.30pm (and by appointment)*

One of several top-class antiquarian dealers in the Bond Street area, this one carries a general antiquarian stock but specialises in economics, science, medicine, women, philosophy, social sciences, humanities, technology and engineering. The shop is up on the first floor above the street at present, but is destined to move to a new address in the same area at the time of writing. Please phone before making a journey to confirm their new location. They also publish regular catalogues.

Popular Book Centre

- 87 Rochester Row, SW1P 1LJ
- ☎ 020 7821 0631
- Victoria LU/Rail
- 🕐 *Mon-Thurs 9.30am-5.30pm, Fri 9.30am-6pm, Sat 9.30am-3.45pm*

Long-standing second-hand shop with a considerable selection of mostly popular paperback fiction but with some non-fiction and literary fiction as well. There are loads of magazines from serious titles like the 'Arts Review' through to 'girlie' mags, discreetly hidden at the back, as well as posters, gifts and vinyl records. There are plenty of bargain boxes for those on a budget.

Henry Pordes

- 58-60 Charing Cross Road, WC2H 0BB
- ☎ 020 7836 9031
- ✆ 020 7240 4232
- *www.henrypordesbooks.com*
- *info@henrypordesbooks.com*
- Leicester Square LU
- 🕐 *Mon-Sat 10am-7pm*

Located in the book-buying hub of Charing Cross Road, this shop sells second-hand, out-of-print, antiquarian and remaindered books in all subject areas. It has an enormous selection of all of these arranged floor-to-ceiling over two floors. The basement is extensive and includes an excellent selection of bargains, especially paperback fiction.

Henry Pordes

Portobello Books

⬜ *328 Portobello Road, W10 5RU*

☎/✆ *020 8964 3166*

✉ *sales@portobello-books.com*

🚌 *Ladbroke Grove LU*

🕐 *Tues-Fri 11am-5pm, Sat 9am-5pm*

This shop has an excellent out-of-print and second-hand stock covering every subject but which caters particularly well to those interested in art, photography, design, architecture, film history, militaria, black studies and the Orient. There are some great Portuguese cafés on Golborne Road.

Jonathan Potter

⬜ *125 New Bond Street, W1S 1DY*

☎ *020 7491 3520*

✆ *020 7491 9754*

✉ *www.jpmaps.co.uk*

🚌 *Bond Street & Oxford Circus LU*

🕐 *Mon-Fri 10am-6pm*

The first floor showroom is home to this specialist seller of maps, charts, atlases plus books on the history of cartography and travel. Jonathan Potter is the author of 'Collecting Antique Maps' which provides a useful overview of the subject.

Arthur Probsthain – see p.115

Q

Bernard Quaritch

⌨ *8 Lower John Street, Golden Square, W1F 9AU*

☏ *020 7734 2983*

✉ *020 7437 0967*

🖱 *www.quaritch.com*

🚌 *Piccadilly Circus LU*

🕐 *Mon-Fri 9.30am-5.30pm*

One of the longest established (they set up in London in 1847) and most well respected antiquarian booksellers in the capital. The range of books here is impressive, as is the collection of rare manuscripts. The quality of the stock is extraordinarily high and the knowledge of the staff encyclopedic. All traditional fields of interest can be found on their shelves.

Bernard
QUARITSCH

*Antiquarian booksellers
since 1847*

8 LOWER JOHN STREET
GOLDEN SQUARE
LONDON W1F 9AU

*Telephone (020) 7734 2983
Fax (020) 7437 0967
e-mail: rarebooks@quaritsch.com
Web site: www.quaritsch.com*

Quinto of Charing Cross Road

🖂   *48a Charing Cross Road, WC2H 0BB*
☎   *020 7379 7669*
✆   *020 7836 5977*
🖳   *www.haycinemabookshop.co.uk*
🚌   *Leicester Square LU*
🕐   *Mon-Sat 9am-9pm, Sun 12noon-8pm*

On the corner of Great Newport Street, this shop is everything a second-hand bookshop should be, with towering shelves, a dusty atmosphere and a labyrinthine basement. The stock covers pretty much every subject imaginable and is changed totally at the beginning of every month – the shop closes on the Sunday afternoon, re-opening on the Tuesday at 2pm – queues can go around the block.

Also at:

Quinto of Great Russell Street

🖂   *63 Great Russell Street, WC1B 3BF*
☎   *020 7430 2535*
✆   *020 7430 2566*
🚌   *Holborn and Tottenham Court Road LU*
🕐   *Mon-Sun 10am-7pm*

Floor to ceiling bookshelves house the 50,000 volumes that make this the biggest second-hand bookshop in Bloomsbury, if not the whole of London. To reach the top shelves customers use a cross between scaffolding and a step ladder on wheels. Every subject is covered but the shop is probably strongest on history, travel, art and military subjects. There are often special promotions and every September sees special student deals. Beware – a ten minute browse here can easily become several hours.

Second-Hand & Antiquarian Bookshops

R

Ripping Yarns
- *355 Archway Road, N6 4EJ*
- *020 8341 6111*
- *020 7482 5056*
- *www.rippingyarns.co.uk*
- *yarns@rippingyarns.co.uk*
- *Highgate LU*
- *Tues-Fri 11am-5pm, Sat 10am-5pm, Sun 11am-4pm*

Ignore the ghastly traffic rumbling outside (but not the bargain boxes) and the interior of this shop can turn up all sorts of delights. Children's books are the main thing here with row upon row of books of all ages, type and provenance, including some very rare and expensive old volumes, but also plenty of 'Beano', 'Rupert' and 'Dandy' annuals to bring back childhood memories. There is also an excellent and extensive range of general stock to keep adults amused including some good quality fiction, plays and poetry.

Charles Russell Rare Books
- *239A Fulham Road, SW3 6HY*
- *020 7351 5119*
- *020 7376 7227*
- *www.russellrarebooks.com*
- *South Kensington LU*
- *Mon-Fri 2am-6pm (these times can vary, please call before making a special journey)*

Delightful little antiquarian bookshop just at the junction with Old Church Street. You need to ring to get in but don't be put off, staff are welcoming. Specialisms are natural history, travel, colour plate books and books with fine bindings. There are also some prints. Book prices start at £50.

S

St James's Art Books - see p.122

Bernard Shapero
- 🖃 *32 St George Street, W1S 2EA*
- ☎ *020 7493 0876*
- ✆ *020 7229 7860*
- ✐ *www.shapero.com*
- 🚌 *Bond Street, Green Park or Oxford Circus LU*
- 🕐 *Mon-Fri 9.30am-6.30pm, Sat 11am-5pm*
  (phone for opening times in August)

This shop is located in the area around Bond Street which has several rare booksellers. Specialising in travel, natural history, guidebooks, colour plate books and modern first editions, the quality of the books here is high and staff are enthusiastic yet unobtrusive. Although there are some books under £100, most will be significantly higher in price. There are regular catalogues.

Quinto, Great Russell Street

Shipley - see p.125-126

Sims Reed - see p.127

Skoob Russell Square

🖱 *www.skoob.com*

Regrettably, Skoob have recently moved out of the Brunswick Centre and currently are of no fixed abode. Skoob have been part of London's book scene for many years and it would be a sad loss if they were not to return. Refer to their website for further information about their trading status.

Sky Books

🖃 *119 Shepherd's Bush Road, W6 7LP*

☎ *020 7603 5620*

🚇 *Hammersmith LU*

🕐 *Mon-Sat 9am-5pm (ring before making a journey)*

Situated just close to Brook Green, this is an old-style pulp-fiction, second-hand shop selling mostly genre paperbacks. However a root through the racks often throws up some surprisingly literary finds and there are also plenty of magazines, comics and graphic novels.

Sotheran's

🖃 *2 Sackville Street, W1S 3DP*

☎ *020 7439 6151*

🖱 *www.sotherans.co.uk*

🚇 *Piccadilly Circus LU*

🕐 *Mon-Fri 9.30am-6pm, Sat 10am-4pm*

Rare and antiquarian bookseller with a large, well-stocked shop specialising in architecture, fine art, literature, children's, illustrated, natural history and travel titles but with most other subjects covered as well. There is also an eclectic range of discounted remaindered new books and a selection of prints in the downstairs showroom.

SPCK - see p.137

Spink - see p.138

T

The Theosophical Society - see p.144

John Thornton
- 455 *Fulham Road, SW10 9UZ*
- 020 7352 8810
- *Fulham Broadway LU*
- *Mon-Sat 10am-5.30pm*

Although a specialist in second-hand, out-of-print and rare theology books, of which they carry a huge range, John Thornton's is also well-stocked in other areas, especially art and all the humanities. They have some wonderful leatherbound volumes. When the weather is fine there is access to their fabulous little courtyard garden.

Tindley & Chapman
- 4 *Cecil Court, WC2N 4HE*
- 020 7240 2161
- 020 7379 1062
- *Leicester Square LU*
- *Mon-Fri 10am-5.30pm, Sat 11am-4pm*

This small book packed shop specialises in first editions of English and American late nineteenth and twentieth-century fiction and poetry including popular and genre titles.

Tlon Books
- *Unit 316, Ground Floor,*
  Elephant & Castle Shopping Centre, SE1 6TE
- 020 7701 0360
- *Elephant & Castle LU/Rail*
- *Mon-Sat 9am-7.30pm, Sun 11am-6pm*

Gem of a second-hand bookshop in the unpromising surroundings of the pink Shopping Centre. Located on the ground floor, the shop is large but well laid out and organised. The stock is vast and the turnover fast for both academic and general titles. The selection of paperback fiction is particularly impressive and prices are keen. There are regular rumours that the shopping centre is to be re-developed, but this is still some way off. This wonderful bookshop seems safe for now.

Travis and Emery

⌨ *17 Cecil Court, WC2N 4EZ*

☎ *020 7240 2129*

✆ *020 7497 0790*

✎ *bmrk@travis-and-emery.com*

🚌 *Leicester Square LU*

🕐 *Mon-Fri & Sun 11am-2pm & 2.30pm-6pm, Sat 10am-6pm*

Second-hand, antiquarian and out-of-print shop stuffed to the gills with music scores but well worth seeking out for its excellent selection of books. The book stock covers classical music, music history and theory but with small sections on jazz and popular music as well. They publish catalogues twice each year detailing a selection of the books and music on offer.

Treadwells

⌨ *34 Tavistock Street, WC2E 7RB*

☎ *020 7240 8906*

✎ *www.treadwells-london.com*

🚌 *Covent Garden LU*

🕐 *Daily 12noon-7pm*

Second-hand and out-of-print books on myth, history, world religions, paganism, travel, literature, poetry, heresy, witchcraft, philosophy and theosophy make-up the book stock of the fascinating little store in the heart of Covent Garden. Browsers are genuinely welcome and in addition to the books there are plenty of 'curiosities' including gift items and herbs and a full notice board of events of interest.

John Trotter Books

⌨ *The Sternberg Centre, 80 East End Road, Finchley, N3 2SY*

☎ *020 8349 9484*

✆ *020 8346 7430*

✎ *www.bibliophile.net/John-Trotter-Books.htm*

🚌 *Finchley Central LU*

🕐 *Mon-Thurs 9am-5pm, Fri & Sun 9am-1pm*

A specialist second-hand shop, attached to Manor House Books (see p.89) with more than 15,000 second-hand and out-of-print books on Judaism, Bible studies, the Middle East, ancient history and archaeology.

U

Ulysses

- 40 Museum Street, WC1A 1LU
- 020 7831 1600
- ulyssesbooks@fsbdial.co.uk
- Holborn or Tottenham Court Road LU
- Mon-Sat 10.30am-6pm

Neat shop in the heart of the bookselling enclave near the British Museum, specialising in modern first editions, poetry and illustrated books. The shop has a large glass front and side windows giving the place a light airy atmosphere and the books are well presented, with fine books displayed in large glass fronted cabinets. They produce four catalogues each year detailing stock and there is plenty on offer for around £25.

Unsworths Booksellers

▫ *101 Euston Road, NW1 2RA*

☎ *020 7383 5507*

✎ *www.unsworths.com*

🚇 *King's Cross and St Pancras LU/Rail*

🕐 *Mon-Sat 10am-6.30pm*

Unsworths closed their Bloomsbury store in the autumn of 2005, making this the only outlet for this excellent bookseller. Unsworths is ideal for book worms being located just opposite the British Library, and offering an excellent stock of second-hand, antiquarian, discounted and new books in all subject areas but with a specialist slant towards the arts, social sciences, history and classics. The shop stocks new books concerning bibliography and the classics and carries the complete Loeb Classical Library (possibly the only bookshop in the country to do so).

V

Vintage Magazine Shop

- 🖳 *39/43 Brewer Street, W1R 3SD*
- ☎ *020 7439 8525*
- ✆ *020 7439 8527*
- 🖉 *www.vinmag.com*
- 🚇 *Piccadilly Circus LU*
- 🕐 *Mon-Wed 10am-7pm, Thurs 10am-8pm,*
  Fri & Sat 10am-10pm, Sun 12noon-8pm

Their basement is stocked to overflowing with more than 200,000 back issues of magazines of every genre. Just as an indication of their scope, they have 'Beano', 'Life', 'Vogue', 'Playboy', 'Petticoat', 'Picture Show', 'The Face' and 'Picture Post'. The stocks dates from as far back as the 1930's – it's a collector's paradise. The rather less interesting ground floor specialises in movie postcards, photographs, posters and other movie memorabilia.

W

Walden Books

- 🖳 *38 Harmood Street, NW1 8DP*
- ☎ *020 7267 8146*
- ✆ *020 7267 8147*
- 🖉 *waldenbooks@lineone.net*
- 🚇 *Chalk Farm & Camden Town LU*
- 🕐 *Thurs-Sun 10.30am-6.30pm*

A bit hidden away off Chalk Farm Road, this shop is overflowing with second-hand bargains – they literally spill out onto shelves outside the shop. The emphasis is on literature (with plenty of poetry and plays), art, architecture and philosophy, but virtually every subject is covered. There is also a stock of first editions and antiquarian books for collectors. Book lovers will do well to search out this wonderful bookshop – a welcome escape from the bustle of Camden market.

Walthamstow Collector's Centre

    98 Wood Street, Walthamstow, E17 3HX

    020 8520 4032

    Wood Street Rail

    Mon-Sat 10.30am-5.30pm (closed Thurs & Sun)

Note: individual shops have their own opening times

The Collector's Centre is a small covered area packed with tiny shops. There's just one bookshop but a few others mix books into their general stock. Units include:

Antique City Bookshop

⌨ *Unit 2 & 3*
☎ *020 8520 8300*
🕑 *Mon, Tues, Fri & Sat 10.30am-4.30pm*

An exhilarating selection of second-hand books on all imaginable subjects crammed into a tiny shop. The prices are very fair and there are bargain shelves outside.

House of Yesterdays

⌨ *Unit 4, 5 & 6*
🕑 *Mon-Sat 10am-5pm (closed Thurs)*

Specialising in vinyl and 78's from the 1940's and 1950's (there are more than 20,000 of them). They also stock plenty of books on the music and cinema of the same era.

Bustle

☎ *07916 191 466*
🕑 *Tues 10.30am-2.30pm, Fri 11am-3.30pm*

Lots of pre-1980's magazines and programmes plus a few books on film, television and radio, boxing, wrestling, music, theatre and football.

Waterstones

⌨ *82 Gower Street, WC1E 6EQ*
☎ *020 7636 1577*
✆ *020 7580 7680*
🚌 *Goodge Street LU*
🕑 *Mon, Wed-Fri 9.30am-8pm, Tues 10am-8pm,*
   Sat 9.30am-7pm, Sun 12noon-6pm

The best academic bookshop in London, just around the corner from the University of London, has an extensive, well-organised second-hand department, with some antiquarian stock, that encompasses the full range of academic subjects – the '-ology's' are well represented. They also stock new discounted titles, so drop in here first before you buy in other departments. There's a window-seat that's a magnet for browers and a coffee shop downstairs in the basement.

Watkins - see p.158

Wellspring Bookshop - see p.159

213

Wildy & Sons Ltd – see p.161

Nigel Williams

⌨ *25 Cecil Court, WC2N 4EZ*
☎ *020 7836 7757*
✆ *020 7379 5918*
✎ *www.nigelwilliams.com*
🚇 *Leicester Square LU*
🕐 *Mon-Sat 10am-6pm*

Specialising in first editions of ninteenth and twentieth-century literature especially P G Wodehouse, detective fiction, children's and illustrated books. The price range runs the gamut, from an Enid Blyton reprint for £18 to an early edition of The Hobbit for £18,000. Catalogues are issued about eight times annually detailing recent acquisitions.

Woburn Books / Porcupine Bookcellar

⌨ *5 Caledonian Road, N1 9DX*
☎ *020 7713 1717*
✎ *woburn@burgin.freeserve.co.uk*
🚇 *King's Cross LU/Rail*
🕐 *Mon-Fri 10am-6.30pm, Sat 10am-6pm*

Set in the basement underneath Houseman's (see p.75), Woburn/Porcupine regards itself as the best left-wing bookshop in London featuring second-hand, review and remaindered books on social history, Socialism, labour history and cultural studies.

Worlds End Bookshop

⌨ *357 King's Road, SW3 5ES*
☎ *020 7352 9376*
🚇 *Fulham Broadway & Sloane Square LU*
🕐 *Mon-Sat 10am-6.30pm, Sun 10am-7pm*

A small but superb second-hand shop at the Fulham end of the King's Road. Outside there are bargain shelves and tables and inside a wide-ranging general stock that is especially strong on fiction, history, art, travel, poetry and media. There is also a small antiquarian stock. The shop is well worth a visit with discounts on Saturday, Sunday and Monday.

1,2,3...

30th Century Comics – see p.164

Antiquarian Bookdealers

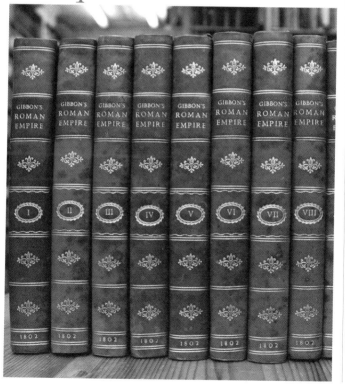

ANTIQUARIAN BOOKDEALERS

In addition to the shops listed above, a great many book dealers operate businesses from their own home. These are not shops, and business is mainly by mail order, via the internet or through books fairs (see page 229). In some cases dealers are willing to allow potential customers to browse their stock in their homes but in all the cases listed below, this is strictly by appointment only, and arrangements should be made beforehand.

Ash Rare Books

    43 Huron Road, SW17 8RE
☎   020 8672 2263
    www.ashrare.com
🕐   Appointment only

Long term London bookdealers who have moved out of their shop in the City. They deal in literary first editions, modern poetry, bibliography, London and general antiquarian books plus prints and maps of London. Catalogues are issued.

Allsworth Rare Books

    P.O.Box 134, 235 Earls Court Road, SW5 9FE
☎   020 7377 0552
✆   020 7377 0552
    www.allsworthbooks.com
🕐   By appointment only at Central London premises

Voyages, travel, exploration and big game hunting.

Beaumont Travel Books

    33 Couthurst Road, SE3 8TN
☎   020 8293 4271
✆   020 8293 4271
    JohnGabrielB@aol.com
🕐   Appointment only

Travel books from 1850 to the present, as well as history, anthropology and the military. Their stock can be checked via ABE.

Robin de Beaumont

🖃 *25 Park Walk, Chelsea, SW10 0AJ*

☎ *020 7352 3440*

✆ *020 7352 1260*

✉ *rdebooks.@aol.com*

🕒 *Appointment only*

Colour printing, design, fin de siecle, Victorian illustrated.

J & S L Bonham

🖃 *Flat 14, 84 Westbourne Terrace, W2 6QE*

☎ *020 7402 7064*

✆ *020 7402 0955*

✉ *www.bonbooks.dial.pipex.com*

🕒 *Appointment only*

Africa, Asia, Australasia, exploration, mountaineering, travel and Polar.

Books & Things

🖃 *PO Box 17768, W8 6ZD*

☎ *020 7370 5593*

✆ *020 7370 5593*

✉ *www.booksandthings.co.uk*

🕒 *Book fairs and postal only*

Fine and decorative art, children's books, modern first editions and photography.

Fiona Campbell

🖃 *158 Lambeth Road, SE1 7DF*

☎ *020 7928 1633*

✆ *020 7928 1633*

✉ *fcampbell@britishlibrary.net*

🕒 *Appointment only*

Specialising in books about Italy plus travel.

Chelsea Rare Books

🖃 *9 Elmstead Close, Totteridge, N20 8ER*

☎ *020 8445 9492*

✆ *020 8492 0470*

✉ *crb@talk21.com*

🕒 *Appointment only*

English literature and illustrated books from the eighteenth to the twentieth-century.

Elton Engineering Books
📖 *27 Mayfield Avenue, W4 1PN*
☎ *020 8747 0967*
✍ *elton_engineering_books@compuserve.com*
🕐 *Appointment only*
Fine and rare eighteenth and nineteenth-century engineering books.

Fishburn Books
📖 *43 Ridge Hill, NW11 8PR*
☎ *020 8455 9139*
✉ *020 8922 5008*
✍ *www.fishburnbooks.com*
🕐 *Appointment only*
Specialists in Judaica, Hebraica and books of Jewish interest.

Nancy Sheiry Glaister Fine and Rare Books
📖 *18 Huntingdon Street, N1 1BS*
☎ *020 7609 1605*
✉ *020 7607 2641*
✍ *glaisterbooks@btinternet.com*
🕐 *Appointment only*
Architecture, urban design, town planning, garden history and allied arts. Occasional catalogues.

Nicholas Goodyer
📖 *8 Framfield Road, Highbury Fields, N5 1UU*
☎ *020 7226 5682*
✉ *020 7354 4716*
✍ *www.nicholasgoodyer.com*
🕐 *Aapointment only*
Colour plate books, illustrated books, natural history, applied arts, architecture, fashion and costumes. Regular catalogues.

Michael Graves-Johnston
📖 *PO Box 532, 54 Stockwell Park Road, SW9 0DR*
☎ *020 7274 2069*
✉ *020 7738 3747*
✍ *www.graves-johnston.com*
🕐 *Appointment only*
Africana, the Americas, Oceania, ethnology, tribal cultures, travel, archaeology and the ancient world. Catalogues are issued.

Robin Greer

☒ *434 Fulham Palace Road, SW6 6HX*
☎ *020 7381 9113*
✆ *020 7381 6499*
✍ *www.rarerobin.com*
🕑 *Appointment only*

Children's, illustrated and original drawings.

Rebecca Hardie

☒ *28 Pavilion Terrace, W12 0HT*
☎ *020 8749 3675*
✆ *020 8749 3675*
✍ *rebecca.hardie@btopenworld.com*
🕑 *Appointment only*

Scientific and medical books from the sixteenth-century onwards. Books about women and family medicine are a speciality. Catalogues issued.

Hesketh & Ward Ltd

☒ *31 Britannia Road, SW6 2HJ*
☎ *020 7736 5705*
✍ *www.bibliopoly.com/dealers/hesketh*
🕑 *Appointment only*

Continental (especially Italian) books and those up to 1800.

Hünersdorff Rare Books

☒ *PO Box 582, SW10 9RP*
☎ *020 7373 3899*
✆ *020 7370 1244*
✍ *huner.rarebooks@dial.pipex.com*
🕑 *Appointment only*

Continental books in rare editions, natural and military history, language and literature, science and medicine, Latin America and subject collections. Search a selection of their stock on ABE.

Sheila Markham

☒ *P.O.Box 214, SE3 9XS*
☎ *020 8852 6309*
✍ *www.sheila-markham.com*
🕑 *Mail order only*

The Ancient Near East, Christian Orient, Far East, exotic printing, calligraphy and general antiquarian.

Barrie Marks Ltd
🖃 *24 Church Vale, N2 9PA*
☎ *020 8883 1919*
🕑 *Appointment only*
Illustrated books, private press, children's books and colour printing.

Nicholas Morrell (Rare Books) Ltd
🖃 *77 Falkland Road, Kentish Town, NW5 2XB*
☎ *020 7485 5205*
📠 *020 7485 5205*
🖉 *www.morbook.com*
🕑 *Appointment only*
Foreign travel and exploration.

Nicolas Books
🖃 *59 Fallowcourt Avenue, N12 0BE*
☎ *020 8445 9835*
📠 *020 8446 9615*
🖉 *www.nicolasrarebooks.com*
🕑 *Appointment only*
Travel, history, illustrated and atlases and a specialism in all Mediterranean countries and islands especially Greece, Cyprus, Malta, the Ottoman Empire and the General Levant.

Hugh Pagan Ltd
🖃 *PO Box 4325, SW7 1DD*
☎ *020 7589 6292*
📠 *020 7589 6303*
🖉 *www.hughpagan.com*
🕑 *Appointment only*
Architecture and the applied arts including town planning, interior decoration and garden design.

Diana Parikian
🖃 *3 Caithness Road, W14 0JB*
☎ *020 7603 8375*
🖉 *dparikian@aol.com*
🕑 *Appointment only*
Continental books 1500-1800, early printed books, emblemata & iconology.

Nigel Phillips

⌨ *Suite 230, Hill House, 210 Upper Richmond Road, SW15 6NP*

☏ *020 8788 2664*

✆ *020 8780 1989*

⊘ *www.nigelphillips.com*

🕑 *Appointment only*

Antiquarian medicine, technology and science.

Edmund Pollinger

⌨ *27D Bramham Gardens, SW5 0JE*

☏ *020 7244 8498*

⊘ *etpollinger@hotmail.com*

⊘ *www.etpollinger.com*

🕑 *Appointment only*

Specialist in books concerning big game hunting, birds, bees and botany. Regular catalogues are produced.

John Price

⌨ *8 Cloudsley Square, N1 0HT*

☏ *020 7837 8008*

✆ *020 7278 4733*

⊘ *books@jvprice.com*

⊘ *www.JohnPriceAntiquarianBooks.com*

🕑 *Appointment only*

Specialist in books from the hand press era i.e pre-1820 with an emphasis on philosophy, literature and the performing arts plus books on music and musicians up to the end of the 19th century.

Paul Rassam

⌨ *Flat 5, 18 East Heath Road, NW3 1AJ*

☏ *020 7794 9316*

✆ *020 7794 7669*

⊘ *paul@rassam.demon.co.uk*

🕑 *Appointment only*

Late nineteenth and early twentieth-century literature, first editions and autograph letters.

Susanne Schulz-Falster Rare Books

- *22 Compton Terrace, N1 2UN*
- *020 7704 9845*
- *020 7354 4202*
- *www.abebooks.com/sfalsterrarebooks/*
- *Appointment only*

Seventeenth and eighteenth-century continental books, economics, political history, social sciences, language and linguistics.

Silver Invicta Books

- *13 Florence street, NW4 1QG*
- *020 8202 2390*
- *www.silverinvicta.com*
- *Mail order and website*

Mainly detective crime fiction and modern firsts but also travel, academic, fishing, history, biography, military and poetry.

Michael Silverman

- *PO Box 350, SE3 0LZ*
- *020 8319 4452*
- *020 8856 6006*
- *www.michael-silverman.com*
- *Appointment only*

Autograph letters, historical documents and manuscripts, specialising in those by English literary figures.

Sokol Books Ltd

- *27 Charles Street, W1J 5DT*
- *020 7499 5571*
- *020 7629 6536*
- *books@sokol.co.uk*
- *Appointment only*

Early printed books mostly from the fifteenth and sixteenth century and all pre-1640.

Benjamin Spademan

- 5A Brackenbury Gardens, W6 0BP
- ☎ 020 8740 6045
- 📠 020 8740 6045
- ✉ benspademan@hotmail.com
- 🕐 By appointment

English and Continental literature and travel.

Rogers Turner

- 87 Breakspears Road, SE4 1TX
- ☎ 020 8692 2472
- 📠 020 8692 2472
- ✉ rogersturner@compuserve.co.uk
- 🕐 By appointment

Horology and the history of science.

Tusculum Rare Books

- 34-36 Maddox Street, W1S 1PD
- ☎ 020 7409 7894
- 📠 020 7409 7894
- ✉ tusculum@tiscali.co.uk

Incunabula, Greek and Latin classics, history, philosophy, literature and fine bindings.

W P Watson Antiquarian Books

- PO Box 29745, NW3 7ZW
- ☎ 020 7431 0489
- 📠 020 7431 0495
- ✉ watsonbooks@dial.pipex.com
- 🕐 Appointment only

Science, medicine, natural history and illustrated books. Annual catalogue available. Check the stock on the Bibliopoly website.

Graham Weiner

- 78 Rosebery Road, N10 2LA
- ☎ 020 8883 8424
- 📠 020 8444 6505
- ✉ graham.weiner@btopenworld.com
- 🕐 Appointment only

Medicine, science, technology and transport.

Alternative Book Outlets

AUCTIONS

All of the major London auction houses hold periodic book sales, and whilst many lots are top quality and regularly fetch tens and sometimes, hundreds of thousands of pounds, if not more (in 1998 Christie's sold a copy of 'The Canterbury Tales' by Geoffrey Chaucer for £4,621,500), many prices are much lower. Viewing days (detailed on the websites) are a great chance for ordinary book lovers to get close to items we'd otherwise only see in our dreams and also to find out what volumes are currently in vogue with collectors. Who knows what we may discover ourselves on market stalls, in jumble sales or charity shops? The sale catalogues are often a fascinating read in their own right and all the auction house websites are lavishly illustrated and fascinating on the subject of fine books.

Bloomsbury Auctions

🖃 *Bloomsbury House, 24 Maddox Street, W1S 1PP*

☎ *020 7495 9494*

✆ *020 7495 9499*

🖋 *www.bloomsburyauctions.com*

🚌 *Bond Street & Oxford Circus LU*

The one specialist book auction house in town and the largest book auctioneers in Europe holds more than 40 specialist and general sales each year which include maps, prints, manuscripts, photographs, coins, medals, fountain pens and general art. Their website is enormously detailed – you can view catalogues online containing guide prices and also see what price the individual items fetched on the day.

Bonhams

🖃 *101 New Bond Street, W1S 1SR*

☎ *020 7447 7447*

✆ *020 7447 7400*

🖋 *www.bonhams.com*

🚌 *Bond Street & Oxford Circus LU*

and

🖃 *Montpelier Street, Knightsbridge, SW7 1HH*

☎ *020 7393 3900*

✆ *020 7393 3905*

🚌 *Knightsbridge LU*

227

Christies

⌨ *8 King Street, St James's, SW1Y 6QT*

☎ *020 7839 9060*

✆ *020 7839 1611*

✎ *www.christies.com*

🚌 *Green Park or Piccadilly LU*

and

⌨ *85 Old Brompton Rd, SW7 3LD*

☎ *020 7930 6074*

✆ *020 7752 3321*

🚌 *South Kensington LU*

Sotheby's

⌨ *34-35 New Bond St, W1A 2AA*

☎ *020 7293 5000*

✆ *020 7293 5989*

✎ *www.sothebys.com*

🚌 *Bond Street & Oxford Circus LU*

and

⌨ *Hammersmith Road, W14 8UX*

☎ *020 7293 5555*

✆ *020 7293 6939*

🚌 *Kensington (Olympia) LU/Rail*

BOOK FAIRS

There are now a huge number of general and specialist book fairs in London, catering for every interest. Many booksellers who otherwise operate a mail order service from their homes (often far from London) have a stall at these fairs, so these events are an excellent opportunity to browse normally unavailable stock and to make contact with booksellers who share your specialist interest. In addition to contacting the major fair organisers listed below, it's worth looking out for flyers in specialist bookshops and advertisements in the weekly London listings magazines 'Time Out' and 'What's On' which also have web listings at *www.timeout.com/london/* and *www.whatsoninlondon.co.uk*.

In addition to the book fairs listed below it is worth bearing in mind the regular London Photograph Fairs (*www.photofair.co.uk*) at Bonnington Hotel which include plenty of exhibitors with photography books and comic fairs which often include cult, genre and pulp fiction (see for example, *www.comicmart.co.uk*).

Amnesty International

✎ *www.aibg.org.uk*

🕐 *June & December*

The Blackheath and Greenwich Group of Amnesty International holds a six-monthly book sale at the Church of the Ascension, Dartmouth Row SE10. There are around 20,000 books on offer each time, both new and second-hand, with prices starting at 50p. Get there early, the bargains get snapped up very fast. All money raised by the sale goes directly to Amnesty International.

The Antiquarian Booksellers' Association

🏠 *Sackville House, 40 Piccadilly, W1J 0DR*
☎ *020 7439 3118*
🖥 *020 7439 3119*
🖊 *www.aba.org.uk*

Anyone seriously interested in collecting antiquarian or rare books will come across the ABA, which is the oldest professional organisation of its kind in the world having been founded in 1906. Many of the antiquarian bookshops and bookdealers listed in this book are members. The ABA organise a large and illustrious international book fair each June at Olympia (*www.olympiabookfair.com*) showcasing more than 150 dealers from across the world. They also hold a national autumn fair at Chelsea Town Hall (*www.chelseabookfair.com*) featuring British dealers.

Artists' Books Fair

🏠 *Enquire at: Marcus Campbell Art Books*
   43 Holland Street, Bankside, SE1 9JR
☎ *020 7261 0111*
🖥 *020 7261 0129*
🖊 *www.marcuscampbell.co.uk*

This fair has been organised by Marcus Campbell Art Books (see p.172) since 1993 in a number of different locations. It's an autumn event which caters for the growing interest in artists' books that has been steadily gathering momentum over the last few years and the fair brings together both national and international exhibitors.

The Provincial Booksellers Fairs Association

🏠 *The Old Coach House, 16 Melbourn Street,*
   Royston, Herts, SG8 7BZ
☎ *01763 248400*
🖥 *01763 248921*
🖊 *www.pbfa.org*

Organisers of more than a hundred book fairs each year across the country. In London there are monthly book fairs at the Hotel Russell, Russell Square WC1, mostly one-day events. There are also larger, international fairs in London in June, around the same time as the big ABA event (see above). Their specialist fairs cover a wide range of interest, for example, Performing Arts, Travel and Exploration, and are often held in London as well.

THE ANTIQUARIAN BOOKSELLERS' ASSOCIATION

CELEBRATES ITS

CENTENARY YEAR

IN 2006

The Edinburgh Book Fair
24th - 25th March 2006
(www.aba.org.uk for
information, and dates in subsequent years)

**The Centenary Antiquarian Book Fair
Olympia**
8th - 11th June 2006
(www.olympiabookfair.com for
information, and dates in subsequent years)

The Chelsea Book Fair
3rd - 4th November 2006
(www.chelseabookfair.com for
information, and dates in subsequent years)
Complimentary tickets are available for
these events by telephoning the

*Antiquarian Booksellers' Association
Sackville House, 40 Piccadilly, London W1J 0DR
Tel: 020 7439 3118   Fax: 020 7439 3119
admin@aba.org.uk   www.aba.org.uk*

CHARITY SHOPS

Charity shops are a book lovers' paradise with the added thrill of serendipity to egg bargain hunters along. Charities have realised that bookselling can bring them a good, solid income and some have now established specialist bookshops or book departments. However, they are totally dependent on the donations they receive – we've selected some shops that are reliably well-stocked with books but don't forget your local branches just a step away – they often repay regular visits.

Bexley Cottage Hospice Shop

⌨ *163 High St, Eltham, SE9 1TW*

☎ *020 8850 6898*

🚍 *Eltham Rail*

🕐 *Mon-Sat 9.30am-4.30pm*

This shop doesn't look huge from the outside but upstairs has a large book area with an excellent range of fiction and non-fiction, all at very competitive prices.

Books For Amnesty

⌨ *241A Eversholt St, NW1 1BE*

☎ *020 7388 0070*

🚍 *Mornington Crescent LU*

🕐 *Mon-Sat 10am-6pm*

A general stock but they are usually strong on art, cinema and film books.

and

⌨ *139B King Street, Hammersmith, W6 9JG*

☎ *020 8746 3172*

🚍 *Hammersmith LU*

🕐 *Mon-Fri 10am-6pm, Sat 10am-4pm*

This well-stocked second-hand shop has a large, good value range in every subject area. There is an Amnesty 'Resource Area' at the back of the shop where visitors can browse Amnesty information, learn more about the organisation and write letters in support of the prisoners of conscience that Amnesty support. The local Amnesty Group meet here at 7.45pm (for 8pm) on the second Monday of each month.

British Heart Foundation

🖅 *19 Powis St, SE18 6LF*

☏ *020 8316 0661*

🚌 *Woolwich Arsenal Rail*

🕐 *Mon-Sat 9.30am-5pm*

An excellent range of books across all subject areas (plus music on CD and tape) make this place an oasis in the book-buying desert of Woolwich. Fiction and non-fiction are equally represented, turnover is good and prices more than fair.

Crusaid

🖅 *19 Churton Street, SW1V 2LY*

☏ *020 7233 8736*

🚌 *Victoria LU/Rail*

🕐 *Mon-Sat 10.30am-5.15pm (Tues opens 11.30am)*

A general charity shop with an excellent selection of very well-priced books covering most subjects but especially good for fiction. The shop is always busy with locals rummaging for a literary bargain.

Geranium Shop for the Blind

🖅 *4 George St, W1M 3DE*

☏ *020 7935 1791*

🚌 *Bond St LU*

🕐 *Mon-Fri 10am-5pm, Sat 10am-4pm*

Not far from the popular shopping area of Marylebone High St, this shop has an excellent range of books all in very good condition. The shop is just around the corner from Marylebone High Street with several other good charity shops including an Oxfam Bookshop (see p.235).

Jambala

🖅 *247 Globe Road, Bethnal Green, E2*

🚌 *Bethnal Green LU*

🕐 *Wed-Fri 2pm-7pm, Sat 12noon-7pm*

Just around the corner from the London Buddhist Centre they sell a great selection of books and vinyl. They are especially strong on fiction, psychology, spirituality, alternative lifestyles and art.

Mind

⌨ *329 Archway, N6 5AA*
☎ *020 8341 1188*
🚌 *Highgate LU*
🕐 *Mon-Sat 10am-5.15pm*

This well organised charity shop is just opposite Highgate tube and nextdoor to another good charity shop run by the RSPCA. Within this shop the book stock is extensive and the prices very fair.

Notting Hill Housing Trust

⌨ *211 Brompton Road, SW3 2EJ*
☎ *020 7581 7987*
🚌 *Knightsbridge LU*
🕐 *Mon-Sat 10am-5.30pm, Sun 12noon-5pm*

The basement beneath this general charity shop is dedicated to books. The stock is huge and all subjects are covered from popular fiction paperbacks up to large format glossy art books via pretty much everything else in between. Prices are good with shelves for as little as 50p and there are chairs for browsers. About 5 minutes walk from Harrods and Patisserie Valerie is a couple of doors away for top-notch cakes and coffee.

Notting Hill Housing Trust

⌨ *High St, W5*
🚌 *Ealing Broadway LU*
🕐 *Mon-Tues & Thurs-Sat 10am-6pm,*
   Wed 9.30am-5.30pm, Sun 12noon-5pm

There's not a huge book section but the stock is generally good quality and reasonably priced. Combine this with a visit to the nearby Oxfam Bookshop on The Green (see p.235).

OXFAM

Oxfam is the largest retailer of second-hand books in Europe, selling more than 11 million books a year. More than 750 Oxfam shops in the UK stock books and they also have many specialist bookshops. Londoners are lucky to have several of these specialist shops. Check *www.oxfam.org.uk* to locate local shops.

Oxfam Bookshops

The stock in these shops (which usually includes music on vinyl, tape and CD) is often extensive including all general and academic subject areas and a good range of fiction. The prices are reasonable without being startling, with Oxfam staff being well aware of the value of their goods. Books are in good condition, well-organised, in attractive surroundings and the turnover of stock is usually high. The shops also have a stock of first editions and collectables and books are well-priced for would-be collectors.

🖃 *1 The Green, Ealing, W5 5DA*
☎ *020 8567 2152*
🚌 *Ealing Broadway LU*
🕐 *Mon-Fri 10am-6pm, Sat 9.30am-6pm, Sun 12noon-5pm*

🖃 *47 Highgate High St, Highgate, N6 5JX*
☎ *020 8347 6704*
🚌 *Highgate LU*
🕐 *Mon & Wed-Sat 10am-5pm, Sun 11am-4pm*

🖃 *91 Marylebone High Street, W1U 4RB*
☎ *020 7487 3570*
🚌 *Baker Street, Bond Street & Regent's Park LU*
🕐 *Mon-Sat 10am-6pm*

🖃 *22 Park Road, Crouch End, N8 8TD*
☎ *020 8347 7942*
🚌 *Crouch Hill Rail*
🕐 *Mon-Sat 10am-5pm*

🖃 *170 Portobello Road, W11 2EB*
☎ *020 7727 2907*
🕐 *Mon-Sat 10am-5.30pm, Sun 12noon-4pm*
Note: Just north of the Elgin Crescent junction with Portobello Road in the heart of the market

🖃 *34 Strutton Ground, SW1P 2HR*
☎ *020 7233 3908*
🚌 *St James's Park LU*
🕐 *Mon, Wed & Fri 9.30am-5pm, Tues & Thurs 10am-5pm*

General Oxfam shops:

⌗ *61 Gayton Road, NW3 1TU*
☎ *020 7794 4474*
🚇 *Hampstead LU*
🕐 *Mon-Sat 10am-5pm*

This is a general charity shop but because of the literary nature of Hampstead it tends to have an extremely good selection of books including recent publications. The fiction section usually has a good mix of contemporary and classic texts. Prices are good value rather than rock bottom.

⌗ *68 Tranquil Vale, SE3 0BN*
☎ *020 8852 6884*
🚇 *Blackheath Rail*
🕐 *Mon-Sat 9am-5.30pm, Sun 12noon-4pm*

There's a bookshop area upstairs above the general shop in the heart of Blackheath village.

⌗ *15 Warwick Way, SW1V 1QT*
☎ *020 7821 1952*
🚇 *Victoria LU/Rail*
🕐 *Mon-Sat 10am-5pm*

One of several good charity shops in the Tachbrook Street area. This is a general shop, but there's usually a good selection of books in stock.

⌗ *202B Kensington High Street, W8 7RG*
☎ *020 7937 6683*
🚇 *High Street Kensington LU*
🕐 *Mon-Sat 10am-5.30pm, Sun 12noon-5pm*

A good selection of books line the wall in this light, airy shop in the heart of the smart Kensington High Street. Prices aren't bargain basement but the quality is good and turnover high. Especially valuable volumes are on show in a glass-fronted display case.

⌗ *149 Putney High Street, SW15 1SU*
☎ *020 8789 3235*
🕐 *Mon-Sat 9.30am-5.30pm, Sun 11am-5pm*
🚇 *East Putney LU*

Excellent book selection, all of it in fine condition and well-displayed. It is especially good for paperback fiction.

Salvation Army Charity Shop

Salvation Army Charity Shop

🖼 *284 Upper Street, N1 8LT*

☎ *020 7359 9865*

🚌 *Highbury & Islington LU/Rail*

🕐 *Mon-Fri 10am-5pm, Sat 11am-5pm*

This friendly, welcoming shop has a good selection of books sold at rock bottom prices. There's a high turn-over of books and anything that doesn't sell finds its way to the bargain boxes outside, where some great bargains can be found. A few doors down Ottolenghi sells cakes and pastries that are beyond description but with a hefty price-tag.

Sudana

🖼 *51 Roman Road, E2 0HU*

🚌 *Bethnal Green LU*

🕐 *Tues-Fri 12noon-6pm, Sun 12noon-5.30pm*

Charity shop attached to the London Buddhist Centre – there's a selection of books and always some on psychology and spirituality. Prices are excellent – many are 50p to £1. Combine a visit here to Jambala around the corner.

Sue Ryder Care

⌗ *35 Warwick Way, SW1 1QS*

☎ *020 7630 0812*

🚉 *Victoria LU/Rail*

🕐 *Mon-Sat 9am-5pm*

One of a clutch of charity shops in the locality that are all good for books. There's a good quality stock here of reasonably priced books with an especially strong paperback fiction section.

Trinity Hospice Bookshop

⌗ *208 Upper Richmond Road, London SW15 6TD*

☎ *020 8780 0737*

🚉 *East Putney LU*

🕐 *Mon-Sat 10am-5pm*

A specialist shop with a vast array of books plus tapes, CDs and vinyl records – this is the only specialist bookshop among more than twenty Trinity Hospice shops in central and southwest London. Combine a visit here with a trip to the general Oxfam Shop around the corner on the High Street.

Trinity Hospice Shop

⌗ *85 Wilton Road, SW1 1DN*

☎ *020 7931 7191*

🚉 *Victoria LU/Rail*

🕐 *Mon-Sat 10.30am-5.30pm*

At 50p for paperbacks and £2 for hardbacks, prices are keen in this general shop and there are lots of other charity shops well worth browsing for books in the area.

Trinity Hospice Shop

⌗ *20A Notting Hill Gate, W11 3JE*

☎ *020 7792 2582*

🚉 *Notting Hill Gate LU*

🕐 *Mon-Tues & Sat 10.10am-6pm, Wed 10.30am-6pm,*
   Thurs-Fri & Sun 10.30am-5.30pm

Just a short walk from the underground station and easy to combine with a visit to Portobello Road market, they have a modern, good-quality stock in all subject areas including plenty of glossy picture books at very good prices.

MARKETS

Southbank Book Market

ALFIE'S ANTIQUE MARKET

⌖ *13-25 Church Street, Marylebone, NW8 8DT*

✐ *www.alfiesantiques.com*

🚌 *Edgware Road LU or Marylebone LU/Rail*

Alfie's is a large antiques market at the corner of Church Street and Ashridge Street with traders selling all kinds of fine things within a rather grand Victorian building. Several stalls offer books among their other items and there are a couple of specialist book dealers within the market:

Bibliopola

⌖ *Stand FO17*

☎ *020 7724 7231*

🕐 *Tues-Sat 10am-4pm*

A sizeable shop on the first floor, specialising in modern first editions, illustrated books and early children's books (up to the 1930's).

East West Antiques and Books

☐ *Stand G113/4/7 on the ground floor*

☎ *020 7723 0564*

✎ *ewa_thomson@hotmail.com*

🕐 *Tues-Sat 10am-4pm*

Alongside a lovely range of ornamental objects this stand carries a general second-hand and antiquarian stock with above average selections of children's books, natural history, typography and nineteenth-century literature plus postcards and ephemera.

BRICK LANE MARKET

☐ *Brick Lane, Cheshire Street and Sclater Street, E1 & E2*

🚇 *Aldgate & Shoreditch LU, Liverpool Street LU/Rail*

🕐 *Sun 6am-1pm*

Brick Lane is a huge and chaotic market and plenty of the junk sellers have books among their stock. A specialist book and magazine stall trades on Cheshire Street and there are usually books on the stalls in the indoor market on that street. The two open air markets on Sclater Street also have a fair mix of books among the merchandise. Combine a trip to the market with a visit to Pathfinder Bookshop (see p.111) and Eastside Bookshop (see p.57).

CAMDEN PASSAGE MARKET

☐ *Camden Passage (opposite Islington Green), N1*

🚇 *Angel LU*

🕐 *Thurs 10am-4.30pm*

Camden Passage is famous for its antiques market, but on Thursdays it also hosts a small book market. The few book dealers that set up here are well stocked, with plenty of books in the 50p-£2 range. Paperback fiction is particularly well represented, but there is also a reasonable stock of travel, history and art titles, as well as academic reference books. The market is busier and has more stalls in the spring and summer, but it always repays a visit.

CAMDEN MARKET

☐ *Camden Lock and Stables, off Camden High Street, NW1*

🚇 *Camden Town LU*

🕐 *Sat-Sun 10am-6pm*

Camden Market is packed with clothes stalls for the young and trendy, but there is a clutch of shops catering for bibliophiles. Book outlets include Black Gull Books (see p.169) in Camden Lock Place and Village Games (see p.151). Also in the area are excellent Walden Books (see p.210) and Offstage (see p.104). There are also several good charity shops on the High Street, south of the tube station.

GREENWICH MARKETS

- ⌨ *Greenwich Church St, SE10*
- ☎ *020 7515 7153*
- 🚇 *Cutty Sark DLR, Greenwich Rail/DLR*
- 🕐 *Sat-Sun 9.30am-5pm (all parts of the market);*
  Thurs 7.30am-5.30pm, Fri 9am-5pm and Bank Holidays
  9.30am-5.30pm (Collector's Market)

Greenwich was once the best market in London for books with a dedicated area for second-hand stalls and several permanent book outlets. All this has changed in the last ten years and now the market is far more like Camden with more of an emphasis on food, arts and crafts, furniture and clothing. Greenwich is still a good place to look for books, but the search is more haphazard and the results less certain than in the past. At the weekend there are still some book stalls around Greenwich Village Market, opposite the Ibis Hotel on Stockwell Street and there are a few stalls in King William Walk Market (an arcade leading off King William Walk). However the best place to look for books is the small market opposite the post office, next to the cinema (Saturday and Sunday 7am-5pm) on Greenwich High Road, where a handful of good stalls can be found. The Collector's Market on Thursday, Friday and Bank Holidays also has a few good book stalls. Combine a market trip with a visit to the excellent Halcyon Books (see p.184), Marcet Books (see p.192) and Greenwich Book Time shops (see p.68).

HAMPSTEAD MARKETS

- ⌨ *Hampstead Community Centre,*
  78 Hampstead High Street, NW3 1RE
- ✆ *020 7794 8313*
- 🚇 *Hampstead LU*
- 🕐 *Sat 10am-6pm and every 3rd Sun (Craft market),*
  2nd Sun of each month 10am-5.30pm (Monthly book fair)

The Saturday market has a regular book stall offering paperbacks at reasonable prices, with the monthly book fair offering a wider range of titles. When visiting the market, don't forget the Oxfam shop just around the corner on Gayton Road (see p.236), they always have a great selection of books donated by the local literati.

HAYNES LANE COLLECTORS MARKET

📺 *Off Westow Street, SE19*

🚌 *Crystal Palace Rail*

🕐 *Sat 11am-5pm, Sun 11am-4pm*

Rather tucked away, this place is definitely worth searching out as there are several book stalls/shops here selling a vast array of books in an extremely wide range of subjects including philosophy, psychology, sociology, history, art, photography and typography alongside plenty of general fiction. Be certain to check out bookshop Crow on the Hill (see p.29) if you are in this part of London.

MERTON ABBEY MILLS

📺 *off Merantum Way, behind the Savacentre, South Wimbledon, SW19*

🚌 *Colliers Wood LU*

🕐 *Sat-Sun & Bank Holidays 10am-5pm*

Although this market is now overlooked by gleaming modern apartments, it still has plenty of character and there are a couple of very good book outlets within the complex in the shape of Books & Lyrics (see p.171) and Abbey Books (see p.166).

PORTOBELLO ROAD MARKET

📺 *Portobello Road and Golborne Road, W11*

📧 *www.portobelloroad.co.uk*

🚌 *Notting Hill Gate and Ladbroke Grove LU*

🕐 *Sat 8am-5.30pm (although many dealers do start packing up in the middle of the afternoon)*

This huge market covers pretty much everything: antiques, clothes, vegetable, junk and of course books. The market extends north along Portobello Road from Lonsdale Road up to and including much of Golborne Road. Saturday is by far the busiest day when all the various parts of the market are open and the streets are awash with shoppers. For those seeking antiquarian and specialist books there are numerous antiques centres many of which house specialist book dealers some of which are listed below. For the best coffee in the area check out Coffee Plant at 180 Portobello Road and the Portuguese cafés on Golborne Road

Demetzy Books

⌨ *Gallery 113, 113 Portobello Road*

✉ *demetzybooks@tiscali.co.uk*

With a large general stock but special strengths in cookery, medical books, travel and some literature.

Don Kelly

⌨ *Admiral Vernon Arcade, 139-147 Portobello Road*

☏ /✆ *020 7731 0482*

✉ *donkellybooks@btinternet.com*

A fine selection reference books on the fine and applied arts. There's a café here too if you need a pick-me-up.

Peter Kennedy

⌨ *First Floor John Dale Antiques, 87 Portobello Road*

☏ *01483 797293*

✆ *01483 488006*

Has a good stock of volumes in a wide range of subjects including travel, typography, architecture, natural history, atlases and general illustrated volumes.

Lipka's Arcade

⌨ *282-290 Westbourne Grove*

Look in the basement here for several stalls with a choice of books among other items; mostly music volumes on the record stall and a stall with film books from the 1950's.

St Swithin's

⌨ *John Dale Antiques, 87 Portobello Road*

☏ /✆ *020 8573 8556*

Specialists in Victorian movable books alongside panoramas, peepshows and ephemera including early cards and juvenilia. There's a good selection of children's books.

Charles Vernon-Hunt

⌨ *Geoffrey Van Arcade, 107 Portobello Road*

☏ *020 8854 1588*

✉ *C.Vernonhunt@btinternet.com*

A superb stock of non-Western art books, especially strong on African, Indian and Islamic art.

SOUTH BANK BOOK MARKET

- *Outside the National Film Theatre, SE1*
- *Waterloo LU and Rail*
- *Daily 11am-7pm (open till later in the summer and with more stalls open at the weekends)*

This open-air book market on the south bank of the Thames has something that no branch of Borders can compete with and that is a sense of romance. Situated under the protection of Waterloo Bridge on a handsome tree lined pedestrian boulevard with a superb view of the Thames and the London skyline, it seems a long way from the hustle and bustle of Charing Cross Road (which is actually only about ten minutes walk from here). This is where Hugh Grant's declaration of love in 'Four Weddings and a Funeral' was filmed and I know of one couple who have conducted a good deal of their courtship here. Even if your interests are strictly literary the market is worth a visit with its fantastic range of fiction, play texts and works concerning film and theatre (as befitting its location on the doorstep of the NFT and National Theatre), biographies and weighty art books. If you are seeking refreshment, the NFT Film Café is right next to the market but the espresso bar just around the corner in the National Theatre is the favourite among the market regulars. The literary appeal of this area has been greatly enhanced by the arrival of a branch of Foyles (see p.62).

SPITALFIELDS MARKET

- *West side of Commercial Street between Folgate Street and Brushfield Street, E1*
- *Enquiries: 020 7247 8556*
- *www.visitspitalfields.com*
- *Liverpool Street LU/Rail*
- *Sun 10am-5.30pm (General market), Mon-Wed & Fri 11am-4pm (collectables), Thurs 8am-3pm (antiques)*

Spitalfields has undergone a major redevelopment which has greatly diminished the area devoted to stalls – the Sunday market is about a third its former size. It is still, however, a useful place to look for books with a number of regular book stalls. The development has harmed the Sunday market but seems to have had a positive effect upon the weekday trading with far more stalls and customers than before and one or two good book dealers finding a place here. There are also a few booksellers at the fortnightly Record and at the weekly Collector's Market.

Libraries

SPECIALIST LIBRARIES

In addition to public and academic libraries, there are a vast number of other specialist libraries located in the capital. These libraries are run by numerous private and public bodies and their policy toward public access is by no means uniform. The more serious libraries often house important collections and restrict access to academics who can demonstrate the necessity of their visit for research purposes. Many other specialist libraries (such as those catering for members of certain associations or groups of professionals) see the provision of information and library facilities for members of the public as very much part of their remit. Nonetheless for all the libraries listed below potential users should telephone in advance to find out the policy on access and if required, to make an appointment. Many of the libraries have quite restricted opening times and sometimes charge access fees.

Africa Centre Library

- 38 King Street, WC2E 8JT
- ☎ 020 7836 1973
- 🖳 www.africacentre.org.uk
- 🚌 Covent Garden LU

Newspapers, journals and books covering all African countries and issues relating to them.

Alpine Club Library`

- 55 Charlotte Street, EC2A 3QF
- ☎ 020 7613 0745
- ✆ 020 7613 0745
- 🖳 www.alpine-club.org.uk
- 🚌 Old Street LU/Rail

One of the largest collections of mountaineering literature in the world, including over 25,000 books from the sixteenth-century onwards, newspaper cuttings from the nineteenth-century onwards, journals, pamphlets, expedition reports, letters and artefacts. The library also keeps the Himalayan Index, a database of all expeditions to Himalayan, Hindu Kush, Chinese and Karakoram peaks over 6000m and over 600 expedition reports.

Alzheimer's Society

- Ann Brown Memorial Library,
  Gordon House, 10 Greencoat Place, SW1P 1PH
- ☎ 020 7306 0835
- ✆ 020 7306 0808
- ✎ www.alzheimers.org.uk
- 🚌 St James's Park LU & Victoria LU/Rail

Specialist library containing literature on medical and social aspects of dementia and dementia care.

Amateur Rowing Association

- 6 Lower Mall, W6 9DJ
- ☎ 0870 060 7100
- ✆ 0870 060 7101
- ✎ www.ara-rowing,org
- 🚌 Hammersmith LU

Historical and current material about the sport of rowing including technique and the history of rowing.

Anti-Slavery International

- Thomas Clarkson House,
  The Stableyard, Broomgrove Road, SW9 9TL
- ☎ 020 7501 8939
- ✆ 020 7738 4110
- ✎ www.antislavery.org
- 🚌 Stockwell LU & Brixton LU/Rail

Contemporary and historical material about slavery, its abolition and related issues. This includes material concerning human rights, a collection of eighteenth and nineteenth-century anti-slavery literature, and collections on modern forms of slavery including child and bonded labour, forced and early marriage, trafficking, and prostitution.

Architectural Association Library

- 36 Bedford Square, WC1B 3ES
- ☎ 020 7887 4035
- ✎ www.aaschool.ac.uk
- 🚌 Tottenham Court Road LU

More than 30,000 volumes on architecture, design, construction and associated subjects, 100 current periodicals, a photo library with more than 150,000 slides of historic and contemporary buildings and an archive of more than 1000 lectures.

Belarusian Francis Skaryna Library

▢ *37 Holden Road, N12 8HS*
☎ *020 8445 5358*
✆ *020 8445 5358*
✎ *www.skaryna.org*
🚌 *Woodside Park LU*

The largest collection of Belarusian books and periodicals outside Belarus. Most are in Belarusian but there are also publications about Belarus in English, Polish, Russian, German and French.

Bishopsgate Institute

▢ *230 Bishopsgate, EC2M 4QH*
☎ *020 7392 9200*
✆ *020 7392 9250*
✎ *www.bishopsgate.org.uk*
🚌 *Liverpool Street LU/Rail*

This is a general reference library dating from 1894 which also has historical collections on London and nineteenth and twentieth-century radical movements.

British Association of Psychotherapists

▢ *37 Mapesbury Road, NW2 4HJ*
☎ *020 8452 9823*
✆ *020 8452 0310*
✎ *www.bap-psychotherapy.org*
🚌 *Kilburn LU*

More than 3,000 books and 20 current journal titles on child and adult psychoanalytic psychotherapy.

British College of Osteopathic Medicine

▢ *Lief House, 120-122 Finchley Road, NW3 5HR*
☎ *020 7435 6464*
✆ *020 7431 3630*
✎ *www.bcom.ac.uk*
🚌 *Finchley Road LU*

Historical and contemporary books and journals on naturopathy, osteopathy and related disciplines together with other resource material such as slides, videos, X-rays, software and anatomical models. The collection is especially strong on historical alternative medicine books.

British Film Institute

- *21 Stephen Street, W1T 1LN*
- ☎ *020 7255 1444*
- ✆ *020 7436 2338*
- ✎ *www.bfi.org.uk/nationallibrary*
- 🚇 *Tottenham Court Road LU*

A major national collection on film and television. The collection includes more than 68,000 books, current journals and unpublished film and television scripts, interviews on audiotape and assorted ephemera. The SIFT database (accessible in the Reading Room) contains references and other filmographic material for over a million film/TV titles, personalities, organisations and film festivals.

The British Library

- *96 Euston Road, NW1 2DB*
- ☎ *Switchboard: 0870 444 1500*
  Reader admissions: 020 7412 7677
- ✎ *www.bl.uk*
- 🚇 *St Pancras LU/Rail*

This is the library for the nation and receives a copy of every publication in UK and Ireland. It currently contains a staggering 150 million items – if you looked at 5 items each day it would take 80,000 years to see them all. However, there's more, the material sweeps across all subject areas and covers all known languages and is often regarded as the world's finest collection of books, journals, manuscripts, maps and printed music. Access to the exhibition galleries (see p.298) is free and unrestricted but as a research library, admission to the reading rooms is only allowed when you can demonstrate no other institution can supply the information you need. The Newspaper Library is at Colindale Ave, NW9 5HE (Tel: 020 7412 7353). This is also the site for the National Sound Archive and Philatelic Collection.

British Medical Association

- *BMA House, Tavistock Square, WC1H 9JP*
- ☎ *020 7383 6625*
- ✆ *020 7383 6400*
- ✎ *www.library.bma.org.uk*
- 🚇 *Russell Square LU, Euston LU/Rail*

One of the largest medical information services in the UK specialising in current clinical practice, medical ethics and health information.

British Museum

- Great Russell Street, WC1B 3DG
- Paul Hamlyn Library 020 7323 8907
  Central Library 020 7323 8491
- www.thebritishmuseum.ac.uk
- Russell Square LU

The Paul Hamlyn Library is a public reference library housed in the restored Reading Room at the heart of the museum. It houses a wide-ranging selection of material covering all aspects of the museum collections for the general reader. The Central Library is a highly specialised, academic library, also covering all aspects of the museum holdings but for use by curatorial staff and with some access for individual advanced researchers.

British Music Information Centre

- 1st Floor, Lincoln House, Westminster Bridge Road, SE1 7HS
- 020 7928 1902
- 020 7928 2957
- www.bmic.co.uk
- Lambeth North LU

This is a resource centre for contemporary British classical music. It includes a collection of more than 40,000 scores by more than 2,600 British composers dating from 1900 but with most of it post-1960. Recordings and listening facilities are the other main part of the library. About 2,500 extracts and scores are available online alongside a thousand or so audio samples.

British Olympic Association

- 1 Wandsworth Plain, SW18 1EH
- 020 8871 2677
- 020 8871 9104
- www.olympics.org.uk
- East Putney LU

Information about sport and the Olympics including the Olympic Games and competitors. They have International Olympic Committee reports and host city bidding documents plus material on issues associated with the Games, for example, drugs and political issues.

British Psychoanalytical Society

- 📖 *The Library, Institute of Psychoanalysis,*
  Byron House, 112A Shirland Road, W9 2EQ
- ☎ *020 7563 5008*
- 📠 *020 7563 5001*
- 🖰 *www.psychoanalysis.org.uk*
- 🚌 *Maida Vale LU*

An enormous collection (almost 22,000 volumes) of material on psychoanalysis dating from the mid-19th century.

Campaign Against Arms Trade

- 📖 *11 Goodwin St, N4 3HQ*
- ☎ *020 7281 0297*
- 📠 *020 7281 4369*
- 🖰 *www.caat.org.uk*
- 🚌 *Finsbury Park LU*

Information on the arms trade especially as it relates to the UK. There's information on individual countries and companies (including brochures) who produce arms. CAAT also publishes Fact sheets and a regular Newsletter.

Centre for Armenian Information and Advice

- 📖 *105A Mill Hill Road, W3 8JF*
- ☎ *020 8992 4621*
- 📠 *020 8993 8953*
- 🖰 *www.caia.org.uk*
- 🚌 *Acton Town LU*

Material in English and Armenian about Armenia, its affairs, culture and history. There are also CDs, records and audio visual materials and an Archive of the bi-lingual quarterly newsletter, 'The Armenian Voice'.

Centre for Independent Transport Research in London

- 📖 *Room 208 The Colourworks,*
  2 Abbot Street, E8 3DP
- ☎ *020 7275 9900*
- 📠 *020 7254 9123*
- 🖰 *www.cilt.dial.pipex.com*
- 🚌 *Dalston Kingsland Rail*

Transport, land use planning, accessibility and any issues that have relevance to making public transport more safe, accessible and efficient.

Centre for Information on Language Teaching and Research

⌨ *20 Bedfordbury, WC2N 4LB*

☎ *020 7379 5110*

✆ *020 7379 5082*

✐ *www.cilt.org.uk*

🚇 *Charing Cross LU/Rail & Leicester Square LU*

Large, comprehensive library on all aspects of language teaching and learning for all ages and levels. It includes almost 14,000 books, audio, video and software titles. There are facilities to allow visitors to use the video and audio material on site.

Centre for Policy on Ageing

⌨ *25-31 Ironmonger Row, EC1V 3QP*

☎ *020 7553 6500*

✆ *020 7553 6501*

✐ *www.cpa.org.uk*

🚇 *Barbican LU*

Unique collection of material on social gerontology whose books and journals comprise of more than 40,000 items including 400 journals.

Chatham House (Royal Institute of International Affairs)

⌨ *10 St James's Square, SW1Y 4LE*

☎ *020 7957 5723*

✆ *020 7957 5710*

✐ *www.chathamhouse.org.uk*

🚇 *Green Park & Piccadilly Circus LU*

The Royal Institute of International Affairs is on of the foremost organisations analysing international affairs. Their library at Chatham House contains around 150,000 books, 300 periodicals and 30 newspapers covering all aspects of international affairs.

Christian Aid Information Resources centre

⌨ *35 Lower Marsh, SE1 7RT*

☎ *020 7620 4444*

✆ *020 7620 0719*

✐ *www.christian-aid.org.uk*

🚇 *Waterloo LU/Rail*

More than 5,000 books and journals are held at this library concerning Third-World development, politics, economics and aid.

Civic Trust Library

- 🖃 *Essex Hall, 1 Essex Street, WC2R 3HU*
- ☎ *020 7539 7900*
- ✆ *020 7539 7901*
- ✎ *www.civictrust.org.uk*
- 🚌 *Charing Cross LU/Rail*

Small collection of books and periodicals on most aspects of the built environment including town planning, architecture, conservation, landscaping, housing, transport, waterways, tourism and leisure.

Confraternity of St James

- 🖃 *Stephen Badger Library of Pilgrimage,*
  27 Blackfrairs Road, SE1 8NY
- ☎ *020 7928 9988*
- ✎ *www.csj.org.uk*
- 🚌 *Southwark LU*

Material on the pilgrimage to the church of St James of Compostela in Santiago in Spain including routes through France and Spain and associated art, architecture, music and history.

Congregational Library

- 🖃 *14 Gordon Square, WC1H 0AR*
- ☎ *020 7387 3727*
- 🚌 *Euston LU/Rail; Goodge St, Euston Square,*
  Russell Square & Warren Street LU

Sharing premises with the Dr Williams's Library (see p.278), this collection has been established since 1831 as the main library for the Congregational denomination.

Crafts Council

- 🖃 *44 Pentonville Road, N1 9BY*
- ☎ *020 7806 2510*
- ✆ *020 7837 6891*
- ✎ *www.craftscouncil.org.uk*
- 🚌 *Angel LU*

The Reference Library provides information (more than 5,000 books plus journals and magazines) on all major crafts and applied arts including technique, theory, criticism and biographies. The National Register of Makers is a database of more than 4,000 UK Crafts people and their work. The Photostore is a visual database of more than 40,000 images of modern craftwork.

The Dicken's House Library

- 📠 *48 Doughty Street, WC1N 2LX*
- ☎ *020 7405 2127*
- ⌨ *www.dickensmuseum.com*
- 🚌 *King's Cross LU/Rail; Russell Square, Chancery Lane & Holborn LU*

Located in, but mostly separate from the Dickens House Museum, the library houses books by and about Dickens and his contemporaries plus letters, photographs and other ephemera such as postcards and newspaper cuttings relevant to the study of Dickens.

Drugscope

- 📠 *32-36 Loman Street, SE1 0EE*
- ☎ *08707 743 682*
- ✎ *020 7928 1771*
- ⌨ *www.drugscope.org.uk*
- 🚌 *Southwark & Borough LU*

Drugscope is an independent centre of excellence on drugs. The library holds books, journals and reports on all aspects of the subject.

Egypt Exploration Society

- 📠 *3 Doughty Mews, WC1N 2PG*
- ☎ *020 7242 2266*
- ✎ *020 7404 6118*
- ⌨ *www.ees.ac.uk*
- 🚌 *Russell Square, Holborn, & Chancery Lane LU*

This is one of the best resources on Egyptology in the country with 20,000 books, journals and pamphlets on the subject.

English Folk Dance And Song Society

- 📠 *Vaughan Williams Memorial Library,*
  Cecil Sharp House, 2 Regent's Park Road, NW1 7AY
- ☎ *020 7485 2206*
- ✎ *020 7284 0523*
- ⌨ *www.efdss.org*
- 🚌 *Camden Town LU*

Multimedia archive on British folk music and culture including printed material dating from the seventeenth century. The emphasis is on English folk, but there is some material held on other folk traditions.

The Evangelical Library

- 78A Chiltern Street, W1U 5HB
- 020 7935 6997
- www.elib.org.uk
- Baker Street LU

Around 80,000 items of evangelical literature covering the history and development of the movement from the seventeenth-century Puritans through to modern times.

FPA (formerly the Family Planning Association)

- 2-12 Pentonville Road, N1 9FP
- 020 7923 5228
- 020 7837 3042
- www.fpa.org.uk
- Angel LU

All aspects of contraception and sexual health.

Fan Museum

- 12 Crooms Hill, SE10 8ER
- 020 8305 1441
- www.fan-museum.org
- Greenwich Rail/DLR

An archive covering anything related to the history and collecting of fans plus associated subjects such as costume.

Feminist Library

- 5 Westminster Bridge Road, SE1 7XW
- 020 7928 7789
- www.feministlibrary.org.uk
- Waterloo and Elephant & Castle LU/Rail, Lambeth North LU

Books and journals on feminism worldwide, including sections on working-class women, women of colour, Jewish, Irish and lesbian women and women with disabilities.

Geffrye Museum

- *Kingsland Road, E2 8EA*
- ☎ *020 7739 9893*
- ✆ *020 7729 5647*
- ✐ *www.geffrye-museum.org.uk*
- 🚇 *Liverpool Street LU/Rail*

There's a reading room in the museum containing titles relating to interior design and decoration, architecture, social history, applied arts and London. The curatorial library is available to researchers with specific requirements and there's also an archive of mostly trade catalogues from the late nineteenth-century to the present day.

Geological Society

- *Burlington House, Piccadilly, W1J 0BG*
- ☎ *020 7432 0999*
- ✆ *020 7439 3470*
- ✐ *www.geolsoc.org.uk*
- 🚇 *Green Park & Piccadilly LU*

Hundreds of thousands of books, maps and journals, including rare books and manuscripts about earth sciences and palaeontology collected since the founding of the library in 1809.

Goethe-Institut

- *50 Prince's Gate, Exhibition Road, SW7 2PH*
- ☎ *020 7596 4044*
- ✆ *020 7594 0230*
- ✐ *www.goethe.de/gr/lon/enbib.htm*
- 🚇 *South Kensington LU*

German and English material about Germany and German culture including, literature, film and theatre, fine arts, photography and social studies. The library also carries German newspapers, periodicals and journals, CDs, audio cassettes, DVDs and videos.

German Historical Institute

- *17 Bloomsbury Square, WC1A 2NJ*
- ☎ *020 7309 2019*
- ✆ *020 7309 2069*
- ✐ *www.ghil.ac.uk*
- 🚇 *Tottenham Court Road LU*

More than 60,000 books and 180 current periodicals on German history (written in German and other languages) especially during the nineteenth and twentieth centuries with particular emphases on 1933-45, post-war development and German unification after 1989.

Goldsmiths' Company

⌨ *Goldsmiths' Hall, Foster Lane, EC2V 6BN*

☏ *020 7606 7010*

✆ *020 7606 1511*

✐ *www.thegoldsmiths.co.uk*

🚌 *St Paul's LU*

More than 7,500 books and 30 periodicals plus journals, photographs, slides, press cuttings, films and videotapes on jewellery, regalia, assaying and hallmarking and anything related to the precious metals of gold, silver and platinum.

Halley Stewart Library

⌨ *St Christopher's Hospice,*
51-59 Lawrie Park Road, SE26 6DZ

☏ *020 8768 4500*

✆ *020 8659 8680*

✐ *www.stchristophers.org.uk*

🚌 *Penge West Rail*

A specialist library covering subjects related to hospice and palliative care, death, dying and bereavement.

Highgate Literary and Scientific Institution

⌨ *11 South Grove, N6 6BS*

☏ *020 8340 3343*

✆ *020 8340 5632*

✐ *www.hlsi.net*

🚌 *Archway & Highgate LU*

A general library with a bias towards biography, literature, history, science and fiction. There are special collections about London with particular emphasis on Highgate, Islington and Hampstead and local writers John Betjeman and Samuel Taylor Coleridge.

Hispanic and Luso Brazilian Council

⌨ *Canning House Library,*
   2 Belgrave Square, SW1X 8PJ
☏ *020 7235 2303*
✆ *020 7235 3587*
✎ *www.canninghouse.com*
🚌 *Hyde Park Corner LU*

Large collection on every imaginable aspect of Spanish and Portuguese-speaking countries including history, culture, current affairs, geography, language and politics. This includes about 60,000 books and some 100 current periodicals on Latin America, the Caribbean, Portugal and Spain.

Horniman Library

⌨ *Horniman Museum & Gardens,*
   100 London Road, SE23 3PQ
☏ *020 8699 1872*
✎ *www.horniman.ac.uk*
🚌 *Forest Hill Rail*

Specialist library for ethnography, natural history and musical instruments. It includes more than 20,000 books, currently subscribes to over 100 journals and also houses records, audio tapes, CDs and videos.

Imperial War Museum

⌨ *Lambeth Road, SE1 6HZ*
☏ *020 7416 5342 (Printed books)*
   020 7416 5221 (Documents)
   020 7416 5294 (Film and Video)
   020 7416 5333 (Photographs)
   020 7416 5363 (Sound archive)
✎ *www.iwm.org.uk*
🚌 *Lambeth North LU*

The museum specialises in all aspects of twentieth-century warfare which have affected Britain and other Commonwealth countries. It has an almost unimaginable amount of research material which is held in separate departments but includes 270,000 printed items, 120 million feet of cine film, 6 million photographs and negatives and 36,000 hours of sound archives. Log onto the website for further details about visiting the library.

INFORM
(Information Network Focus on Religious Movements)

⌨ Z25, St Philip's Building, North Block,
London School of Economics, Sheffield Street, WC2A 2AE

☎ 020 7955 7654

✆ 020 7955 7679

✍ www.inform.ac

🚇 Holborn LU

Affiliated to and housed in the London School of Economics, this charity aims to provide up-to-date information on new and alternative religious movements. Their library contains books, journals, academic studies, material from the religions themselves and from the media on more than 1,500 groups worldwide.

INIVA - Institute of International Visual Arts

⌨ 6-8 Standard Place,
Rivington Street, EC2A 3BE

☎ 020 7729 9616

✆ 020 7729 9509

✍ www.iniva.org

🚇 Old Street LU/Rail

An arts and cultural studies institute with the focus on contemporary art from Africa, Asia, Latin America and British artists from many cultural backgrounds. The printed collection includes more than 4,000 exhibition catalogues, 1,000 monographs and more than 150 periodical titles including many that are not readily available in the UK. There's also a collection of more than 4,500 slides of contemporary art.

Institut Francais (French Institute)

⌨ Multimedia Library, 17 Queensberry Place, SW7 2DT
and
Children's Library, 32 Harrington Road, SW7 3ES

☎ 020 7073 1350

✍ www.institut-francais.org.uk

🚇 South Kensington LU

Extremely well-stocked and popular adult and children's French language libraries. As well as books, the libraries carry a comprehensive range of videos, DVDs, CDs, recorded music and magazines.

Institute for Indian Art and Culture

🔲 *Bharatiya Vidya Bhavan, 4a Castletown Road, W14 9HQ*
☎ *020 7381 3086*
✎ *020 7381 8758*
🖉 *www.bhavan.net*
🚌 *West Kensington LU*

Reference library on Indian philosophy, religion, literature, art and history.

Institute of Alcohol Studies

🔲 *Alliance House, 12 Caxton Street, SW1H 0QS*
☎ *020 7222 4001*
✎ *020 7799 2510*
🖉 *www.ias.org.uk*
🚌 *St James's Park LU*

Specialist reference library on all aspects of alcoholism. The library contains a collection relating to the Temperance Movement which is one of only two in the country.

Instituto Cervantes

🔲 *102 Eaton Square, SW1W 9AN*
☎ *020 7201 0757*
✎ *020 7235 0329*
🖉 *www.londres.cervantes.es /*
🚌 *Sloane Square LU, Victoria LU/Rail*

Spanish and Latin American literature, history, art, travel and audio-visual material.

Islamic Cultural Centre

🔲 *London Central Mosque*
  146 Park Road, NW8 7RG
☎ *020 7724 3363*
✎ *020 7724 0493*
🖉 *www.iccuk.org*
🚌 *Baker Street & St John's Wood LU*

Books and journals in English, Arabic and other languages on all aspects of Islam including theology, history, culture, the Arab/Muslim world and Muslim minorities in Europe.

Italian Cultural Institute Library

- 39 Belgrave Square, SW1 8NX
- ☎ 020 7235 1461
- ✆ 020 7235 4618
- ⌨ www.italcultur.org.uk
- 🚌 Hyde Park Corner LU

Containing around 25,000 books plus journals and newspapers in Italian with an emphasis on literature, history and culture plus a collection of audiovisual material.

Japanese Information and Cultural Centre

- Embassy of Japan, 101-104 Piccadilly, W1J 7JT
- ☎ 020 7465 6543
- ⌨ www.uk.emb-japan.go.jp
- 🚌 Piccadilly & Green Park LU

Japanese literature, education, history and culture, in both Japanese and English. There are more than 100 videos covering a wide range of subjects, from business to classical Japanese theatre. Daily newspapers, periodicals and Government papers are also available.

Kennel Club Library

- 1 Clarges Street, Piccadilly, W1J 8AB
- ☎ 020 7518 1009
- ✆ 020 7518 1058
- ⌨ www.the-kennel-club.org.uk
- 🚌 Green Park LU

Books, journals, audiovisual and multimedia material relating to everything canine. This is Europe's largest collection of canine information and includes Kennel Club Breeding Records from 1880 and Kennel Club Stud Books from 1873.

King's Fund Library

- 11-13 Cavendish Square, W1G 0AN
- ☎ 020 7307 2568
- ✆ 020 7307 2805
- ⌨ www.kingsfund.org.uk
- 🚌 Oxford Circus LU

This is an independent charitable foundation whose goal is to improve health, especially in London. The library reflects this and is the only specialist health and social care library in the UK open to the public.

Laban
- *Creekside, SE8 3DZ*
- *020 8691 8600*
- *020 8691 8400*
- *www.laban.co.uk*
- *Cutty Sark DLR*

The largest and most varied collection on dance and associated subjects in the UK. There are books, journals, videos, CDs and software plus various archive collections relating to the history of dance.

Lambeth Palace
- *Lambeth Palace, SE1 7JU*
- *020 7898 1400*
- *020 7928 7932*
- *www.lambethpalacelibrary.org*
- *Westminster & Lambeth North LU*

Lambeth Palace Library is the main library and record office for the Church of England. There is a vast collection of archives, books and manuscripts covering ecclesiastical history and geneology.

Linacre Centre for Healthcare Ethics
- *60 Grove End Road, NW8 9NH*
- *020 7806 4088*
- *020 7266 5424*
- *www.linacre.org*
- *St John's Wood LU*

This organisation exists to help Catholics and others explore the Church's position on bioethical issues. There are over 6,000 books and 50 current journals on bioethics.

The Linnean Society of London
- *Burlington House, Piccadilly, W1J 0BF*
- *020 7434 4479*
- *020 7287 9364*
- *www.linnean.org*
- *Green Park & Piccadilly Circus LU*

Containing 40,000 volumes from 1483 to the present day on all aspects of biology but with an emphasis on plant and animal classification. The library has a particularly strong collection of books concerning Charles Darwin and Evolutionary Theory.

London's Buddhist Vihara

🏠 *The Avenue, W4 1UD*

☎ *020 8995 9493*

✉ *020 8994 8130*

🖰 *www.londonbuddhistvihara.co.uk*

🚌 *Turnham Green LU*

Books (more than 26,000) and periodicals on all schools of Buddhism and related subjects.

London Contemporary Dance School

🏠 *The Place, 17 Duke's Road, WC1H 9PY*

☎ *020 7387 0161*

✉ *020 7383 4851*

🖰 *www.theplace.org.uk*

🚌 *Euston LU/Rail*

Books, periodicals, videos, CDs and CD-ROMs on contemporary modern dance.

The London Library

🏠 *14 St James's Square, SW1Y 4LG*

☎ *020 7930 7705*

✉ *020 7766 4766*

🖰 *www.londonlibrary.co.uk*

🚌 *Piccadilly Circus & Green Park LU*

Founded in 1841 as a subscription library, the London Library now has over one million volumes in all European languages and is the largest independent lending library in the world. Its emphasis is on the humanities (particularly literature, biography and history) with good coverage on fine and applied art, architecture, philosophy, religion and travel. The annual membership fee is currently £180.

London Society

🏠 *Mortimer Wheeler House,*
   46 Eagle Wharf Road, N1 7ED

☎ *020 7253 9400*

🖰 *www.LondonSociety.org.uk*

🚌 *Old Street LU/Rail*

Books, maps and newspaper cuttings on the history and development of London.

London Transport Museum

⊡ *Covent Garden Piazza, WE2E 7BE*

☎ *020 7379 6344*

✎ *www.ltmuseum.co.uk*

🚌 *Covent Garden LU*

The open access Learning Centre offers resources to all visitors who wish to follow up their museum visit with more detailed information. The Reference Library offers access to researchers and holds more than 12,000 books, pamphlets and reports about the history of transport in London and London's development. There are substantial holdings on the art, architecture and design of London Transport and more than 100 journals on all aspects of urban transport. A redevelopment of the Museum is due to be finished in 2007, so access may be interrupted during the work.

Marx Memorial Library

⊡ *37a Clerkenwell Green, EC1R 0DU*

☎ *020 7253 1485*

✉ *020 7251 6039*

✎ *www.marxmemoriallibrary.sageweb.co.uk*

🚌 *Farringdon LU/Rail*

More than 150,000 volumes (including books, pamphlets and periodicals) on all aspects of Marxism, the history of socialism and the history of working-class movements.

Marylebone Cricket Club Library

⊡ *Lord's Cricket Ground,*
   St John's Wood Road, NW8 8QN

☎ *020 7289 1611*

✉ *020 7616 8659*

🚌 *St John's Wood LU*

Specialist cricket and real tennis reference library.

Model Railway Club

⊡ *Keen House, 4 Calshot Street, N1 9DA*

☎ *020 7837 2542*

✎ *www.themodelrailwayclub.org*

🚌 *King's Cross LU/Rail*

There are about 5,000 books and an extensive video collection related to railways, model railways.

Museum of London Library

- 150 London Wall, EC2Y 5HN
- ☎ 0870 444 3851
- www.museumoflondon.org.uk
- 🚌 Moorgate LU/Rail; Barbican, St Paul's & Bank LU

Books, periodicals, journals and pamphlets on all aspects of London history.

Museum in Docklands

- Sainsbury Study Centre, No 1 Warehouse
  West India Quay, Hertsmere Road, E14 4AL
- ☎ 0870 444 3856
- www.museumindocklands.org.uk
- 🚌 Canary Wharf LU/DLR, West India Quay DLR

Material covering the history of the Port of London from 1770 to the present day and the regeneration of the Docklands. The collection includes the Port of London Archive and Sainsbury Archive.

National Army Museum

- Royal Hospital Road, SW3 4HT
- ☎ 020 7730 0717
- www.national-army-museum.ac.uk
- 🚌 Sloane Square LU, Victoria LU/Rail

Books, pamphlets, manuscripts and pictures on the history of the British Army from 1485.

National Art Library

- Victoria & Albert Museum,
  Cromwell Road, SW7 2RL
- ☎ 020 7942 2400
- 📠 020 7942 2401
- www.nal.vam.ac.uk
- 🚌 South Kensington LU

The largest library of fine and applied art and design in UK covering fine and decorative arts of many countries (including the Far East, India and South East Asia) and historical ages. There are more than a million items in the library with material on ceramics, woodwork, metalwork, glass, furniture and textiles as well as fine art. The library also holds a large number of special collections including early printed books, calligraphy and comics and graphic novels.

National Autistic Society

- 🖥 *393 City Road, EC1V 1NG*
- ☎ *0845 070 4004*
- ✆ *020 7833 9666*
- 🖱 *www.nas.org.uk*
- 🚌 *Angel LU, King's Cross & Euston LU/Rail*

Books, journals and audio-visual material about autism plus a research information database with more than 15,000 references from journals, reports and books.

National Childbirth Trust

- 🖥 *Alexandra House, Oldham Terrace, W3 6NH*
- ☎ *0870 770 3236*
- ✆ *0870 770- 3237*
- 🖱 *www.nctpregnancyandbabycare.com*
- 🚌 *Acton Central Rail*

Information on pregnancy, birth and early parenthood. The library is open to members with an appointment.

National Children's Bureau

- 🖥 *8 Wakley Street, EC1V 7QE*
- ☎ *020 7843 6008*
- ✆ *020 7843 6007*
- 🖱 *www.ncb.org.uk*
- 🚌 *Angel LU*

All issues relating to children and young people, including health and disability, child protection, rights, family law, children in care, sex education, special education, poverty and social exclusion, health, and drug education and misuse. There are more than 30,000 publications and 300 journal titles.

National Gallery Library

- 🖥 *Trafalgar Square, WC2N 5DN*
- ☎ *020 7747 2542*
- ✆ *020 7747 2892*
- 🖱 *www.national gallery,org.uk*
- 🚌 *Charing Cross LU/Rail*

Highly specialised library with more than 75,000 volumes (a significant number dating from before 1850) relating to the history of Western European painting.

National Maritime Museum

🖾 *Caird Library, Park Row, SE10 9NF*

☎ *020 8312 6673*

✆ *020 8312 6632*

🖱 *www.nmm.ac.uk*

🚌 *Cutty Sark DLR*

The largest maritime reference library in the world covering all aspects of maritime history. There are over 100,000 books dating from 1474, more than 20,000 pamphlets and 200 current periodical titles.

National Philatelic Society

🖾 *British Philatelic Centre,*
    107 Charterhouse St, EC1M 6PT

☎ *020 7490 9610*

✆ *020 7490 4253*

🚌 *Barbican LU, Farringdon LU/Rail*

Catalogues, books, monographs, newspapers, periodicals and multimedia material of interest to stamp collectors.

National Portrait Gallery

🖾 *Heinz Archive and Library,*
    St Martin's Place, WC2H 0HE

☎ *020 7306 0055 ext 257*

✆ *020 7306 0056*

🖱 *www.npg.org.uk*

🚌 *Charing Cross LU/Rail, Leicester Square LU*

The primary centre for all research into British portraiture, dating back to the gallery's foundation in 1856. The holdings include 35,000 books, plus engravings, reproductions and over 150,000 prints and negatives of portraits. The Heinz Archive and Library is located behind the main gallery in Orange Street.

Natural History Museum

⌨ *Cromwell Road, SW7 5BD*

☎ *General and Zoology: 020 7942 5460*
  Botany: 020 7942 5220 5685
  Entomology: 020 7942 5251
  Earth Sciences: 020 7942 5476
  Ornithology: 020 7942 6156

✍ *www.nhm.ac.uk*

🚇 *South Kensington LU*

Over a million books and periodicals on the biological and earth sciences, divided into several libraries.

NSPCC

⌨ *Weston House, 42 Curtain Road, EC2A 3NH*

☎ *020 7825 2500*

✆ *020 7825 2525*

✍ *www.nspcc.org.uk/inform*

🚇 *Liverpool Street LU/Rail*

Books, articles, reports and journals relating to child protection and child welfare.

Office for National Statistics

⌨ *1 Drummond Gate, SW1V 2QQ*

☎ *020 7533 6266*

✍ *www.ons.gov.uk*

🚇 *Pimlico LU*

Statistics and publications from the Office for National Statistics. A great deal of the information is available online.

Order of St John

⌨ *St John's Gate, St John's Lane, Clerkenwell, EC1M 4DA*

☎ *020 7324 4070*

✍ *www.sja.org.uka*

🚇 *Farringdon LU/Rail*

The largest collection outside Malta on the history of the Knights Hospitallers (the Order of the Hospital of St John of Jerusalem) and the history of the St John Ambulance Association in this country.

Paul Mellon Centre for Studies in British Art

⌨ *16 Bedford Square, WC1B 3JA*

☎ *020 7580 0311*

✆ *020 7636 6730*

✍ *www.paul-mellon-centre.ac.uk*

🚌 *Tottenham Court Road & Goodge Street LU*

British art (painting, sculpture, drawing and architecture) from the mid-sixteenth to mid-twentieth centuries including 12,000 books, 120 periodicals, exhibition and auction catalogues and a photographic archive of more than 80,000 images of British paintings, sculpture, drawings and prints.

The Poetry Library

⌨ *Level 5, Royal Festival Hall, SE1 8XX*

☎ *020 7921 0943/0664*

✆ *020 7921 0939*

✍ *www.poetrylibrary.org.uk*

🚌 *Waterloo LU/Rail*

Note: The Library is currently closed to visitors as part of the re-development of the South Bank. It is due to re-open in the Summer of 2007, meanwhile many of its activities continue – see the website or call for more details

The most comprehensive collection of modern poetry in Britain, with free membership to all. Founded in 1953 to support modern British poetry, the library now has more than 80,000 volumes, including almost all the poetry published in Britain since 1912. The huge collection of poetry magazines dates from 1960's and comes from all over the English speaking world. An audiovisual collection of poetry on video, cassette, CD and record, supplements the library's printed material. This is one of the most remarkable libraries in London and it deserves to be far better known.

The Polish Library

⌨ *238-246 King Street, W6 0RF*

☎ *020 8741 0474*

✍ *bibliotekapolska@posklibrary.fsnet.co.uk*

🚌 *Ravenscourt Park LU*

Established since 1942, this lending and reference library is one of the biggest libraries of its kind outside Poland with around 150,000 books and pamphlets and more than 4,500 journal titles. The vast majority are in the Polish language.

Puppet Centre Trust

⌨ *Battersea Arts Centre, lavender Hill, SW11 5TN*

☎ *020 7228 5335*

✎ *020 7228 8863*

🖱 *www.puppetcentre.com*

🚋 *Clapham Junction Rail*

Hundreds of books plus videos, photographs and slides on the art of puppets and puppetry.

RAF Museum Library

⌨ *Grahame Park Way, Hendon, NW9 5LL*

☎ *020 8205 2266*

🖱 *www.rafmuseum.com*

🚋 *Colindale LU*

Tens of thousands of printed works dating from 1783 on all aspects of aviation. The library's holdings include around 100,000 Air Publications from the RAF including books, technical manuals, journals, air diagrams and aeronautical maps.

Religious Society of Friends (Quakers)

⌨ *Friend's House, 173-177 Euston Road, NW1 2BJ*

☎ *020 7663 1000*

✎ *020 7663 1001*

🖱 *www.quaker.org.uk*

🚋 *Euston LU/Rail*

One of the largest and most important collections in the world of material relating to Quakers. It includes Quaker thought and history as well as issues of special interest to the Friend's, such as peace, relief work and anti-slavery.

Royal Academy of Arts

⌨ *Burlington House, Piccadilly, W1J 0BD*

☎ *020 7300 8000*

🖱 *www.royalacademy.org.uk*

🚋 *Green Park & Piccadilly Circus LU*

The oldest fine arts library in the UK specialises in the history of British art and the Royal Academy, its exhibitions and members. The holdings include a complete set of summer exhibition catalogues from 1769.

Royal Academy of Dance

- 36 Battersea Square, SW11 3RA
- 020 7326 8000
- 020 7585 0640
- www.rad.org.uk
- Clapham Junction Rail

All aspects of dance, but ballet in particular, including books and journals and videos/DVDs. Viewing and listening facilities are available.

Royal Aeronautical Society

- 4 Hamilton Place, W1J 7BQ
- 020 7670 4362
- 020 7670 4359
- www.aerosociety.com
- Green Park & Hyde Park Corner LU

Books, pamphlets, journals, reports, photographs, letters, posters and lithographs make up the oldest aeronautical library in the world. The archives contain material relating to the early pioneers of flight – such as a collection of letters from the Wright Brothers.

Royal Asiatic Society

- 60 Queens Gardens, W2 3AF
- 020 7724 4741
- 020 7706 4008
- www.royalasiaticsociety.org
- Bayswater & Lancaster Gate LU, Paddington LU/Rail

More than 100,000 books, manuscripts, journals and art works relating to Asia over the last 2,000 years (but not the last 50 years). Most of the material relates to the humanities.

Royal Entomological Society

- 41 Queen's Gate, SW7 5HR
- 020 7584 8361
- 020 7581 8505
- www.royensoc.co.uk
- Gloucester Road & South Kensington LU

General biology but especially insect taxonomy. Almost 1,000 of the books are pre-1850 and the archives contain material from eminent entomologists.

Royal Geographical Society

🖳 *1 Kensington Gore, SW7 2AR*

☎ *020 7591 3000*

✎ *020 7591 3001*

✐ *www.rgs.org*

🚌 *South Kensington LU*

Maps, books, photographs, artwork and documents, including expedition reports, which together form one of the most important geographical collections in the world. The collection includes more than 150,000 books (dating from as far back as 1830), a map room and a picture library holding more than 500,000 images from around the world. There's also an Expedition Advisory Centre for those thinking of heading off on an adventure.

Royal Horticultural Society

🖳 *Lindley Library, 80 Vincent Square, SW1P 2PE*

☎ *020 7821 3050*

✐ *www.rhs.org.uk*

🚌 *St James's Park & Pimlico LU, Victoria LU/Rail*

Probably the world's foremost horticultural library. It includes more than 50,000 books, over 300 current journals and 22,000 botanical drawings.

Royal Institute of British Architects (RIBA)

🖳 *66 Portland Place, W1B 1AD*

☎ *020 7580 5533*

✎ *020 7255 1541*

✐ *www.riba-library.com*

🚌 *Oxford Circus, Regent's Park & Great Portland St LU*

The largest and most comprehensive resource in the UK for information on all aspects of architecture.

Royal National Institute for the Blind Research Library

🖳 *105 Judd Street, WC1H 9NE*

☎ *020 7391 2052*

✎ *020 7388 2034*

✐ *www.rnib.org.uk*

🚌 *King's Cross LU/Rail*

Europe's most comprehensive and diverse collection of material covering all aspects of partial sight and blindness.

Royal National Institute for the Deaf

Institute of Laryngology & Otology,
Royal National Throat, Nose and Ear Hospital,
330-332 Gray's Inn Road, WC1X 8EE

☎ *020 7915 1553*

✆ *020 7915 1443*

✎ *www.rnid.org.uk*

🚌 *King's Cross LU/Rail*

The largest library on deafness and hearing loss in Europe – and open to everyone.

The Royal Society

6-9 Carlton House Terrace, SW1Y 5AG

☎ *020 7451 2500*

✆ *020 7930 2170*

✎ *www.royalsoc.ac.uk*

🚌 *Charing Cross LU/Rail, Piccadilly Circus LU*

The Royal Society is the UK's national academy of science and was founded in 1660. Its library also dates from that time and covers the history of science and science policy from the 1470's to the present day.

Royal Society for Asian Affairs

2 Belgrave Square, SW1X 8PJ

☎ *020 7235 5122*

✎ *www.rsaa.org.uk*

🚌 *Hyde Park Corner & Knightsbridge LU*

Around 7,000 books covering Asian history, geography, politics and travel in Asia mostly in the twentieth-century. There are also archives of glass slides and photographs from the 1920's to 1950's.

St Bride Library

Bride Lane, EC4Y 8EE

☎ *020 7353 4660*

✆ *020 7583 7073*

🚌 *Blackfriars LU/Rail*

Printing and allied subjects including paper binding, graphic design, typefaces, calligraphy, illustration, publishing and bookselling. This is one of the largest collections of its kind in the world with more than 40,000 books and pamphlets and 2,000 periodical titles.

St Paul's Cathedral Library

⌨ *EC4M 8AE*
☎ *020 7246 8345*
✆ *020 7248 3104*
✎ *www.stpauls.co.uk*
🚇 *St Paul's LU*

Housed in a chamber designed by Sir Christopher Wren, this library covers theology, church history, Wren and the building of the Cathedral.

Science Museum Library

⌨ *Imperial College Road, SW7 5NH*
☎ *020 7942 4242*
✆ *020 7942 4243*
✎ *www.sciencemuseum.org.uk*
🚇 *South Kensington LU*

Sharing a building with the Imperial College library, this is a major British library for science and technology and includes material on the history of science, technology and medicine since the eighteenth century.

Society for Co-operation in Russian and Soviet Studies

⌨ *320 Brixton Road, SW9 6AB*
☎ *020 7274 2282*
✆ *020 7274 3230*
✎ *www.scrss.org.uk*
🚇 *Brixton LU/Rail*

More than 35,000 books, journals and pamphlets about Russia and the former Soviet Union mostly from Russian publishers.

Society of Genealogists

⌨ *14 Charterhouse Buildings,*
   Goswell Road, EC1M 7BA
☎ *020 7251 8799*
✎ *www.sog.org.uk*
🚇 *Barbican LU, Farringdon LU/Rail*

This is the foremost library in the UK for anyone involved in the study of genealogy. The collection includes professional and education records, family histories, census material and more than 9,000 copies of Parish Registers.

South London Botanical Institute

- 323 Norwood Road, SE24 9AQ
- ☎ 020 8674 5787
- ✎ www.slbi.org.uk
- 🚌 Tulse Hill & Herne Hill Rail

The Institute exists to encourage the study of plants. The library holds books journals and slides including British and European floras, botany, mycology and horticulture.

South Place Ethical Society

- Conway Hall, 25 Red Lion Square, WC1R 4RL
- ☎ 020 7242 8037
- ✆ 020 7242 8036
- ✎ www.ethicalsoc.org.uk
- 🚌 Holborn LU

This library claims to be the UK's largest Humanist research library and contains over 10,000 books relating to philosophy and ethics.

Rudolf Steiner House Library

- Rudolf Steiner House,
  35 Park Road, NW1 6XT
- ☎ 020 7724 8398
- ✆ 020 7724 4364
- ✎ www.anth.org.uk
- 🚌 Baker Street LU

This is the library of the Anthroposophical Society in Great Britain and contains material on all aspects of the work of Rudolf Steiner and anthroposophical thought.

Swedenborg Society

- 20-21 Bloomsbury Way, WC1A 2TH
- ☎ 020 7405 7986
- ✆ 020 7831 5848
- ✎ www.swedenborg.org.uk
- 🚌 Holborn & Tottenham Court Road LU

The library contains books by and about Emanuel Swedenborg including journals and archival material.

Tate Gallery

🖃 *Hyman Kreitman Research Centre,*
   Tate Britain, Millbank, SW1P 4RG

☎ *020 7887 8838*

🖉 *www.tate.org.uk*

🚌 *Pimlico LU*

The Tate's library and archive collections are combined in this research centre. The library material covers British art from 1500 and international art from 1900. The library includes more than 40,000 books, more than 2,000 journals and over 140,000 art exhibition catalogues.

Theatre Museum Study Room

🖃 *1E Tavistock Street, WC2E 7PR*

☎ *020 7943 4700*

✆ *020 7943 4777*

🖉 *www.theatremuseum.org*

🚌 *Covent Garden LU*

This is the largest collection of its kind in the world. The emphasis is on theatre, dance, opera and musical theatre but also includes puppetry, circus and theatre architecture. This is also the home of the National Video Archive of Performance.

Theosophical Society

🖃 *50 Gloucester Place, W1U 8EA*

☎ *020 7935 9261*

🖉 *www.theosophical-society.org.uk*

🚌 *Baker Street LU*

Theosophy, world religions, philosophy, psychology, myth, parapsychology, astrology and related fields.

Tourism Concern

🖃 *Stapleton House,*
   277-281 Holloway Road, N7 8HN

☎ *020 7133 3330*

✆ *020 7133 3331*

🖉 *www.tourismconcern.org.uk*

🚌 *Holloway Road LU*

Resource area containing books, articles, reports and documents about travel and tourism and their impacts throughout the world.

Wallace Collection Library

⌖ *Hertford House, Manchester Square, W1U 3BN*

☏ *020 7563 9500*

✆ *020 7224 2155*

✎ *www.wallacecollection.org*

🚇 *Bond Street LU*

Material on all areas of this famous art collection encompassing European fine and decorative art up to the late nineteenth-century.

Wellcome Library for the History & Understanding of Medicine

⌖ *210 Euston Road, NW1 2BE*

☏ *020 7611 8722*

✆ *020 7611 8369*

✎ *www.library.wellcome.ac.uk*

🚇 *Euston LU/Rail, Euston Square LU*

This is one of the world's major resources for the study of the history of medicine. The collection includes more than 600,000 books and journals, over 100,000 pictures plus manuscripts, archives and films.

Wellcome Library

Westminster Abbey Library

- *East Cloister, Westminster Abbey, SW1P 3PA*
- *020 7654 4830*
- *www.westminster-abbey.org*
- *Westminster LU*

Home of the extensive collections of books, manuscripts and archives of the Dean and Chapter of Westminster and a research centre for all aspects of the history of the Abbey. It includes many historic books, medieval manuscripts as well as printed and manuscript music.

Wiener Library

- *4 Devonshire Street, W1W 5BH*
- *020 7636 7247*
- *020 7436 6428*
- *www.wienerlibrary.co.uk*
- *Great Portland Street & Regent's Park LU*

The library specialises in modern Jewish history with particular reference to the Holocaust and the Third Reich. It also covers Middle-Eastern history, post-war Germany and anti-semitism.

Dr Williams's Library

- *14 Gordon Square, WC1H 0AR*
- *020 7387 3727*
- *Euston LU/Rail*

Theological library with more than 300,000 items dating from the earliest years of printing to modern times plus a collection of manuscripts. It is the pre-eminent research library of English Protestant nonconformity. Premises are shared with the Congregational Library (see p.253).

Kenneth Ritchie Wimbledon Library

- *Wimbledon Lawn Tennis Museum, Church Road, SW19 5AE*
- *020 8946 6131*
- *www.wimbledon.org/museum*
- *Southfields & Wimbledon LU*

Worldwide material about lawn tennis.

Women's Health

- 52 Featherstone Street, EC1Y 8RT
- 0845 125 5254
- 020 7250 4152
- www.womenshealthlondon.org.uk
- Old Street LU/Rail

Around a 1,000 books, 150 journals and 3,500 folders containing information on all aspects of women's health.

Women's Library

- Old Castle Street, E1 7NT
- 020 7320 2222
- 020 7320 2333
- www.thewomenslibrary.ac.uk
- Aldgate East LU

The library covers a huge number of topics about women, including women's rights, suffrage, health, sexuality, education, employment, reproductive rights, the home and the family. There is some international material but the emphasis is on women in Britain. The libraries holdings comprise of books and pamphlets (more than 60,000), periodicals, newspaper cuttings, ephemera, visual materials and archival collections.

Zoological Society of London

- London Zoo, Regent's Park, NW1 4RY
- 020 7722 3333
- 020 7586 5743
- www.zsl.org
- Baker Street & Regent's Park LU

This is one of the major zoological libraries in the world. Founded in 1826 it includes more than 200,000 books and 5,000 journal titles (1,300 of which are current) covering all aspects of the subject.

ACADEMIC LIBRARIES

Each of the universities and higher education establishments in London maintains its own library, all of which are serious academic resources existing primarily for their own students. Regulations on access for individual researchers vary enormously; in many cases there is leniency towards students at other London or British universities but in others access is allowed only for reference rather than borrowing and fees are often charged. Anyone interested in using one of these libraries is advised to telephone first to find out the exact entrance criteria. It's also worth remembering that university libraries tend to have different opening hours outside term time.

Central School of Speech & Drama
Embassy Theatre, 64 Eton Avenue, NW3 3HY
Tel: 020 722 8183
Website: www.cssd.ac.uk
Transport: Swiss Cottage LU
Art, design, theatre, education.

University of the Arts
Website: www.arts.ac.uk

Camberwell College of Arts,
Peckham Road, SE5 8UF
Tel: 020 7514 6349
Transport: Peckham Rye or Denmark Hill Rail
Arts, film, photography, history of printing.

Central St Martin's College of Art and Design
Website: www.csm.arts.ac.uk

Three libraries:
102 Charing Cross Road, WC2H 0DU
Tel: 020 7514 7190
Transport: Tottenham Court Road LU
Arts, design, photography.

Byam Shaw School of Art
2 Elthorne Road, N19 4AG
Tel: 020 7281 4111
Transport: Archway LU
Arts.

Southampton Row, WC1B 4AP
Tel: 020 7514 7307
Transport: Holborn LU
Arts, design, film, theatre.

Chelsea College of Art & Design
Millbank, SW1P 4RJ
Tel: 020 7514 7773
Transport: Pimlico LU
Architecture, arts, design.

Drama Centre
Back Hill, EC1R 5LQ
Tel: 020 7514 8747
Transport: Farringdon LU/Rail
Theatre.

London College of Fashion
20 John Princes Street, W1G 0BJ
Tel: 020 7514 7453
Transport: Oxford Circus LU
Specialising in fashion from Business, management to costume history.

London College of Communication
Elephant and Castle, SE1 6SB
Tel: 020 7514 6527
Transport: Elephant & Castle LU/Rail
Arts, business studies, design, film, media, photography and printing.

City University
Website: www.city.ac.uk/library

Cass Learning Resource Centre
Sir John Cass Business School,
106 Bunhill Row, EC1Y 8TZ
Tel: 020 7040 8787
Transport: Old Street or Moorgate LU/Rail
Accountancy, business studies, finance and management.

Inns of Court School of Law Library
4 Gray's Inn Place, WC1R 5DX
Tel: 020 7400 3605
Transport: Chancery Lane LU
Law.

Radiography Library
Rutland Place,
Charterhouse Square, EC1M 6PA
Tel: 020 7040 5653
Transport: Barbican LU,
Farringdon LU/Rail
Medical applications of radiography.

The Resource Centre
Department of Cultural Policy and Management, School of Arts,
Northampton Square, EC1V 0HB
Tel: 020 7040 8752
Transport: Angel LU, Farringdon LU/Rail
The arts.

University Library
Northampton Square, EC1V 0HB
Tel: 020 7040 8191
Transport: Angel LU, Farringdon LU/Rail
General academic library.

West Smithfield Library
School of Nursing and Midwifery,
5th floor, 20 Bartholomew Close,
EC1A 7BE
Tel: 020 7040 5759
Transport: Barbican LU,
Farringdon LU/Rail
Nursing.

Whitechapel Library
School of Nursing and Midwifery,
4th Floor, Philpot St, E1 2EA
Tel: 020 7040 5859
Transport: Whitechapel LU
Nursing.

University Of East London
Website: www.uel.ac.uk/lss
The university has libraries at:

Barking Campus
Longbridge Road, Essex, RM8 2AS
Tel: 020 8223 2614
Transport: Barking LU
General academic library.

Docklands Campus
University Way, E16 2RD
Tel: 020 8223 3434
Transport: Cyprus DLR
Arts and the humanities.

Duncan House
High Street, Stratford, E15 2JB
Tel: 020 8223 3346
Transport: Stratford LU
Business studies, management and law.

Stratford Campus
Romford Road, E15 4LZ
Tel: 020 8223 4224
Transport: Maryland Rail
Health studies, life sciences, psychology.

University Of Greenwich
Website: www.gre.ac.uk
The university has libraries at:

Avery Hill Campus
Bexley Road, Eltham, SE9 2PQ
Tel: 020 8331 8484
Transport: Falcon Wood or
New Eltham Rail
Architecture, building, education, health studies, nursing, psychology, sport and leisure.

Maritime Greenwich Campus Library
Dreadnought Library,
30 Park Row, SE10 9LS
Tel: 020 8331 9604
Transport: Cutty Sark DLR
Computing, law, maths, maritime studies, humanities, business, economics and sociology.

Medway Campus
Nelson Building, Central Avenue,
Chatham Maritime, ME4 4AW
Tel: 020 8331 9617
Transport: Chatham Rail
Agriculture, earth, environmental and life sciences, chemistry, pharmacy, pharmacology, sport, leisure, geography, and engineering (civil, electronic and mechanical).

Guildhall School Of Music and Drama
Silk Street, Barbican, EC2Y 8DT
Tel: 020 7628 2571
Website: www.gsmd.ac.uk
Transport: Barbican LU,
Moorgate LU/Rail
Music, theatre, drama criticism, stagecraft, costume, music therapy. Also a collection of plays, poetry, scores and video and sound recordings.

London Metropolitan University
Website: www.londonmet.ac.uk
The university has libraries at:

Calcutta House
Old Castle St, E1 7NT
Tel: 020 7320 1185
Transport: Aldgate & Aldgate East LU
Computing, information systems, language studies, law, politics, modern history, psychology and sociology.

Integrated Learning Resource Centre
41 Commercial Road, E1 1IA
Tel: 020 7320 1869
Transport: Aldgate East LU
Art, design, communication, media, photography, silversmithing, jewellery, film and video.

Moorgate
84 Moorgate, EC2M 6SQ
Tel: 020 7320 1563
Transport: Moorgate LU/Rail
Business, accountancy, banking, civil aviation, economics, insurance, management, marketing, transport, travel, tourism and shipping.

Ladbroke House
62-66 Highbury Grove, N5 2AD
Tel: 020 7133 5149
Transport: Highbury & Islington LU/Rail
Accounting, bibliography, government, law, health, media, nursing, politics, social sciences, psychology, cultural studies, information and knowledge management.

The Learning Centre
236-250 Holloway Road, N7 6PP
Tel: 020 7133 2371
Transport: Holloway Road LU
A general library, it is also the location of the TUC Libraries Collection

which has collections in all areas in which the Trades Union Congress has been involved since the second half of the nineteenth-century.
Tel: 020 7133 2260
Website: www.unionhistory.info

University of London
The University of London is made up of a large number of colleges and specialist schools and institutes, each with its own specialist library. Admission regulations are set by each individual establishment and vary enormously between libraries. The university has libraries at:

University of London Library
Senate House, Malet Street, WC1E 7HU
Tel: 020 7862 8500
Fax: 020 7862 8480
Website: www.ull.ac.uk
Transport: Russell Square LU, Goodge Street LU
Huge academic library with over two million books and five thousand current journals. Specialisms are humanities and social sciences but the library's material also covers basic reference material on the history of science and medicine.

Birkbeck College
Malet Street, WC1E 7HX
Tel: 020 7631 6239
Website: www.bbk.ac.uk
Transport: Goodge Street, Russell Square, Euston Square LU.
General academic library.
and
Extra-Mural Library
(Faculty of Continuing Education
39 Gordon Square, WC1H 0PD
Tel: 020 7631 6167
Transport: Euston & Russell Square LU

British Library of Political and Economic Science
Lionel Robbins Building,
10 Portugal Street, WC2A 2HD
Tel: 020 7955 7229
Website: www.lse.ac.uk/library/
Transport: Holborn, Temple LU
This is one of the largest social science collections in the world. The holdings comprise of around a million bound volumes and 28,000 journals.

Courtauld Institute of Art
Somerset House, Strand, WC2R 0RN
Tel: 020 7848 2701
Website: www.courtauld.ac.uk
Transport: Charing Cross LU/Rail, Temple LU
An estimated 140,000 titles, including 60,000 exhibition catalogues, on arts & architecture. The Coutauld also has the Conway Library consisting of almost a million photographs and cuttings and the Witt Library housing reproductions of art.

Goldsmiths College
New Cross, SE14 6NW
Tel: 020 7919 7150
Website: www.libweb.gold.ac.uk
Transport: New Cross & New Cross Gate LU/Rail
General academic library holding more than a quarter of a million books and subscriptions to 1,500 journals. There are special strengths in the creative and performing arts, humanities, social sciences and education.

Heythrop College
Kensington Square, W8 5HQ
Tel: 020 7795 4250
Website: www.heythrop.ac.uk/library/
Transport: High Street Kensington LU
History, philosophy, psychology, religion and Jewish studies with more than 200,000 volumes.

Imperial College
Central Library,
Imperial College and Science Museum
Libraries Building,
Prince Consort Road, SW7 2AZ
Tel: 020 7594 8820
Website: www.imperial.ac.uk
Transport: South Kensington LU
All aspects of science and technology. The library shares its site and services with the Science Museum Library. Each of the departments of the College has a departmental library; refer to the website for details.

Institute of Education
20 Bedford Way, WC1H 0AL
Tel: 020 7612 6080
Website: www.ioe.ac.uk
Transport: Russell Square LU
All aspects of education.

King's College
Website: www.kcl.ac.uk
Main Library, Maughan Library,
Chancery Lane, WC2A 1LR
Tel: 020 7848 2424
Website: www.kcl.ac.uk
Transport: Chancery Lane & Temple LU
Main academic library for the college with more than a quarter of a million items, especially in law, humanities, physical science, public policy and social science.

Franklin–Wilkins Information Service
Franklin-Wilkins Building,
150 Stamford Street, SE1 9NN
Tel: 020 7848 4378
Transport: Waterloo LU/Rail
Health, life sciences, nursing, midwifery, education, management.

London Business School
Sussex Place, Regent's Park, NW1 4SA
Tel: 020 7262 5050
Website:
www.london.edu/theschool783.html
Transport: Baker Street LU
Accountancy, business studies, economics, finance and management.

London School of Economics and Political Science
See the British Library of Political and Economic Science (page 283).

London School of Hygiene and Tropical Medicine
Keppel Street, WC1E 7HT
Tel: 020 7927 2276
Website: www.lshtm.ac.uk
Transport: Goodge Street LU
Health studies, life sciences, medicine and nutrition, especially international public health and tropical medicines.

London School of Jewish Studies
Schaller House, 44a Albert Road,
NW4 2SJ
Tel: 020 8203 6427
Website: www.brijnet.org/lsjs
Transport: Hendon Central LU

Queen Mary and Westfield College
Main Library, Mile End Road, E1 4NS
Tel: 020 7882 3300
Website: www.library.qmul.ac.uk
Transport: Mile End, Stepney Green LU
General academic library.

Royal Academy of Music
Marylebone Road, NW1 5HT
Tel: 020 7873 7321
Website: www.ram.ac.uk
Transport: Baker Street LU
A vast stock of more than 125,000 books, recordings, sheet music, manuscripts and sound recordings.

Royal Veterinary College
Royal College Street, NW1 0TU
Tel: 020 7468 5162
Website: www.rvc.ac.uk
Transport: King's Cross LU/Rail, Mornington Crescent LU

School of Advanced Studies
Website: www.sas.ac.uk
The following eight establishments are all part of the School of Advanced Study, itself a part of the University of London. Only post-graduate students and lecturers can gain access.

Institute of Advanced Legal Studies
17 Russell Square, WC1B 5DR
Tel: 020 7862 5790
Website: www.ials.sas.ac.uk
Transport: Euston LU/Rail, Russell Square LU
The UK National law library with a world class collection of legal material.

Institute of Classical Studies
Senate House, Malet Street, WC1E 7HU
Tel: 020 7862 8709
Website: www.sas.ac.uk/icls
Transport: Euston Rail/LU, Russell Square LU
All aspects of research in classical studies.

Institute of Commonwealth Studies
28 Russell Square, WC1B 5DS
Tel: 020 7862 8842
Website: www.sas.ac.uk/commonwealth-studies
Transport: Euston Rail/LU & Russell Square LU
The Commonwealth as a whole and any of its member states.

Institute of English Studies
Room 304, Senate House,
Malet Street, WC1E 7HU
Tel: 020 7862 8675
Website: www.sas.ac.uk/ies
Transport: Russell Square & Goodge Street LU
The Centre for Manuscript and Print Studies is based here.

Institute of Germanic & Romance Studies
29 Russell Square, WC1B 5DP
Tel: 020 7862 8967
Website: www.sas.ac.uk/igrs
Transport: Euston LU/Rail, Russell Square LU
Mostly German language and literature.

Institute of Historical Research
Senate House, Malet Street, WC1E 7HU
Tel: 020 7862 8760
Website: www.history.ac.uk
Transport: Russell Square & Goodge Street LU
History.

Institute For the Study of the Americas
31 Tavistock Square, WC1H 9HA
Tel: 020 7862 8501
Website: www.americas.sas.ac.uk
Transport: Euston LU/Rail & Russell Square LU
Latin American studies.

Warburg Institute
Woburn Square, WC1H 0AB
Tel: 020 7862 8935
Website: www.sas.ac.uk/warburg
Transport: Russell Square, Goode Street,
Euston Square & Warren Street LU;
Euston LU/Rail
Archaeology, bibliography, classics,
history, history of science, literature,
religion, philosophy.

School of Oriental & African Studies
Thornhaugh St, Russell Sq, WC1H 0XG
Tel: 020 7898 4163
Website: www.soas.ac.uk
Transport: Russell Square &
Goodge Street LU
Material relating to the study of Asia
and Africa. There are around 850,000
books and 4,500 periodicals plus an
extensive archive and manuscript
collection.

University College London
Website: www.ucl.ac.uk/library/
A large number of libraries and institutes are incorporated within this
college. The libraries with public
access are featured below:

School of Pharmacy
29-39 Brunswick Square, WC1N 1AX
Tel: 020 7753 5833
Website: www.ulsop.ac.uk
Transport: Russell Square LU,
King's Cross LU/Rail
Pharmacy and pharmacology.

Main Library
Wilkin's Building, Gower Street,
WC1E 6BT
Tel: 020 7679 7793
Transport: Euston Square & Warren
Street LU, Euston LU/Rail
General academic library covering
arts, humanities, economics, public
policy and law.

School of Slavonic and East European Studies
Senate House, Malet Street, WC1E 7HU
Tel: 020 7862 8523
Transport: Goodge Street, Euston Square
& Russell Square LU; Euston LU/Rail
Languages, literature, history, politics,
economics, geography and bibliogra-
phy of Eastern Europe.

Science Library
DMS Watson Building,
Malet Place, WC1E 6BT
Tel: 020 7679 7789
Transport: Euston LU/Rail, Euston
Square & Warren Street LU
Engineering, life sciences mathemati-
cal and physical sciences, anthropol-
ogy, geography and management.

Special Collections
140 Hampstead Road, NW1 2BX
Tel: 020 7679 5197
Transport: Warren Street &
Mornington Crescent LU
Manuscripts, archives and rare books
covering a vast number of subject
areas. The George Orwell Archive is
among the collection.

Middlesex University
Website: www.ilrs.mdx.ac.uk
The university has libraries at:

Cat Hill Campus
Cat Hill, Barnet, EN4 8HT
Tel: 020 8411 5042
Transport: Cockfosters LU
Art and design learning resources.

Enfield Campus
Queensway, Enfield, EN3 4SA
Tel: 020 8411 5334
Transport: Southbury Rail
A humanities library catering for
campus students but with access for
the public.

Royal College of Music
Prince Consort Road, SW7 2BS
Tel: 020 7591 4325
Fax: 020 7589 7740
Website: www.rcm.ac.uk
Transport: South Kensington LU
One of the foremost music libraries
in the UK with more than 250,000
items and material dating from the
fifteenth-century.

South Bank University
Website: www.lisa.sbu.ac.uk
The university has libraries at:

Perry Library
250 Southwark Bridge Road, SE1 6NJ
Tel: 020 7815 6604
*Transport: Elephant & Castle, Waterloo,
London Bridge LU/Rail*
The main university library, with
reference facilities for member of the
public.

Trinity College of Music
*Jerwood Library of the Performing Arts
King Charles Court, Old Royal Naval
College, SE10 9JF*
Tel: 020 8305 4444
Fax: 020 8305 9444
Website: www.tcm.ac.uk
Transport: Cutty Sark DLR
Music library with more than 70,000
books, scores and sound recordings.
Especially strong on twentieth-
century music.

PUBLIC LIBRARIES

All of the 32 London boroughs plus the Corporation of London provide free public libraries for the use of the public. The figures are staggering; there are 395 public libraries in London, open for over 15,000 hours each week. 51.5 million visits are made to London's public libraries each year and ten times more people use their public library than visit league football matches. Each borough usually has a main lending and reference library and then a spread of smaller, local libraries which typically feature more restricted stock, fewer facilities and shorter opening hours. The range of facilities available in libraries is increasing and many now offer public internet access, DVDs and audio material in addition to books. Below are details for each of the main libraries, followed by telephone numbers for branch libraries. Opening hours vary enormously so do give the smaller libraries a call before making a special journey.

Idea Store, Whitechapel

Barking and Dagenham

Central Library
- Barking, IG11 7NB
- ☎ 020 8227 3604
- ✆ 020 8227 3625
- ✐ www.barking-dagenham.gov.uk

Also at:
Fanshawe 020 8270 4244
Marks Gate 020 8270 4165
Markyate 020 8270 4137
Rectory 020 8270 6233
Rush Green 020 8270 4304
Thames View 020 8270 4164
Valence 020 8270 6864
Wantz 020 8270 4169
Whalebone (Chadwell Heath)
020 8270 4305
Woodward 020 8270 4166

Barnet

Hendon Library
- The Burroughs, NW4 4BQ
- ☎ 020 8359 2628
- ✐ www.barnet.gov.uk

Also at:
Burnt Oak 020 8959 3112
Childs Hill 020 8455 5390
Chipping Barnet 020 8359 4040
Church End 020 8346 5711
East Barnet 020 8440 4376
East Finchley 020 8883 2664
Edgware 020 8359 2626
Friern Barnet 020 8368 2680
Golders Green 020 8359 2060
Grahame Park 020 8200 0470
Hampstead Garden Suburb
020 8455 1235
Mill Hill 020 8959 5066
North Finchley 020 8445 4081
Osidge 020 8368 0532
South Friern 020 8883 6513

Bexley

Central Library
- Townley Rd, Bexleyheath, DA6 7HJ
- ☎ 020 8301 1066
- ✐ www.bexley.gov.uk

Also at:
Barnehurst Mobile Library Service
020 8309 4165
Bexley Village 01322 522168
Blackfen 020 8300 3010
Bostall 020 8310 1779
Crayford 01322 526050
Erith 01322 336582
North Heath 01322 333663
Sidcup 020 8303 7777 ext 5100
Slade Green 020 8319 9640
Thamesmead 020 8310 9944
Upper Belvedere 01322 439760
Welling 020 8303 2788

Brent

Willesden Green Library
- 95 High Street, NW10 2SF
- ☎ 020 8937 3400
- ✐ www.brent.gov.uk

Also at:
Barham Park 020 8937 3550
Cricklewood (includes local history
library & archives) 020 8937 3540
Ealing Road 020 8937 3560
Harlesden 020 8965 7132
Kensal Rise 020 8969 0942
Kilburn 020 89937 3530
Kingsbury 020 8937 3520
Neasden 020 8937 3580
Preston 020 8937 3510
Tokyngton 020 8937 3590
Town Hall 020 8937 3500

Bromley

Central Library

- High Street, Bromley, BR1 1EX
- ☎ 020 8460 9955
- 📠 020 8313 9975
- 🖎 www.bromley.gov.uk

Also at:
Anerley 020 8778 7457
Beckenham 020 8650 7292
Biggin Hill 01959 574468
Burnt Ash 020 8460 3405
Chislehurst 020 8467 1318
Hayes 020 8462 2445
Mottingham 020 8857 5406
Orpington 01689 831551
Penge 020 8778 8772
Petts Wood 01689 821607
St Paul's Cray 020 8300 5454
Shortlands 020 8460 9692
Southborough 020 8467 0355
West Wickham 020 8777 4139

Camden

Swiss Cottage Library

- 88 Avenue Road, NW3 3HA
- ☎ 020 7974 6522
- 📠 020 7974 6532
- 🖎 www.camden.gov.uk

Also at:
Belsize 020 7974 6518
Camden Town 020 7974 1563
Chalk Farm 020 7974 6526
Heath (Hampstead) 020 7974 6520
Highgate 020 7974 5752
Holborn 020 7974 6345
Kentish Town 020 7974 6253
Kilburn 020 7974 1965
Queen's Crescent 020 7974 6243
Regent's Park 020 7974 1530
St Pancras 020 7974 5833
West Hampstead 020 7974 6610

Corporation of London

Guildhall Library

- Aldermanbury, EC2P 2EJ
- ☎ 020 7332 1868
- 📠 020 7332 3384
- 🖎 www.cityoflondon.gov.uk

The original library at Guildhall was founded in the 1420's under the terms of Richard Whittington's will. It is a major public reference library specialising in the history of London and with many other significant collections.

Also at:
Barbican 020 7638 0569
Camomile Street 020 7247 8895
City Business Library 020 7600 1461
Shoe Lane 020 7583 7178

Croydon

Central Library

- Croydon Clocktower, Katharine Street, CR9 1ET
- ☎ 020 8760 5400
- 📠 020 8253 1004
- 🖎 www.croydon.gov.uk

Also at:
Ashburton 020 8656 4148
Bradmore Green 01737 553267
Broad Green 020 8684 4829
Coulsdon 020 8660 1548
New Addington 01689 841248
Norbury 020 8679 1597
Purley 020 8660 1171
Sanderstead 020 8657 2882
Selsdon 020 8657 7210
Shirley 020 8777 7650
South Norwood 020 8653 4545
Thornton Heath 020 8684 4432
Upper Norwood 020 8670 2551
(Upper Norwood Library is jointly funded by Croydon and Lambeth and a separate library card is needed to borrow from it)

Ealing

Central Library
- 103 Ealing Broadway Centre, The Broadway, W5 5JY
- ☎ 020 8567 3670
- ✆ 020 8840 2351
- ✑ www.ealing.gov.uk

Also at:
Acton 020 8752 0999
Greenford 020 8578 1466
Hanwell 020 8567 5041
Jubilee Gardens 020 8578 1067
Northfields 020 8567 5700
Northolt 020 8845 3380
Perivale 020 8997 2830
Pitshanger 020 8997 0230
Southall 020 8574 3412
West Ealing 020 8567 2812
Wood End 020 8422 3965

Enfield

Central Library
- Cecil Road, Enfield, EN2 6TW
- ☎ 020 8379 8366
- ✆ 020 8379 8401
- ✑ www.enfield.gov.uk

Also at:
Bowes Road 020 8379 1707
Bullsmoor 020 8379 1723
Bush Hill Park 020 8379 1709
Edmonton Green 020 8379 2600
Enfield Highway 020 8379 1710
Merryhills 020 8379 1711
Ordnance Road 020 8379 1725
Palmer's Green 020 8379 2711
Ponder's End 020 8379 1712
Ridge Avenue 020 8379 1714
Southgate Circus 020 8350 1124
Weir Hall 020 8379 1717
Winchmore Hill 020 8379 1718

Greenwich

Woolwich Library
- Calderwood Street, SE18 6QZ
- ☎ 020 8921 5750
- ✑ www.greenwich.gov.uk

Also at:
Abbey Wood 020 8310 4185
Blackheath 020 8858 1131
Charlton 020 8319 2525
Claude Ramsey (Thamesmead) 020 8310 4246
Coldharbour 020 8857 7346
East Greenwich 020 8858 6656
Eltham 020 8850 2268
Ferrier 020 8856 5149
New Eltham 020 8850 2322
Plumstead 020 8854 1728
Slade 020 8854 7900
West Greenwich 020 8858 4289

Hackney

Hackney Central Library
- Hackney Technology & Learning Centre, 1 Reading Lane, E8 1GQ
- ☎ 020 8356 2542
- ✆ 020 8356 2531
- ✑ www.hackney.gov.uk

Also at:
Clapton 020 8356 1620
C L R James Library, Dalston Lane 020 8356 1665
Homerton 020 8356 1690
Shoreditch 020 8356 4350
Stamford Hill 020 8356 1700
Stoke Newington 020 8356 5230

Hammersmith and Fulham

Hammersmith Library
- Shepherd's Bush Road, W6 7AT
- ☎ Lending 020 8753 3820
- ✆ 020 8753 3815
- ✑ www.lbhf.gov.uk

Also at:
Askew Road 020 8753 3863
Barons Court 020 8753 3888
Fulham 020 8753 3876
Sands End 020 8753 3885
Shepherd's Bush 020 8753 3853

Haringey
Central Library
🖳 *High Rd, Wood Green, N22 6XD*
☎ *020 8489 2780*
🖰 *www.haringey.gov.uk*

Also at:
Alexandra Park 020 8489 8770
Bruce Castle Museum (archive and
local history) 020 8808 8772
Coombes Croft 020 8489 8771
Highgate 020 8489 8772
Hornsey 020 8489 1118
Marcus Garvey 020 8489 5309
Muswell Hill 020 8489 8773
St Ann's 020 8489 8775
Stroud Green 020 8489 8776

Harrow
Central Library
🖳 *Gayton Road, Harrow, HA1 2HL*
☎ *020 8427 6012*
🖰 *www.harrow.gov.uk*

Also:
Bob Laurence, Edgware
020 8952 4140
Civic Centre 020 8424 1055
Hatch End 020 8428 2636
Kenton 020 8907 2463
North Harrow 020 8427 0611
Pinner 020 8866 7827
Rayners Lane 020 8866 9185
Roxeth 020 8422 0809
Stanmore 020 8954 9955
Wealdstone 020 8420 9333

Havering
Central Library
🖳 *St Edward's Way,*
   Romford, Essex, RM1 3AR
☎ *01708 432389*
🖰 *01708 432391*
🖰 *www.havering.gov.uk*

Also at:
Collier Row 01708 760063
Elm Park 01708 451270
Gidea Park 01708 441856
Harold Hill 01708 342749
Harold Wood 01708 342071
Hornchurch 01708 452248
Rainham 01708 551905
South Hornchurch 01708 554126
Upminster 01708 251052

Hillingdon
Uxbridge Central Library
🖳 *14-15 High St, Uxbridge,*
   UB8 1HD
☎ *01895 250600*
🖰 *01895 239794*
🖰 *www.hillingdon.gov.uk*

Also at:
Eastcote 020 8866 3668
Harefield 01895 822171
Harlington 020 8569 1612
Hayes 020 8573 2855
Hayes End 020 8573 4209
Ickenham 01895 635945
Kingshill 020 8845 3773
Manor Farm 01895 633651
Northwood Hills 01923 824595
Oak Farm 01895 234690
Oaklands Gate 01923 826690
Ruislip Manor 01895 633668
South Ruislip 020 8845 0188
West Drayton 01895 443238
Yeading 020 8573 0261
Yiewsley 01895 442539

Hounslow

Hounslow Library
- 🖳 *Treaty Centre, High St, TW3 1ES*
- ☎ *0845 456 2800*
- 📠 *0845 456 2880*
- 🖉 *www.hounslow.info*

Also at:
Beavers 0845 456 2800
Bedfont 020 8890 6173
Brentford 020 8560 8801
Chiswick 020 8759 1008
Cranford 020 8759 0641
Feltham 020 8890 3506
Hanworth 020 8898 0256
Heston 020 8570 1028
Isleworth 020 8560 2934
Osterley 020 8560 4295

Islington

Central Library
- 🖳 *2 Fieldway Crescent, N5 1PF*
- ☎ *020 7527 6900*
- 🖉 *www.islington.gov.uk*

Also at:
Archway 020 7527 7820
Finsbury 020 7527 7960
John Barnes Library,
Camden Road 020 7527 7900
Lewis Carroll 020 7527 7936
Mildmay 020 7527 7880
N4 Library, 020 7527 7800
North Library, Manor Gardens
020 7527 7840
South Library, Essex Road
020 7527 7860
West Library, Bridgeman Road
020 7527 7920

Kensington and Chelsea

Central Library
- 🖳 *Phillimore Walk, W8 7RX*
- ☎ *020 7937 2542*
- 📠 *020 7361 2976*
- 🖉 *www.rbkc.gov.uk*

Also at:
Brompton 020 7373 3111
Chelsea 020 7352 6056
Kensal 020 8969 7736
Norh Kensington 020 7727 6583
Notting Hill Gate 020 7229 8574

Kingston upon Thames

Kingston Library
- 🖳 *Fairfield Road, Kingston upon Thames, KT1 2PS*
- ☎ *020 8547 6400*
- 📠 *020 8547 6401*
- 🖉 *www.kingston.gov.uk*

Also at
Hook & Chessington. Temporarily located in Coppard Gardens, until 2006 020 8547 6480
New Malden 020 8547 6540
Old Malden 020 8547 6467
Surbiton 020 8547 6444
Tolworth 020 8547 6470
Tudor Drive 020 8547 6456

Lambeth

Brixton Central Library (Tate Library)
- 🖳 *Brixton Oval, SW2 1JQ*
- ☎ *020 7926 1056*
- 📠 *020 7926 1070*
- 🖉 *www.lambeth.gov.uk*

Also at:
Carnegie Library,
Herne Hill Road 020 7926 6050
Clapham 020 7926 0717
Durning, Kennington Lane 020 7926 8682
Minet, Knatchbull Rd 020 7926 6073
South Lambeth Road 020 7926 0705
Streatham 020 7926 6768
Waterloo 020 7926 8750
West Norwood 020 7926 8092

Lewisham

Lewisham Library

- 199-201 Lewisham High Street, SE13 6LG
- ☎ 020 8297 9677
- ✆ 020 8297 1169
- ⌨ www.lewisham.gov.uk

Also at:

Blackheath Village 020 8852 5309
Catford 020 8314 6399
Crofton Park 020 8692 1683
Forest Hill 020 8699 2065
Grove Park 020 8857 5794
Manor House 020 8852 0357
New Cross 020 8694 2534
Sydenham 020 8778 7563
Torridon Road 020 8698 1590
Wavelengths, Deptford 020 8694 2535

Merton

Three town centre libraries:

Morden Library

- Merton Civic Centre, London Road, Morden SM4 5DX
- ☎ 020 8545 4040
- ⌨ www.merton.gov.uk

Mitcham Library

- 157 London Road, Mitcham, CR4 2YR
- ☎ 020 8648 4070

Wimbledon Library

- 35 Wimbledon Hill Rd, SW19 7NB
- ☎ 020 8946 7432

Also at:

Donald Hope Library,
Colliers Wood 020 8542 1975
Pollards Hill 020 8764 5877
Raynes Park 020 8542 1893
West Barnes 020 8942 2635

Newham

East Ham Library

- High Street South, E6 4EL
- ☎ 020 8430 3648
- ⌨ www.newham.gov.uk

Stratford Library

- 3 The Grove, E15 1EL
- ☎ 020 8430 6890

Also at:

Beckton Globe 020 8430 4063
Canning Town 020 7476 2696
Custom House 020 7476 1565
The Gate 020 8430 3838
Green Street 020 8472 4101
Manor Park 020 8478 1177
North Woolwich 020 7511 2387
Plaistow 020 8472 0420

Redbridge

Central Library

- Clements Road, Ilford, IG1 1EA
- ☎ 020 8708 2414
- ⌨ www.redbridge.gov.uk

Also at:

Aldersbrook 020 8496 0006
Chadwell Heath (Keith Axon Centre)
020 8708 0790
Fullwell Cross 020 8708 9281
Gants Hill 020 8708 9274
Goodmayes 020 8708 7750
Hainault 020 8708 9206
South Woodford 020 8708 9067
Wanstead 020 8708 7400
Woodford Green 020 8708 9055

Richmond

Richmond Lending Library
- 🖾 *Little Green, Richmond, TW9 1QL*
- ☎ *020 8940 0981*
- 🌐 *www.richmond.gov.uk*

Central Reference Library
- 🖾 *Old Town Hall,*
  Whittaker Ave, TW9 1TP
- ☎ *020 8940 5529*

Also at:
Castlenau 020 8748 3837
East Sheen 020 8876 8801
Ham 020 8940 8703
Hampton 020 8979 5110
Hampton Hill 020 8979 3705
Hampton Wick 020 8977 1559
Heathfield 020 8894 1017
Kew 020 8876 8654
Teddington 020 8977 1284
Twickenham 020 8892 8091
Whitton 020 8894 9828

Southwark

Newington Library
- 🖾 *155-157 Walworth Rd, SE17 1RS*
- ☎ *Lending 020 7525 2176*
  Reference 020 7525 2181
- 🌐 *www.southwark.gov.uk*

Also:
Blue Anchor 020 7231 0475
Brandon 020 7735 3430
Camberwell 020 7703 3763
Dulwich 020 7525 6220
East Street 020 7703 0395
Grove Vale 020 8693 5734
Borough High Street (John Harvard Library) 020 7407 0807,
(local studies 020 7403 3507)
Kingswood 020 8670 4803
Nunhead 020 7639 0264
Peckham 020 7525 0200
Rotherhithe 020 7237 2010

Sutton

Central Library
- 🖾 *St Nicholas Way, Sutton, SM1 1EA*
- ☎ *020 8770 4700*
- ✉ *020 8770 4777*
- 🌐 *www.sutton.gov.uk*

Also at:
Beddington 020 8688 5093
Carshalton 020 8647 1151
Cheam 020 8644 9377
Middleton Circle 020 8648 6608
Phoenix Centre 020 8770 6006
Ridge Road 020 8644 9696
Roundshaw 020 8770 4901
Wallington 020 8770 4900
Worcester Park 020 8337 1609

Tower Hamlets

Bethnal Green Library
- 🖾 *Cambridge Heath Road, E2 0HL*
- ☎ *020 8980 3902*
- 🌐 *www.ideastore.co.uk*

There are Idea Stores at:
Bow
- 🖾 *1 Gladstone Place, Roman Road*
  E3 5ES
- ☎ *020 7364 4332*

Chrisp Street
- 🖾 *1 Vesey Path*
  East India Dock Road, E14 6BT
- ☎ *020 7364 4332*

Whitechapel
- 🖾 *319 - 331 Whitechapel Road,*
  E1 1BU
- ☎ *020 7364 4332*

An Idea Store is a combined library, learning centre and arts centre with extended opening hours. Future ones are planned for Canary Wharf, Isle of Dogs, Watney Market and Bethnal Green

Libraries at:
Bancroft 020 8980 4366
Cubitt Town 020 7987 3152
Dorset 020 7739 9489
Stepney 020 7790 5616
Wapping 020 7488 3535
Watney Market 020 7790 4039
Whitechapel 020 7247 5272

Waltham Forest
Central Library
- *High St, Walthamstow, E17 7JN*
- *020 8496 1100*
- *020 8496 1150 (Information & Reference Service)*
- *020 8496 1101*
- *www.lbwf.gov.uk*

Also at:
Friday Hill 020 8529 6660
Hale End 020 8496 1050
Harrow Green 020 8496 1063
Higham Hill 020 8496 1173
Lea Bridge 020 8496 1152
Leyton 020 8496 1090
Leytonstone 020 8496 1190
North Chingford 020 8496 1070
St James St 020 8496 1165
South Chingford 020 8496 1079
Wood Street 020 8496 1155

Wandsworth
Battersea Library
- *265 Lavender Hill, SW11 1JB*
- *020 8871 7466*
- *020 7978 4376*
- *www.wandsworth.gov.uk*

Also at:
Alvering 020 8871 6398
Balham 020 8871 7195
Battersea Park 020 8871 7468
Earlsfield 020 8871 6389
Northcote 020 8871 7469
Putney 020 8871 7090
Roehampton 020 8871 7091
Southfields 020 8871 6388
Tooting 020 8871 7175
West Hill 020 8871 6386
York Gardens 020 8871 7471

City of Westminster
- *www.westminster.gov.uk*
- *020 7641 1300 (for all library enquiries in the borough)*

Westminster Reference Library
- *35 St Martin's Street, WC2H 7HP*

Marylebone Information Service
- *109-117 Marylebone Road, NW1 5PS*

Also at:
Charing Cross
Church Street
Maida Vale
Marylebone
Mayfair
Paddington
Pimlico
Queen's Park
St James's
St John's Wood
Victoria

Public Libraries

Museums, Galleries & Historic Houses of Literary Interest

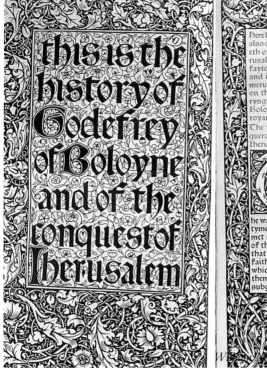

Here begynneth the boke
also of Godefrey of Bol
eth of the conquest of
rusalem, conteynyng di
faytes of Armes made i
and in the contrees adi
meruayllous werkes hap
on this syde, as in tho
ryng, and how the valy
Boloyne conquerd wit
royamme, and was kyn
The first chapitre treat
querd Perse & slewe Co
Iherusalem the very ero

HER
ye th
cryst
of th
in bi
ben,
of th
pepl
he was a prophete sent
tyme of Eracles was th
met sowen and sprad a
of thoryent, & namely
that the prynces of the l
faith to his secte that
whiche is cursed and et
them by force and by
subgets to obeye to hi

The places listed below are a good way for book lovers to get a more intimate knowledge of their literary heroes and heroines. Those who don't see the point in such shrines and prefer to explore the works should read Julian Barnes', *Flaubert's Parrot*, a wonderful account of walking in the footsteps of a great writer.

The British Library

- 96 Euston Road, NW1 2DB
- ☎ 020 7412 7332
- ✎ www.bl.uk
- 🚇 Euston, King's Cross and St Pancras LU/Rail
- ⏰ Mon-Fri 9.30am-6pm (Tues until 8pm), Sat 9.30am-5pm, Sun & Bank Holidays 11am-5pm
- 💷 Admission free (audio tours of the John Ritblat Gallery or an Architectural Tour of the building are available £3.50)

This is the undoubted highlight for any book lover in London – a place to savour and visit again and again. As well as holding the twelve million books (on three hundred and fifty kilometres of shelving!) which make up the national library of Britain (see p.249 for details about reading rights), there are exhibition galleries for visitors. The real delight is the John Ritblat Gallery: Treasures of the British Library, which displays some incredible texts, manuscripts, maps and musical scores. Here you can view the likes of the Lindisfarne Gospel, a First Folio of Shakespeare, the Magna Carta and Leonardo da Vinci's notebooks plus some extremely old, sacred texts from the great religions of the world. Many of the most valuable books can now be viewed on screen. The interactive screens are located in the John Ritblat Gallery or on the library's website.

The 'Workshop of Words, Sounds and Images' looks at book production from the earliest written material to modern digital methods and there are regular demonstrations of book-binding, calligraphy and printing. The Pearson Gallery hosts temporary exhibitions, always with a literary theme and generally lasting a few months.

A visit to the café or to the restaurant is a grand experience, located as they are beside the stunning King's Library, the collection of around 65,000 books collected by King George III and given to the nation in 1823 by his son, King George IV. The stack of sumptuous leatherbound volumes stretches upwards, housed in a six storey, seventeen-metre high glass tower situated at the centre of the library.

There are guided tours of the public areas of the building (£6) on

Mon, Wed, Fri and Sat and tours which also include a visit to one of the reading rooms on Sun and Bank Holidays (£7). Booking is advisable, either at the Information Desk or by ringing the number above.

Carlyle's House

⌨ *24 Cheyne Row, SW3 5HL*
☎ *20 7352 7087*
🚌 *Sloane Square LU*
🕐 *Wed-Sun & Bank Hol Mon 11am-5pm (April-end October)*
⚓ *£4 (adults), £2 (children)*

Although he is no longer a well-known figure, the Victorian historian, Thomas Carlyle (1795-1881) was hugely influential and famous in his own lifetime. He lived at this house from 1834 until his death. Most revered for works such as 'The French Revolution' and 'Frederick the Great', Carlyle was also a founder of The London Library (see p.263).

He was visited at this house by many of the great names of the day including Dickens, Tennyson, Chopin, Browning, George Eliot, Darwin, Thackeray, John Stuart Mill and John Ruskin. The house still contains its original furniture as well as Carlyle's books and belongings. However, don't get too carried away imagining domestic tranquillity – the Carlyles had a notoriously volatile relationship. A statue of Carlyle stands in nearby Cheyne Walk.

The Dickens House Museum

⌨ *48 Doughty Street, WC1 2LX*
☎ *020 7405 2127*
✍ *www.dickensmuseum.com*
🚌 *Russell Square, Holborn & Chancery Lane LU*
🕐 *Mon-Sat 10am-5pm, Sun 11am-5pm*
⚓ *£5 (adults), £4 (concessions), £3 (children), £14 (family ticket)*

Charles Dickens (1812-1870) lived in this late-Georgian terrace between 1837 and 1839. During his time here he wrote parts of 'The Pickwick Papers' and 'Barnaby Rudge' and all of 'Nicholas Nickleby' and 'Oliver Twist'. Dickens lived at around fifteen London addresses but this is the only house which survives. Laid out over four floors, some of the rooms are furnished as they would have been in his time while others hold displays including family portraits (it includes the earliest known portrait of the author, painted by his aunt in 1830), an extensive family tree, letters, papers, furniture and first editions of Dickens' books.

The Freud Museum

- 20 Maresfield Gardens, NW3 5SX
- ☎ 020 7435 2002
- ✆ 020 7431 5452
- ✑ www.freud.org.uk
- 🚇 Finchley Road LU
- 🕐 Wed-Sun 12noon-5pm
- 💷 £5 (adults), £2 (concessions), free (children under 12 years)

In 1938 Sigmund Freud fled from Nazi Vienna with enough belongings to recreate a replica of his Austrian home in London, including his famous couch which is in the centrepiece of the museum – the Library and Study. When Freud arrived in London he was already sick with cancer and he died here in 1939 but Anna, Freud's daughter (herself a psychoanalyst), lived on in the house until her death in 1982. The house remains as it was in Freud's time and it contains many of the ancient Egyptian, Greek, Roman and Oriental antiquities that he avidly collected. He admitted that his passion for collecting such items was second only to his passion for cigars! There is a portrait of the man himself painted by Salvador Dali and video footage from the Freud family home movies is also on show.

Dr Johnson's House

- 17 Gough Square, EC4A 3DE
- ☎ 020 7353 3745
- ✑ www.drjh.dircon.co.uk
- 🚇 Blackfriars LU/Rail; Chancery Lane, Temple & Holborn LU
- 🕐 Mon-Sat 11am-5.30pm (May-Sept), Mon-Sat 11am-5pm (Oct-April)
- 💷 £4.50 (adults), £3.50 (concessions), £1.50 (children)

Dr Samuel Johnson (1709-1784) is famous as the compiler of the first dictionary of the English Language and for his many sayings – carefully recorded by his biographer, James Boswell. He moved to this house, built around 1700, with the advance that he got for his dictionary and it was during his time here (1748-1759) that he and his six scribes, standing at high desks in the attic, compiled the enormous work (containing over 40,000 definitions and over one hundred thousand quotations), which was published in 1755. The house has been restored to its original condition and furnished with eighteenth-century pieces, including Johnson memorabilia and a first edition of the dictionary. There are portraits of Dr Johnson in the National Portrait Gallery (see p.302). Johnson is buried in Westminster Abbey.

Freud Museum

Keats' House

- *Keat's Grove, NW3 3RR*
- *020 7435 2062*
- *www.cityoflondon.gov/keats*
- *Belsize Park or Hampstead LU*
- *Tues-Sun 1pm-5pm (April-Oct)*
- *£3 (adults), £1.50 (concessions), free (children under 16), tickets are valid for a year*

The Romantic poet (1795-1821) John Keats lived in this Regency house from 1818 to 1820 and is said to have written his famous 'Ode to a Nightingale' under a plum tree in the garden. The Brawne family lived next door and Keats fell in love with and became engaged to Fanny Brawne, the daughter of the house. Sadly, they never got married as Keats died from TB at the age of just twenty five. The house contains many mementos of their love, including her garnet engagement ring and a lock of hair. There is a portrait of Keats in the National Portrait Gallery (see below). A Poetry Reading Group meets regularly in the house. Keats is buried in the Protestant Cemetery in Rome; there is no name on the tombstone but the quote 'Here lies one whose name was writ in water'. Fanny Brawne wore her engagement ring until she died in 1865 despite marriage to Louis Lindon and the birth of three children. She is buried in Brompton Cemetery.

National Portrait Gallery

- *St Martin's Place, WC2H 0HE*
- *020 7312 2463*
- *www.npg.org.uk*
- *Charing Cross LU/Rail, Leicester Square LU*
- *Daily 10am-6pm (Thurs & Fri until 9pm)*
- *Admission free (admission charges for some temporary exhibitions)*

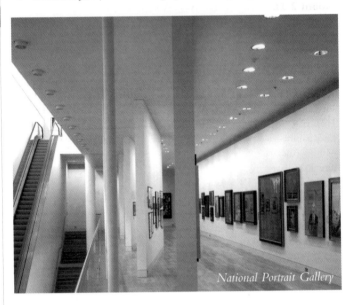

National Portrait Gallery

The National Portrait Gallery is a wonderful institution and an excellent way for book lovers to discover what their literary heroes actually looked like. It's fascinating to see images of favourite writers for perhaps the first time and to try to square their picture with what may be in your mind's eye. Remember it is a collection of national portraits so, don't expect to see any writers from outside Britain.

Visitors should note that displays do change and portraits may not be on regular display. Either ring the Gallery or access the database via the website if you intend travelling here to see a particular portrait.

A Sound Guide is available to take around the gallery with you and provides more detailed information about the exhibits while the IT Gallery on the Mezzanine Floor is a database of tens of thousands of the portraits owned by the Gallery and which helpfully indicates whether and where they are on display and provides high-quality illustrations of a good percentage of them. This can also be accessed via the website.

The oldest portraits are on the second floor and so for a chronological visit, start from the top and work your way down. We've listed the rooms where you'll find most writers but, of course, there is plenty in the intervening rooms to enjoy as well:

Room 2 The Elizabethan Age: Amidst several famous paintings of Queen Elizabeth I and her courtiers there's one of Sir Walter Raleigh, a writer and poet as well as explorer plus the famous portrait of William Shakespeare attributed to John Taylor (the painter's identity has never been fully established). It is especially important as it is the only portrait of Shakespeare to have a valid claim to being painted from life.

Room 4 The Jacobean Court: Among the great intellects of Jacobean England is Francis Bacon, lawyer, philosopher, scientist and essayist.

Room 6 Science and the Arts in the 17th Century: Here you'll find paintings of philosopher and poet Thomas Hobbes, poets John Milton, Andrew Marvell, George Herbert, Anne Finch and Aphra Behn plus John Bunyan, author of Pilgrim's Progress, and philosopher John Locke. There's also a small engraving of John Donne, poet and orator.

Room 7 Charles II The Restoration of the Monarchy: This room features John Dryden, poet, dramatist and literary critic and the famous diarist Samuel Pepys.

Room 8 Later Stuarts: A large portrait of the philosopher John Locke is here and one of the scientist Isaac Newton.

Room 9 The Kit-Cat Club: This was a group of influential Whigs who helped bring William III to the throne. This room contains portraits of dramatists William Congreve and Sir John Vanbrugh, the essayist and poet Joseph Addison, physician and poet Sir Samuel Garth and Sir Richard Steele, dramatist and essayist.

Room 10 The Arts in the Early 18th Century: Hanging here are the writers, Jonathan Swift, Alexander Pope, Samuel Richardson, Horace Walpole and Thomas Gray.

Room 11 Britain in the Early 18th Century: The religious writer Elizabeth Burnet can be found in this room alongside miniatures of poets Alexander Pope, William Somerville, Stephen Duck, William Mason and dramatist Sir Richard Steele.

Room 12 The Arts in the Later 18th Century: There are rich pickings here for book lovers including Laurence Sterne, Samuel Johnson, Oliver Goldsmith, Alexander Pope and Fanny Burney.

Room 18 Art, Invention and Thought. The Romantics: This room has a host of noteworthy literary portraits, including those of John Clare, John Keats, Samuel Taylor Coleridge, Mary Shelley, William Wordsworth, Percy Bysshe Shelley, Robert Southey, Mary Wollstonecraft, Charles Lamb and Walter Scott. One of the most famous pictures here is of George Gordon, Lord Byron (1788-1824) painted by Thomas Phillips in 1835 with Byron wearing a suitably flamboyant Albanian costume. There's also the small pencil and watercolour portrait of Jane Austen drawn in around 1810 by her sister Cassandra. It is believed to be the only portrait of the author that was drawn from life.

Room 20 The Road to Reform: Edmund Burke, William Cobbett, Sydney Smith plus busts of Walter Scott and Felicia Dorothea Hemans, poet and playwright.

Room 24 Early Victorian Arts: This room contains some of the best known Victorian portraits held by the Gallery. There is the famous oil painting of all three Brontë sisters painted by Patrick Branwell Brontë in 1834. Other paintings include Charles Dickens, Charles Kingsley, Robert Browning, George du Maurier, Elizabeth Barrett Browning, George Eliot and Wilkie Collins.

Room 26 Portraits by G F Watts: Algernon Charles Swinburne, John Stuart Mill, Thomas Carlyle, William Morris and Matthew Arnold.

Room 28 Late Victorian Arts: Robert Louis Stevenson (a painting and a bronze head).

Room 29 The Turn of the Century: Henry James and a bust of Joseph Conrad.

Room 30 The First World War: Lytton Strachey

Room 31 The Armistice to the New Elizabethans: This room contains a mixture of paintings, sculptures and photographs, including likenesses of Kingsley Amis, Antony Powell, Dame Freya Stark, Bertrand Russell, E. M. Forster, D. H. Lawrence, Ian Fleming, J.G.Ballard, Beatrix Potter, James Joyce, H. G. Wells, Laurie Lee, T. S. Eliot, Dylan Thomas, Dorothy L. Sayers, Virginia Woolf, T. H. White, T. E. Lawrence and Bertrand Russell.

Balcony Gallery Britain 1960-90: Philip Larkin, Iris Murdoch, William Golding, Steven Berkoff are pictured here and there is a bronze plaque of Ted Hughes.

Ground Floor: Britain Since 1990: Writers in this room include Harold Pinter, Samuel Beckett, John Mortimer, Kazuo Ishiguro, Seamus Heaney, Salman Rushdie and Germaine Greer. This floor seems especially prone to changes.

St Bride Library

- *Bride Lane, EC4Y 8EE*
- *020 7353 4660*
- *020 7583 7073*
- *Blackfriars LU/Rail*
- *Tues-Thurs 12noon-5.30pm, Wed 12noon-8.30pm*
- *Admission free*

The exhibition rooms here hold a changing series of exhibitions that relate to the subjects covered by the Library – printing and the printing trades.

Shakespeare's Globe Theatre

- *New Globe Walk, SE1 9DT*
- *020 7902 1400*
- *020 7902 1401*
- *www.shakepeares-globe.org*
- *Cannon Street & Southwark LU, London Bridge LU/Rail*
- *Daily 10am-5pm (1st Oct-5th May); daily 9am-12noon & 12.30pm-5pm (6th May-2nd Oct)*
- *£9 (adults), £7.50 (concessions), £6.50 (children), £25 (family)*

Note: There is no theatre tour access to the auditorium on the afternoons of matinee performances

This theatre is a reconstruction of The Globe Theatre in which Shakespeare was an actor and shareholder, and where many of his greatest plays were first performed (including 'Hamlet', 'Othello', 'King Lear' and 'Macbeth'). The Globe opened in 1599, and was one of four theatres on Bankside – known in those days as an area of rough and bawdy entertainment. It is thought that at that time, London had a population of around one hundred thousand and that an estimated forty thousand people went each week to one of the Bankside theatres. The original site of The Globe was in fact in what is now Park Street (about two hundred metres away), but this was the closest piece of land available for the project, right on the river with fine views across to St Paul's Cathedral. The original Globe was burned down on 29th June 1613 started by a stray spark from a cannon fired in a performance. By that time Shakespeare had retired to Stratford-upon-Avon a rich man. The theatre was rebuilt the next year but eventually shut when, under the regime of the Puritans, all entertainment was deemed unacceptable.

American actor, Sam Wanamaker was the moving force behind the current Globe, a remarkable building constructed of green (unseasoned) oak, held together with nine thousand five hundred tapered oak pegs (rather than nuts and bolts), and topped by a thatch roof (the first in London since 1666). Partly open to the elements, the theatre only stages performances from May to September but a visit to the exhibition and a tour of the theatre is worthwhile at any time of the year. You'll see excellent displays about Elizabethan theatre, costumes and special effects, learn how the Elizabethans spoke English and learn about the reconstruction of the theatre.

This is, quite rightly, an extremely popular tourist attraction and if you need a break from the crowds, the restaurant/café offers good food and windows that look out across the river.

The Globe

The Sherlock Holmes Museum

🖃 *221b Baker Street, NW1 6XE*
☎ *020 7935 8866*
✎ *www.sherlock-holmes.co.uk*
🚌 *Baker Street LU*
🕐 *Daily 9.30am-6pm (except Christmas Day)*
💰 *£6 (adults), £4 (children)*

This is a reconstruction in a building with no known connection to Holmes or to his inventor, Sir Arthur Conan Doyle. It is intended to show how Holmes and Watson could have lived in the nineteenth-century had they not been creations of Conan Doyle's over active imagination. According to his creator, Holmes lived at this address from 1881-1904. It's an interesting idea for Sherlock Holmes fans, but builds fiction on top of fiction.

The Type Museum

🖃 *100 Hackford Road, SW9 0QU*
☎ *020 7735 0055*
✎ *www.typemuseum. org*
🚌 *Oval LU*

This is one of the world's best typographic collections and covers the technical and aesthetic developments in printing since the sixteenth-century. The museum is still under development and currently the only open days are on the first Wednesday of each month; these include demonstrations relevant to printing. Contact the museum for more details.

William Morris Gallery

Lloyd Park, Forest Road, E17 4PP

020 8527 3782

020 8527 7070

www.lbwf.gov.uk.uk/wmg

Walthamstow Central LU

Tues-Sat and the first Sun of each month 10am-1pm and 2-5pm

Admission free

Designer, craftsman, writer and Socialist, William Morris (1834–1896), lived in this house as a young man, from 1848–1856. It is now a celebration of his life, work and influence and that of some of his contemporaries such as Edward Burne-Jones, Philip Webb, Rossetti and Ford Madox Ford, and features paintings, drawings, fabrics, rugs, carpets, wallpaper, stained glass and tiles. As well as an involvement in the Arts and Crafts Movement and with the Pre-Raphaelites, Morris was also involved in the Socialist League and published several political works. For book lovers, the items of most interest relate to the Kelmscott Press – the very beautiful Kelmscott edition of Chaucer (published in 1896), is on display here.

Women's Library

Old Castle Street, E1 7NT

020 7320 2222

020 7320 2333

www.thewomenslibrary.ac.uk

Aldgate East LU

The library is the most extensive collection of material on women's history in the UK and the schedule of exhibitions mounted here use items from the collection to demonstrate and illustrate that history.

Places of Literary Interest

The literary heritage of London is indisputably rich: Chaucer's pilgrims departed from the Tabard Inn in Southwark, Shakespeare's plays were first performed in the theatres of Bankside, Dickens' novels were steeped in both the author's love of and contempt for the Victorian capital in which he lived, and more recently, the Bloomsbury area (around the British Museum) became inextricably linked to the eponymous literary group.

However, in addition to the illustrious writers most closely associated with the city, London has played host to numerous other literary notables. They include Dostoevsky, James Joyce, Emile Zola, T.S Eliot (who became naturalised in 1927), Voltaire, Tolstoy, Henry James (who became naturalised in 1915), Rudyard Kipling, Ezra Pound, Jane Austen, A. E. Houseman and George Eliot. London, has also provided an irresistible backdrop for works by modern and contemporary writers such as Angela Carter, Martin Amis, Peter Ackroyd, Penelope Lively, Anita Brookner, Iain Sinclair and Michael Moorcock. In addition to the literary works, the physical landmarks of literary London take several forms.

GRAVES & MEMORIALS

To check the whereabouts of the grave of a particular person the website *www.findagrave.com* is very useful although it is not restricted to London sites or literary figures.

Brompton Cemetery

- 🏛 *South Gate off Fulham Road,*
  North Gate off Old Brompton Road, SW10
- ☎ *020 7352 1201*
- ✐ *www.theroyalparks.gov.uk*
- 🚌 *West Brompton LU*

Not as illustrious as the other big London cemeteries, although there are more than 200,000 souls buried here, this site nevertheless contains the mortal remains of Fanny Brawne (Keats' fiancée) and Emmeline Pankhurst, the suffragette. The annual Open Day, held every summer, is a great chance to see parts usually closed to the public.

Golders Green Crematorium and Jewish Cemetery

- 🏛 *62 Hoop Lane, NW11 7NL*
- ☎ *020 8455 2374*
- 🚌 *Golders Green LU*

Many famous figures have been cremated here and commemorated with plaques – although finding any particular one isn't easy. The literary figures include T S Eliot, Enid Blyton, Rudyard Kipling, George Bernard Shaw, Bram Stoker and Sigmund Freud.

Highgate Cemetery

- 🏛 *Swains Lane, N6 6PJ*
- ☎ *020 8340 1834*
- ✐ *www.highgate-cemetery.org*
- 🚌 *Archway LU*

East Cemetery
- 🕐 *Mon-Fri 10am, Sat & Sun 11am*
  Last admission 4.30pm (1st April to 30th October)
  Last admission 3.30pm (1st November-31st March)
- 🪙 *£2, camera permit £1 (no video cameras allowed)*

West Cemetery - access only on guided tours

☺   *Guided tours: Mon-Fri at 2pm (except Dec, Jan, Feb),*
    Sat & Sun hourly from 11am-4pm (no 4pm tour
    1st November-31st March)

🎫   *£3, camera permit £1 (no video cameras allowed)*

In the nineteenth-century, as a means of coping with the terribly over-crowded city churchyards, a number of cemeteries were opened in what were in those days the green areas outside London. Highgate Cemetery was established in 1839 and with its attractive layout, stone carvings, catacombs and Egyptian obelisks soon became an extremely popular burial place. As a result, the West Cemetery was soon full and the newer, East Cemetery opened in 1854. The cemetery is now considered to contain some of the finest Victorian funerary architecture still in existence.

The most famous grave in the East part of the cemetery is that of Karl Marx (1818-1883). Nearby is the grave of George Eliot (1819-1880), who lived openly with her lover, George Lewes for many years (a state of affairs that outraged the society of the time) – he is buried closeby.

It is only possible to visit the West Cemetery on a guided tour. Christina Rossetti, the poet (1830-1894) is buried in her family tomb, Radclyffe Hall and her lover Mabel Batten is also here, as is the Charles Dickens' family tomb containing the author's wife and daughter. Dickens had wanted to be buried here but Queen Victoria insisted that he be buried in Westminster Abbey.

Kensal Green Cemetery

🏠   *Harrow Road, W10 4RA*

☎   *020 8969 0152*

🚇   *Kensal Green LU*

🎫   *Admission free*

Opened in 1832, this was the first of the large Victorian cemeteries and it soon gained in popularity: Thackeray (1811-1863), Leigh Hunt (1784-1859), Anthony Trollope (1815-1882) and Wilkie Collins (1824-1889) are all buried here.

Places of Literary Interest / Graves & Memorials

St Paul's Cathedral

☎ *020 7236 4128*

✎ *www.stpauls.co.uk*

🚌 *St Paul's LU*

🕐 *Mon-Sat 8.30am-4pm (last admission 4pm)*

🎫 *£8 (adults), £7 (concessions), £19.50 (family)*

There are far fewer memorials to literary figures here than in Westminster Abbey, but John Donne (1572-1631), Dean of St Paul's and preacher and poet is here, as are the philosopher Francis Bacon and Dr Johnson. There is also a commemorative bust to the writer and adventurer T. E. Lawrence in the crypt. An audio tour (£3.50) and guided tour (£2.50) are available.

Westminster Abbey

☎ *020 7654 4900*

✎ *www.westminster-abbey.org*

🚌 *Westminster LU*

🕐 *Mon-Fri 9.30am-3.45pm, Sat 9.30am-3.45pm*
   (last admission 3.45pm, Abbey closes an hour later)

🎫 *£8 (adults), £6 (concessions), £18 (family);*
   verger led tours (£4) and audio guide (£3) are available

Poets' Corner in the South Transept contains a huge number of memorials to literary figures. The first two poets to be buried there were Geoffrey Chaucer (1400) and Edmund Spencer (1599). Other memorials include those for John Dryden, Samuel Johnson, Robert Browning, Tennyson, Thomas Hardy (apart from his heart, which was buried in Dorset) and Dickens. Some statues are simply memorials to major figures who were buried or cremated elsewhere, for example, Shakespeare, Milton, Keats, Rudyard Kipling and Oscar Wilde. This part of the abbey also contains graves of other artistic figures, including the composer Handel, and David Garrick, the eighteenth-century actor. Apparently the overcrowding is now so severe that no further burials will be possible – the actor Laurence Olivier (who died in 1989) was supposedly the last to get a plot.

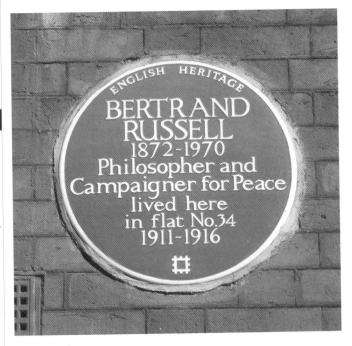

Bloomsbury

Built in the seventeenth-century by the Earl of Southampton, this area of graceful squares, tree-lined streets and attractive houses expanded considerably in the following century as its popularity and fashionable status grew. Over time it has acquired an unmistakable cultural and intellectual atmosphere by virtue of its proximity to the British Museum and the University of London. Many famous people have lived in the area, including the artists Constable and Rossetti, and the writers Dickens and Shaw. However, the name Bloomsbury will be forever associated with the group of writers, artists and thinkers who lived, worked and entertained here in the early twentieth-century. The Stephen sisters who were to become Vanessa Bell and Virginia Woolf moved to 46 Gordon Square when their father died (this caused outrage as the girls were young, unmarried, and unchaperoned), and gradually a group of young, upper-middle class, like-minded friends established a network around them. The Bloomsbury Group's guiding principle was a rejection of the established ideas and morals of the time; members included Woolf and her husband Leonard, Virginia and Vanessa's brothers Thoby and Adrian, Lytton Strachey, artist Duncan Grant, John Maynard Keynes, Clive Bell and Roger Fry. It was said that they lived in squares and loved in triangles! Virginia and Leonard Woolf founded the Hogarth Press in 1917 to champion new literature, and published T. S. Eliot's poem, *The Waste Land* in 1922, and the works of Katherine Mansfield, although they refused to publish James Joyces' *Ulysses*.

Blue plaques mark the houses associated with the group: Lytton Strachey (critic and biographer), 51 Gordon Square; John Maynard Keynes (economist), 46 Gordon Square and Virginia Woolf, 29 Fitzroy Square. She lived at this address between 1907 and 1911 with her brother Adrian, in a house previously occupied by George Bernard Shaw. Other significant buildings not marked by plaques include 24 Russell Square, where T. S. Eliot worked at the publishers Faber and Faber.

Chelsea
Initially a fishing village on the north bank of the River Thames, in the sixteenth-century Chelsea became the home of royal courtiers such as Sir Thomas More. By the early nineteenth-century Chelsea had become fashionable among artistic and literary figures. Shelley and Turner were early residents and later the writers George Eliot, Swinburne, Henry James, Oscar Wilde and the historian Thomas Carlyle (see p.299) lived here.

In the 1950's the focus of interest was The Royal Court Theatre on Sloane Square, where the dramatists who became known as the 'Angry Young Men' (a group which included John Osborne and Arnold Wesker) had their plays staged. The theatre has retained its reputation for showcasing new and original writing. In the 1960's Chelsea became famous for the fashions available in the King's Road and music and media stars moved in.

Cheyne Walk is probably Chelsea's most illustrious street with an impressive roll-call of famous past residents: George Eliot lived at No.4, Dante Gabriel Rossetti at No.16, Hilaire Belloc at No.104, Henry James at Carlyle Mansions, and Mrs Gaskell was born at No.93. Elsewhere in Chelsea, Leigh Hunt lived at 22 Upper Cheyne Row, Tobias Smollett at 16 Lawrence Street, Mark Twain at 23 Tedworth Square and Bram Stoker at 18 St Leonard's Terrace. In the same area, Oscar Wilde lived first at 3 Tite Street and then in 1885 at 34 Tite Street, until he was sent to Reading Jail in 1895. He wrote *The Picture of Dorian Gray* in the house and also first met Lord Alfred Douglas here – it was their relationship which ultimately led to Wilde's downfall. He was arrested at the Cadogan Hotel in 1895, where Jane Austen had stayed around a hundred years earlier.

Thomas Carlyle wrote in a letter in 1834 that 'Chelsea is a single heterogenous kind of spot, very dirty and confused in some places, quite beautiful in others, abounding in antiquities and the traces of great men...' It's a description which still rings true over one hundred and sixty years later.

Hampstead

At one time Hampstead used to be covered in forest, but many of its trees were felled to rebuild London after The Great Fire in 1666. Then in the eighteenth-century, numerous country houses were constructed here as Londoners gravitated towards the open space, fresh air and spring waters of Hampstead Heath. Hampstead still has something of a village feel even though it is now very much part of London. Keats' House (see p.301) is open to the public as a museum celebrating one of the area's most famous inhabitants. Other literary figures associated with Hampstead include William Blake, Dirk Bogarde, John le Carré, Agatha Christie, Ian Fleming, Sigmund Freud (see p.300), Gerald Manley Hopkins, A. A. Milne, George Orwell, Robert Louis Stevenson and John Galsworthy. Today the association of Hampstead with London's writing community is so strong it is almost a cliché and the local supermarket is often awash with well-known literary figures stocking up the Volvo – so much for starving artists in their garrets.

LITERARY PUBS

The Anchor
🏠 *34 Park Street, Bankside, SE1 9EF*
🚇 *London Bridge LU/Rail, Southwark LU*

With fine views across the river to St Paul's Cathedral, this pub is a short walk from Shakespeare's Globe and was frequented by Samuel Pepys. On a less highbrow note, parts of the film Mission Impossible were filmed here.

Fitzroy Tavern
🏠 *16 Charlotte Street, W1*
🚇 *Tottenham Court Road & Goodge Street LU*

Between the 1920s and the 1950s this area, between Soho and Bloomsbury, was named Fitzrovia by the group of artists, sculptors, composers, critics, poets and writers who met in the area and the Fitzroy Tavern became the main Bohemian meeting place of the time. Patrons included Lawrence Durrell, Dylan Thomas (he first met his wife, Caitlin here) and George Orwell.

The Flask
🏠 *Highgate West Hill, N6 6BU*
🚇 *Archway LU*

It is said that Dick Turpin hid from his pursuers here but on a more literary note T. S. Eliot and John Betjeman drank here.

The George Inn
🏠 *77 Borough High Street, SE1 1NH*
🚇 *London Bridge LU/Rail*

This pub dates back at least to 1542 when Shakespeare was a regular. It's also mentioned in 'Little Dorrit'.

The Grapes
🏠 *76 Narrow Street, Limehouse, E14 8BP*
🚇 *Limehouse DLR*

The pub dates back to 1583. Charles Dickens was a customer and fictionalised it in 'Our Mutual Friend'.

Museum Tavern

The Jerusalem Tavern

🖃 *55 Briton Street, Clerkenwell, EC1M 5NA*

This pub has moved three times since it was established in the four-teenth-century. However, this building dates from 1720 and Samuel Johnson used to drink here.

Museum Tavern

🖃 *49 Great Russell Street, WC1*

🚌 *Tottenham Court Road & Holborn LU*

Opposite the entrance to the British Museum – Karl Marx was a regular.

Prospect of Whitby

🖃 *57 Wapping Wall, E1W 3SH*

🚌 *Wapping LU*

Originally called The Devils Tavern when Samuel Pepys was a regular. It dates back to the sixteenth-century and has a gruesome history – it was the site of public executions.

Spaniards Inn

🏠 *Spaniard's Road, NW3*

🚌 *Hampstead LU*

A four hundred year-old pub, located near Kenwood House and Hampstead Heath. Writers Dickens, Shelley, Keats and Byron were all patrons, and it is said that the highwayman Dick Turpin drank here. Mrs Bardell's tea party in Dicken's 'Pickwick Papers' was set here.

Trafalgar Tavern

🏠 *5 Park Row, SE10*

🚌 *Cutty Sark DLR*

Beside the river at Greenwich and mentioned in 'Our Mutual Friend', this pub was supposedly a favourite drinking spot of Charles Dickens.

Ye Olde Cheshire Cheese

🏠 *Wine Office Court, 145 Fleet Street, EC4A 2BU*

🚌 *Blackfriars LU/Rail & Temple LU*

This is the oldest remaining pub on Fleet Street with the most historic parts of the building dating from the mid-seventeenth-century, when the pub was rebuilt after the Great Fire. Many literary greats drank here; Dr Johnson, Thackeray, Sir Arthur Conan Doyle, Dickens, Yeats and Mark Twain.

Ye Olde Cock Tavern

🏠 *22 Fleet Street, EC4*

🚌 *Blackfriars LU/Rail & Temple LU*

T. S. Eliot was a regular here in the 1920's.

LITERARY WALKS

A guided walk is a great way for Londoners as well as visitors to learn some unusual facts about the city and explore some of the areas described above. Many walks are on offer covering a variety of subjects and many have a literary theme.

Both the listings magazines 'Time Out' and 'What's On in London' list the walks available in London each week alternatively contact any of the companies listed below. Participating in a walk is simply a matter of turning up at the specified time and place and paying the guide, but it's advisable to ring beforehand to check it's actually going ahead. Below are listed some of the walks which have literary associations:

Angel Weekend Walks

☎ *020 7226 8333 and 07796 673 846*

✎ *www.angelwalks.co.uk*

Peter Powell's speciality is literary and historic walks in Islington. He offers walks about George Orwell and Charles Dickens and 'The Murder Mile Walk' includes literary figures such as Joe Orton and the Lambs.

City Sidewalks

☎ *020 8449 4736*

✎ *www.citysidewalks.co.uk*

The programme includes 'Printing, Publishing and law'.

Lance Pierson

☎ *020 7731 6544*

✎ *www.lancepierson.org*

Lance's 'London Poetry Walk, Walking with Wordsworth, Strolling with Shakespeare' covers the River Thames from Waterloo to Westminster with performance of relevant poetry on the way. Check for dates, this walk is not weekly.

The Original London Walks

☎ *020 7624 3978*

✎ *www.walks.com*

The huge programme includes walks exploring Dickens, Shakespeare, Oscar Wilde, Sherlock Holmes, Bloomsbury and Hampstead. Their leaflet is available in many central London bookshops.

Streets of London

☎ *020 8906 8657*

✎ *www.thestreetsoflondon.com*

Their walks include Dickens, Sherlock Holmes, 'Plague and Fire: Pepys and Wren' during which extracts from Pepy's diary describe the progress of the plague and fire through the City and 'Palaces, Prisons and print' which takes in stories of printing barons and the journalist's church.

Appendix

LITERARY VENUES

Reading and enjoying books is considered by many to be a rather solitary pastime, and yet the capital plays host to public readings, signings and book events virtually every day of the week. Literary events vary in scale and character tremendously, from local poetry meetings where you might be expected to read your own verse; to a major book reading by a literary star where you will be lucky to get a seat.

For regular information about what is on offer, 'Time Out' and 'What's On in London' have sections devoted to literary events and the websites *www.poetrylondon.co.uk*, *www.poetrylibrary.org.uk* and *www.poetrykit.org* have thorough listings of poetry events. Independent bookshops host readings, but the famous literary names tend to limit their appearances to large branches of the major chains. Generally these events are free, but tickets may need to be reserved. Look out particularly for events in Books etc, Borders and Waterstones.

As well as the major bookshops there are many other venues hosting regular literary events some of which are listed below:

Bath House Pub

📖 *96 Dean Street, Soho, W1*
☎ *020 8340 3566*
✎ *www.ambitmagazine.co.uk*
🚌 *Leicester Square & Tottenham Court Road LU*
Monthly poetry.

The British Library

📖 *96 Euston Road, NW1 2DB*
☎ *020 7412 7332*
✎ *www.bl.uk*
🚌 *Euston, King's Cross and St Pancras LU/Rail*
A programme of evening talks and lectures, often by very prominent literary figures.

Brixton Art Gallery

- *35 Brixton Station Road, SW9*
- ☎ *020 7733 6957*
- ✉ *brixart@brixtonartgallery.co.uk*
- 🚆 *Brixton LU/Rail*

Monthly spoken word and open mic.

Camden Head

- *Camden Walk, Islington, N1*
- ✉ *www.20six.co.uk/shortfuse*
- 🚆 *Angel LU*

Weekly poetry

Centerprise

- *136-138 Kingsland High Street, E8 2NS*
- ☎ *020 7254 9632*
- ✆ *020 7923 1951*
- ✉ *www.centerprisetrust.org.uk*
- 🚆 *Dalston Kingsland Rail*

Programme of readings and workshops.

Charterhouse Bar

- *38 Charterhouse Street, EC1*
- ☎ *020 7608 0858*
- ✉ *www.x-about.com/aroma*
- 🚆 *Farringdon LU/Rail*

Twice monthly spoken word and open mic.

Enterprise

- *2 Haverstock Hill, NW3 2BL*
- ☎ *020 7485 2659*
- ✉ *www.expressexcess.co.uk*
- 🚆 *Chalk Farm LU*

Weekly comedy, poetry and storytelling.

The Foundry

- *Great Eastern Street, Shoreditch, EC2*
- ☎ *020 7736 6900*
- 🚆 *Old Street LU/Rail*

Weekly open mic and spoken word.

Pleasure Unit Bar

   ⬚   *359 Bethnal Green Road, E2*

   🚌 *Bethnal Green LU*

Monthly spoken word and poetry.

The Plough

   ⬚   *Museum Street, WC1*

   ☏ *020 8882 7892*

   🚌 *Holborn LU*

Monthly open mic, spoken word and performance poems.

Poetry Society

   ⬚   *22 Betterton Street, WC2H 9BX*

   ☏ *020 7420 9880*

   ✆ *020 7240 4818*

   ✎ *www.poetrysociety.org.uk*

   🚌 *Covent Garden LU*

The Poetry Society is engaged in a huge range of activities aimed at promoting poetry throughout Britain. The Poetry Café (Mon-Fri 11am-11pm, Sat 6.30-11pm) is a great place for poetry-lovers to meet, eat and relax and there's a vibrant programme of poetry events.

Royal Society of Literature

   ⬚   *Somerset House, Strand, WC2R 1LA*

   ☏ *020 7845 4676*

   🚌 *Temple LU*

Regular lectures, discussions and readings often by big names. Anybody interested in literature can join.

The South Bank Centre

   ⬚   *Belvedere Road, SE1 8XX*

   ☏ *0870 382 8000*

   ✎ *www.rfh.org.uk*

   🚌 *Waterloo LU/Rail*

The South Bank hosts plenty of events in spaces big and small by well-known names and the less familiar but also arranges numerous visits by internationally renowned writers. This is also the location for the Poetry Library (see p.269) and hosts 'Poetry International', a biennial event which is the biggest poetry festival in Britain, involving a huge number of poets from here and abroad.

Torriano Meeting House

🖼 *99 Torriano Avenue, NW5*

☎ *020 7281 2867*

🚌 *Kentish Town LU*

Weekly poetry.

Troubador Coffee House

🖼 *265 Old Brompton Road, SW5*

☎ *020 8354 0660*

🚌 *Earl's Court LU*

Regular coffee-house poetry.

FESTIVALS

London plays host to a burgeoning array of annual arts festivals, some are dedicated to literature and others feature literary events among a wide programme of music, theatre, dance, art and other events. For a countrywide 'Literature Festivals' list contact The British Council (see below) enclosing a stamped addressed envelope. The list is also available at *www.literaryfestivals.britishcouncil.org/* where it can be searched by date, area and subject matter.

Another useful source of information is British Arts Festivals:

✍ *www.artsfestivals.co.uk*

The Literature Department

⌨ *The British Council, 10 Spring Gardens, SW1A 2BN*

☎ *020 7389 3166*

✎ *020 7389 3175*

MAJOR LONDON FESTIVALS

Book Now! Richmond's Literature Festival

☎ *020 8831 6494*

✍ *www.richmond.gov.uk*

A November festival with a broad range of literature events.

Chelsea Festival

☎ *020 7351 1005 (March to July)*

✍ *www.chelseafestival.org.uk*

A general arts festival held annually in June. There are usually talks and events of literary interest among the music, ballet and visual arts events.

City of London Festival

☎ *020 7377 0540*

✍ *www.colf.org*

An annual summer (June/July) festival that embraces the full range of the arts and includes plenty of literary events.

Crime Scene
☎ *020 7928 3232*
✍ *www.bfi.org.uk/crimescene*
An annual festival, usually held over a weekend in July, at the National Film Theatre on the South Bank which celebrates crime film and fiction. There are author appearances, signings, events and a book fair alongside the screenings.

Dulwich Festival
☎ *020 8693 7556*
✍ *www.dulwichfestival.co.uk*
Community arts festival held every May, which includes the work of amateur and professional locals. It encompasses literary events as well as theatre, film, music and art.

Hampstead and Highgate Festival
☎ *020 7722 1414*
✍ *www.hamandhighfest.co.uk*
Mainly a classical music festival but, as befits this most literary part of London, literary events are also programmed.

Imagine: Writers and Writing for Children
☎ *08703 800 400*
✍ *www.rfh.org.uk*
This is usually a biennial festival of children's literature although the redevelopment of the Royal Festival Hall has disturbed the schedule, the next Imagine is due in late 2006. It usually alternates at the Royal Festival Hall with Poetry International (see p.328). Plenty of appearances by authors and storytelling events for children are included .

International Playwriting Festival
☎ *020 8681 1257*
✍ *www.warehousetheatre.co.uk*
Based in the Warehouse Theatre in Croydon, this long-running annual festival (2005 was its 20th year) promotes new and aspiring playwrights. The first part of the festival takes place from the beginning of the year until the end of June when entries to the playwriting competition are accepted from all over the world. Following judging, there is a showcase of the winning entries at the theatre over three or four days at the end of November.

Jewish Book Week

☎ *020 8343 4675*

✐ *www.jewishbookweek.com*

This is a major festival of Jewish writing drawing interest and participants from around the world, many of them extremely well-known. It takes place annually in Spring/Summer.

London International Poetry and Song Festival

✐ *www.epiberen.com/lips/*

A weekend of poetry and music in October

Poetry International

☎ *08703 800 400*

✐ *www.rfh.org.uk*

Biennial festival (it usually alternates with Imagine – see p.327) in October/November; it is the biggest poetry festival in the UK attracting poets from across the globe. Readings, workshops, debates and lectures are all part of the heady mix. The refurbishment of the Royal Festival Hall has disturbed schedules – it is currently uncertain when the next Poetry International will take place.

Sable LitFest

✐ *www.sablelitmag.org*

A long weekend of events in April including readings, performances, storytelling and workshops.

Spitalfields Festival

☎ *020 7377 0287*

    020 7377 1362 (Box office from 1st April)

✐ *www.spitalfieldsfestival.org*

Annual summer (June) and winter (December) festivals mostly dedicated to music but including a selection of walks and talks of literary interest.

Spit-Lit: The Spitalfields Literary Festival

✐ *www.alternativearts.co.uk*

Held annually in March covering the full range of literature.

Streatham Festival

☎ *020 7926 5905*

✐ *www.streathamfestival.info*

General local festival – literature isn't a large part but there may be something of interest.

SW11 Literary Festival

Ottakar's, St John's Road

☎ *020 7978 5844*

✐ *www.ottakars.co.uk*

In September, a fortnight of literary events in and around the Calpham Junction area.

Wandsworth Arts Festival

☎ *020 8871 8711*

✐ *www.wandsworth.gov.uk*

A general arts festival held annually in October/November featuring some literary events.

The Word

Polka Theatre Wimbledon

☎ *020 8545 8354*

✐ *www.polkatheatre.com*

A celebration of everything to do with childrens' books in October.

OUTSIDE LONDON

The following festivals are all easily accessible from London and can be visited on an excursion from the city.

Brighton Poetry and Book Festival

☎ *07810 272 791*

✐ *www.thesouth.org.uk*

Week long festival dedicated to all aspects of poetry and books. It takes place in December so is ideal if you like the seaside in winter.

cambridgewordfest

☎ *01223 503333*

✐ *www.cambridgewordfest.co.uk*

It's only a weekend but is jam-packed with literature events (for writers and readers) in April. Cambridge is lovely in spring.

Charleston Festival

☎ *01323 811265*

✑ *www.charleston.org.uk*

An annual literary festival usually held over a week or so, which is usually staged as part of the Brighton Festival in May. Charleston is a brilliant setting, seven miles east of Lewes, and was the home and country meeting place for the Bloomsbury Group.

Essex Book Festival

☎ *01245 244953*

✑ *www.essexbookfestival.org.uk*

A month-long festival throughout the county in March with a vast number of events, many held in libraries and many featuring big names.

Essex Poetry Festival

✑ *www.come.to/the-essex-poetry-festival*

Held in Chelmsford in October with a vast range of poetry events including readings, open mic sessions, competitions and workshops.

Hay-on-Wye Festival

☎ *01497 821 299 (festival box office)*

✑ *tickets@hayfestival.co.uk*

✑ *www.hayfestival.co.uk*

The largest and most famous literary festival in the UK and one that attracts literary stars such as Sebastian Faulks and Germain Greer. Bill Clinton was a recent visitor here describing the festival as "...a Woodstock for books".

Henley Festival

☎ *01491 843400*

✑ *www.henley-festival.co.uk*

A general programme with a literary thread running through it. The event usually takes place in July.

The Sunday Times Oxford Literary Festival

☎ *01865 514149*

✑ *www.sundaytimes-oxfordliteraryfestival.co.uk*

Held each year in March or April, this festival is one of the largest literary festivals in UK drawing big names and big crowds.

COURSES

London offers a vast number of full and part-time courses of interest to anyone who loves books. The spectrum stretches from craft courses like bookbinding and papermaking through to the creative writing, scriptwriting or playwriting. Classes run during academic terms: the autumn term runs from September to December, the spring term from January to Easter and the summer term from Easter to June. Many institutions offer one-day intensive courses throughout the year and short courses at a 'Summer School'. Contact the college enrollment office for detailed information about course content, cost, enrollment dates and location.

There are also two useful publications for those looking for a course. 'Floodlight' (*www.floodlight.co.uk*) and 'Hot Courses' (*www.hotcourses.com*) are produced each summer and list the courses for the next academic year, they are available in larger newsagents.

Book Arts including Bookbinding, Conservation and Restoration of Books and Papers

Adult Education College for Bexley
Brent Adult and Community Education Service
Camberwell College of Arts
Central St Martins College of Art and Design
City Lit
Greenwich Community College
Hampstead Garden Suburb Institute
Kingston Adult Education and Training
Community Education Lewisham
London College of Communication
Mary Ward Centre
Morley College
Richmond Adult Community College

Literature

General Literature Courses:

Pretty much every institution in London operates English Literature courses that lead to exams and qualifications – usually GCSE or A Level. Here are the colleges who operate general English literature courses for pleasure and recreation.

Birkbeck
Brent Adult and Community Education Service
Bromley Adult Education College
City Lit
Greenwich Community College
Kensington and Chelsea College
Kingston Adult Education
Mary Ward Centre
Merton Adult College
Middlesex University
Morley College
Richmond Adult Community College
South Thames College
Sutton College of Learning for Adults
Westminster Adult Education Service
Westminster Kingsway College
Workers' Educational Association

Courses that cover a defined subject area include:
American Literature (Birkbeck, City Lit, Richmond Adult
Community College, Workers' Educational Association)
Chinese Literature (Morley College, SOAS)
Detective Fiction (Birkbeck, Hampstead Garden Suburb Institute)
French Literature (Morley College)
Historical Novels (Workers' Educational Association)
Italian Literature and Culture 12th-14th century (Morley College)
Russian Literature (Morley College)
Pulped Crime Fiction (Waltham Forest Community Learning and
Skills Service)
Victorian Novels (City Lit))
South Asian Fiction (City Lit)
Virginia Woolf and the Bloomsbury Set (Richmond Adult
Community College)
Women Writers (Birkbeck, City Lit, Workers Educational Association)
World Literature (Richmond Adult Community College, South
Thames College)

Courses that concentrate on just one author, or even one work include:
Margaret Atwood (Morley College)
Chaucer (Birkbeck)
Chekov (Morley College)
Canterbury Tales (Hillinghdon Adult Education Services)
Dante's Divine Comedy (Morley College)
George Eliot (Morley)
Thomas Hardy (City Lit)
Ben Johnson (Richmond Adult Community College)
Philip Larkin (Morley College)
D.H.Lawrence (Birkbeck)
Keats (Birkbeck)
Andrew Marvell (City Lit)
Arthur Miller (City Lit)
Milton (City Lit, Richmond Adult Community College)
Sylvia Plath (Richmond Adult Community College)
Shakespeare (Birkbeck, City Lit, Hampstead Garden Suburb Institute, Richmond Adult Community College, Sutton College of Learning for Adults)
Oscar Wilde (City Lit)
Wuthering Heights (Morley Colege)

Papermaking
Bromley Adult Education College
City Lit
Greenwich Community College
Community Education Lewisham
Mary Ward Centre
Morley College

Publishing
These include courses in areas such as proof-reading, sub-editing, magazine publishing, design and publishing practice.
Central St Martins College of Art and Design
Hampstead Garden Suburb Institute
City University
London College of Communication
Middlesex University
Richmond Adult Community College
Southgate College
University College London

Writing, Playwriting and Scriptwriting

Some of the courses under this heading are general creative writing courses while others specialise in a specific form of writing such as poetry, screenwriting, novels, plays or short stories.

Birkbeck
Bromley Adult Education College
Central Saint Martin's College of Art and Design
City and Islington College
City Lit
City University
City of Westminster College
Goldsmiths College
Greenwich Community College
Hammersmith and Fulham
Hampstead Garden Suburb Institute
Hounslow Adult and Community Education
Kensington and Chelsea College
Kingston Adult Education
Lambeth College
London Academy of Radio, Film and TV
London College of Communication
London Jewish Cultural Centre
London School of Journalism
Mary Ward Centre
Merton Adult College
Middlesex University
Morley College
Richmond Adult Community College
South Thames College
St Francis Xavier Sixth Form College
Sutton College of Learning for Adults
Tower Hamlets College
Waltham Forest Community Learning and Skills Service
Westminster Kingsway College

Contacts

If the institution is at a single location we have given the address in addtion to the other contact details. If it is one of the many colleges that operate classes at several different sites, we've given the telephone number and web address.

Adult Education College for Bexley
Tel: 020 8309 5570
Website: www.adultedbexley.org

Birkbeck University of London
Faculty of Continuing Education
26 Russell Square, WC1B 5DQ
Tel: 020 7631 6651
Website: www.bbk.ac.uk

Brent Adult and Community
Education Service
Tel: 020 8937 1200
Website: www.brent.gov.uk/baces

Bromley Adult Education College
Tel: 020 8460 0020
Website:
www.bromleyadulteducation.ac.uk

Camberwell College of Arts
Peckham Road, SE5 8UF
Tel: 020 7514 6311
Website:
www.camberwell.arts.ac.uk/short-courses

Central Saint Martin's
College of Art and Design
Southampton Row, WC1B 4AP
Tel: 020 7514 7015
Website: www.csm.arts.ac.uk

City and Islington College
Tel: 020 7700 9200
Website: www.candi.ac.uk

City Lit
Keeley Street, WC2B 4BA
Tel: 020 7831 7831
Website: www.citylit.ac.uk

City University
Northampton Square, EC1V 0HB
Tel: 020 7040 5060
Website: www.city.ac.uk/conted/cfa

City of Westminster College
Tel: 020 7723 8826
Website: www.cwc.ac.uk

Community Education Lewisham
Tel: 020 8691 5959
Website: www.cel.lewisham.gov.uk

Enfield College
Tel: 020 8443 3434
Website: www.enfield.ac.uk

Goldsmiths College
(University of London)
New Cross, SE14 6NW
Tel: 020 7919 7766
Website: www.goldsmiths.ac.uk

Greenwich Community College
Tel: 020 8488 4800
Website: www.gcc.ac.uk

Hammersmith and Fulham
Tel: 020 8600 9191
Website: www.lbhf.gov.uk

Hampstead Garden Suburb Institute
Tel: 020 8455 9951
Website: www.hgsi.ac.uk

Hillingdon Adult Education Service
Tel: 01895 676690
Website: www.hillingdon.gov.uk

Hounslow Adult and Community
Education
Tel: 020 8583 2755
Website: www.hounslow.gov.uk

Kensington and Chelsea College
Tel: 020 7573 5333
Website: www.kcc.ac.uk

Kingston Adult Education
Tel: 020 8547 6758
Website: www.kingston.gov.uk/adult-education

Lambeth College
Tel: 020 7501 5000
Website: www.lambethcollege.ac.uk

London Academy of Radio,
Film and TV
1 Lancing Street, NW1 1NA
Tel: 0870 381 4303
Website: www.media-courses.com

London College of Communication
Elephant & Castle, SE1 6SB
Tel: 020 7514 6569
Website: www.lcctraining.co.uk

London Jewish Cultural Centre
Old House
c/o King's College
Kidderpore Avenue, NW3 7SZ
Tel: 020 7431 0345
Website: www.ljcc.org.uk

London School of Journalism
126 Shirland Road, Maida Vale,
W9 2EP
Tel: 020 7289 7777
Website: www.home-study.com

Mary Ward Centre
42 Queen Square, WC1N 3AQ
Tel: 020 7269 6000
Website: www.marywardcentre.ac.uk

Merton Adult College
Tel: 020 8543 9292
Website: www.merton-adult-
college.ac.uk

Middlesex University
Tel: 020 8411 5555
Website: www.mdx.ac.uk

Morley College
Tel: 020 7450 1889
Website: www.morleycollege.ac.uk

Richmond Adult
Community College
Tel: 020 8843 7921
Website: www.racc.ac.uk

St Francis Xavier Sixth Form College
Malwood Road, SW12 8EN
Tel: 020 8772 6060
Website: www.sfx.ac.uk

SOAS
(School of Oriental and African
Studies)
Thornhaugh St, Russell Sq, WC1H
0XG
Tel: 020 7637 2388
Website: www.soas.ac.uk

Southgate College
Tel: 020 8982 5050
Website: www.southgate.ac.uk

South Thames College
Tel: 020 8918 7000
Website: www.south-thames.ac.uk

Sutton College of Learning for Adults
Tel: 020 8770 6901
Website: www.scola.ac.uk

Tower Hamlets College
Tel: 020 7510 7777
Website: www.tower.ac.uk

University College London
Gower Street, WC1E 6BT
Tel: 020 7679 2000
Website: www.ucl.ac.uk

Waltham Forest Community
Learning and Skills Service
Tel: 020 8523 9355
Website: http://class.lbwf.gov.uk

Westminster Adult Education Service
Tel: 020 7297 7297
Website: www.waes.ac.uk

Westminster Kingsway College
Tel: 0870 060 9800
Website: www.westking.ac.uk

Workers' Educational Association
Tel: 020 7613 7550
Website: www.wea.org.uk

Working Men's College
44 Crowndale Road, NW1 1TR
Tel: 020 7255 4700 or 0800 358 1854
Website: www.wmcollege.ac.u

BOOKBINDERS ·

Bookbinders are a very diverse group and those included below range from individuals making one-off handmade books at a very high price to industrial binders who will take on individual projects alongside more mundane work. There are two main professional organisations Designer Bookbinders (*www.designerbookbinders.org.uk*) and the Society of Bookbinders. Many bookbinders, however, don't belong to either of these groups.

Kathy Abbott

⌦ *12 Chippenham Mews, W9 2AW*
☎ /✏ *0207286 9890*
✎ *kathyabbott34@hotmail.com*

Gorgeous one-off contemporary fine bindings and restoration and rebinding of Islamic manuscripts. Kathy is part of the *Tomorrow's Past* group who get together each year to display their work at the ABA International Bookfair at Olympia.

Alinea Bindery

⌦ *46 Porchester Road, London, W2 6ET*
☎ *020 7727 6659*
✎ *patrick@alinea.fsnet.co.uk*

This is an imaginative bookbindery that will undertake all kinds of projects and offers a design service. The bindery also works with small publishers to produce small print runs of books with fine bindings. Alinea also do a great deal of restoration work.

Susan J Allix

⌦ *19 Almorah Road, N1 3ER*
☎ *020 7359 2949*

Susan Allix sells handmade books in very small print runs and also makes fine bindings to commission (prices start from around £250); she doesn't do restoration work.

Bardel Bookbinding.com Ltd

⌦ *Unit D2, Aladdin Business Centre,*
   426 Long Drive, Greenford, UB6 8UH
⌦ /✏ *020 8575 2583*

A small bookbinders who specialise in binding theses, photographic and wedding albums and repairs. They don't do restoration work.

Bookbinders of London

⌨ *11 Ronalds Road, N5 1XJ*

☎ *020 7607 3361*

✑ *www.bookbindersoflondon.com*

This is a general, traditional bookbinders who specialises in thesis and leather binding.

Bookends Bindery Ltd

⌨ *1a Orleston Road, N7 8LJ*

☎ *020 7609 2613*

✑ *020 7700 5593*

Bookends are a long established bookbinders who will undertake restoration, preservation and conservation as well as bespoke re-binding.

Collis Bird & Whithey

⌨ *1 Drayton Park, N5 1NU*

☎ *020 7607 1116*

✑ *www.thesisbookbinding.co.uk*

This bookbinding company undertake restoration, repair and original binding work.

Grays (Bookbinders) Ltd

⌨ *Unit 5, 24 Willow Lane, Mitcham, CR4 4NA*

☎ *020 8640 1449*

✑ *020 8687 0937*

✑ *graysbookbinders@aol.com*

Grays are a long-established bookbinders with a staff of twelve who will undertake most bookbinding tasks and who can usually give an accurate quote over the phone. They also make presentation boxes to order.

Keypoint Bookbinders

⌨ *9 Railway Street, Kings Cross, N1 9EE*

☎ *020 7837 4833*

✑ *020 7837 0386*

✑ *keypointlondon@aol.com*

Keypoint largely deal in short-run case bindings and thesis binding, but also work on individual commissions.

Marba Bookbinding

- 63 Jeddo Road, W12 9EE
- ☎ 020 8743 4715
- ✆ 020 8749 4965

Marba bookbinding do all kinds of repair and rebinding and can also make bespoke boxes. They don't do restoration work.

J. Muir & Co. (Bookbinders) Ltd

- 64-68 Blackheath Road, SE10 8DA
- ☎ 020 8692 7565
- ✆ 020 8692 2072
- ✎ jmuirbookbinders@yahoo.com

J Muir are a very well-known bookbinders, established in 1900. Although a lot of their work is for the book trade they also maintain a craft bindery which undertakes commissions and restoration work.

Cathy Robert

- Studio 2, 14-16 Meredith St, EC1R 0AE
- ☎ 020 7837 7557
- ✆ 020 7837 9878
- ✎ www.cathyrobert.com

Cathy will undertake most tasks from original bookbindings to restoration and repair. She also makes fine boxes and folios to order.

Rook's Books

- 9 Coopers Yard, SW19 1TN
- ☎ 020 8766 6398
- ✆ 020 8761 0933
- ✎ www.rooksbooks.com

Gavin Rookledge has acquired a reputation as one of the country's most skilled and imaginative bookbinders. The emphasis here is on one-off, handcrafted books, in some cases incorporating the use of precious metals in collaboration with silversmith Gabriella Lane. Rook's Books are always busy, so it's essential to commission work well in advance to avoid disappointment. Their leather-covered van is a fabulous advert and is regularly spotted around London.

Tracey Rowledge

✉ *12 Chippenham Mews, W9 2AW*

☎ / ✆ *0207286 9890*

✎ *traceyrowledge@hotmail.com*

Lovely one-off fine bindings in contemporary designs from simple materials up to commissions using gold-tooled leather. Tracey is part of the *Tomorrow's Past* group who get together each year to display their work at the ABA International Bookfair at Olympia.

Shepherds Bookbinders

✎ *www.bookbinding.co.uk*

Shop:

✉ *76 Rochester Row, SW1P 1JU*

☎ *020 7620 0060*

and

Bindery and Workshop:

✉ *30 Great Guilford Street, SE1 0HS*

This company specialises in bookbinding, restoration and paper conservation and framing, as well as supplying binding materials (including some fabulous papers). In addition to their specialist services, this is an excellent shop to visit for unusual gifts – they sell wonderful notebooks, address and visitors books.

The Wyvern Bindery

✉ *56-58 Clerkenwell Road, EC1M 5PX*

☎ *020 7490 7899*

✆ *020 7490 1391*

✎ *www.wyvernbindery.com*

Wyvern Bindery has a small, enthusiastic team of bookbinders who will undertake any task. One of their most popular services is the construction of portfolios for photographers, with prices starting from £120.

USEFUL WEBSITES

The internet has emerged as a remarkable resource for the world of books: it's a great way to track down rare books, discover more about events and bookshops, chat to like-minded literary souls and post your own writing. Below is an extremely brief selection of websites for literary surfers:

Metasearch Sites

These are sites which search through numerous websites to provide information, as such they offer a powerful search tool although the disadvantage is that they sometimes provide rather too much information.

www.addall.com

This metasearch site trawls through 40 websites offering the books of over 20,000 bookdealers. It is particularly nifty in that it provides a price table listing the cheapest copy first.

www.bookfinder.com

A powerful and simply designed website with millions of books from which to choose, although with an emphasis on booksellers in the US.

www.usedbooksearch.co.uk

This one details 55 million books from more than 6,000 book stores and it clearly identifies the lowest-priced copy.

Other second-hand, out-of-print and antiquarian websites:

www.abebooks.com

This is the largest independent website listing over 70 million second-hand and out of print books from 13,000 English speaking bookdealers. Beware, this site is highly addictive.

www.alibris.com

This is a large website offering new and used books from thousands of booksellers. The site looks good and is easy to use but is predominantly US oriented.

www.biblion.com
This well designed website is run by Biblion in Mayfair (see p.169).
The site offers millions of second-hand, out-of-print and antiquarian
books from hundreds of dealers. The site is especially user-friendly.

www.biblio.com
Three thousand sellers, plenty from UK, list 20 million second-hand,
rare and out-of-print titles.

www.bibliopoly.com
This is a site run by Bernard Quaritch, antiquarian booksellers in
London (see p.199) but lists the stock from booksellers across the
world. The books listed are all antiquarian and top-quality.

www.ibooknet.com
A website developed by the Independent Booksellers Network, a
cooperative of booksellers in the UK. It's easy to use with an excellent range.

www.ilab-lila.com
This is the website of the International League of Antiquarian
Booksellers and offers antiquarian and rare books from over 2,000
dealers. An important website for serious book collectors.

On-line Literary Magazines & Resources

www.theatlantic.com
The Atlantic Online – This is an on-line version of the US based
literary magazine.

www.barcelonareview.com
The Barcelona Review – An international on-line literary magazine
with lots of new fiction.

www.richmondreview.co.uk
The Richmond Review – This website keeps design frills to a
minimum, but offers some excellent new fiction and poetry.

www.webdelsol.com
Web del Sol – A mixture of extracts, articles, literary news and links to other websites.

www.onlineoriginals.com
This site offers on-line works of fiction and non-fiction for down-loading onto any kind of computer for between £4 and £6.

Reference Sites on the Net

www.ipl.org
The Internet Public Library – An invaluable metasearch reference site offering online access to books and magazines.

Miscellaneous

www.poetrybooks.co.uk
The Poetry Book Society – A unique book club for poetry lovers offering a choice of membership packages from £10 and a website that anyone can enjoy including masses of links to other sites of interest.

www.storycode.co.uk
Story Code – A novel and addictive site that uses readers' coding of books they've enjoyed to suggest more books they might enjoy. One way to answer the question, 'What shall I read next?'

General Index

A

Abbey Books p.166
Abbotts p.8
Adanami Bookshop p.166
Africa Book Centre p.4, 8
Africa Centre Library p.246
Agape Arabic Christian Centre p.8
Al Saqi Books p.9
Alfie's Antiques Market p.239
All Flutes Plus p.3, 9
Allan, Ian p.9
Allsworth Rare Books p.216
Alpine Club Library p.246
Alsenthal, J p.10
Altea Gallery p.5, 167
Alzheimer's Society p.247
Amateur Rowing Association p.247
Amnesty International p.229
Amwell Book Company p.167
Anchor, The p.317
Angel Weekend Walks p.321
Anti-Slavery International p.247
Antiquarian Booksellers' Association
p.230-231
Antique City Bookshop p.212
Antonym Bookshop p.10
Any Amount of Books p.167
Architectural Association Library p.247
Archive Books and Music p.168
Argent's Printed Music p.4, 10
Artists' Books Fair p.230
Artwords p.12
Artwords Bookshop at The Whitechapel
Gallery p.12
Ash Rare Books p.216
Astrology Shop p.4, 13
Atlantis Bookshop p.3, 13
Avalon Comics p.14

B

Banana Bookshop p.4, 14
Barbican Chimes Music p.14
Bardel Bookbinding.com Ltd p.337
Bargain Bookshop p.15
BBC Shops p.4-5, 15
Robin de Beaumont p.217
Beaumont Travel Books p.216

Beaumonts p.16
Beautiful Books p.16
BEBC Bookshop p.5, 16
Beckett's p.17
Beetles, Chris p.17
Belarusian Francis Skaryna Library p.248
Bexley Cottage Hospice Shop p.232
Biblion p.5, 169
Bibliopola p.239
Bishopsgate Institute p.248
Black Gull p.169
Blackwell's Business and Law Bookshop
p.3, 18
Blackwell's Charing Cross Road p.4, 18
Blackwell's University Bookshops:
    Guy's Hospital p.19
    King's College p.19
    London Business School p.18
    London Metropolitan University p.19
    South Bank University p.19
Blenheim Books p.20
Bloomsbury Auctions p.5, 226
Bolingbroke Bookshop p.20
Bonham, J & S L p.217
Bonhams p.5, 226
Bookbinders of London p.338
Bookends Bindery Ltd p.338
Book & Comic Exchange p.170
Book Ends Papercrafts p.22
Book House Nasherketab p.22
Book Now! Richmond's Literature
Festival p.326
Book Warehouse, Notting Hill p.33
Book Warehouse, Regent St p.5, 33
Book Warehouse, Southampton Row
p.3, 33
Book Warehouse, Strutton Ground p.33
Book Warehouse, Waterloo Road p.33
bookartbookshop p.21
Bookcase p.21
Bookends p.4, 21
Bookhouse p.3, 22
Bookmarks p.3, 23
Bookmongers p.170
Books & Things p.217
Books and Lyrics p.171
Books Etc:
    Broadgate p.24
    Canary Wharf p.24

344

General Index

Area Index

Central

Area Index

NORTH

South East

Area Index

South West

Area Index

West

Subject Index

The subject index is not comprehensive but will help you to locate bookshops, libraries and venues specialising in a particular field. There are of course large book stores that will cover all subjects comprehensively, the best of these are:

Blackwell's, Charing Cross Road p.18
Borders p.35
W & G Foyles p.62
Hatchards p.157
Waterstones, Gower Street p.212
Waterstones, Piccadilly p.157

Africa/Orient

Africa Book Centre p.8
Africa Centre Library p.246
Bonham, J & S L p.217
Fine Books Oriental p.180
Fogg, Sam p.180
Graves-Johnston, Michael p.218
Guanghwa p.69
Headstart Books & Crafts p.71
Holland and Holland p.74
INIVA - Institute of International Visual Arts p.259
Maghreb Bookshop p.88
Markham, Sheila p.219
New Beacon Books p.102
Portobello Books p.198
Potter, Jonathan p.198
Probsthain, Arthur p.115
School of Oriental & African Studies p. 124, 286, 336
Vernon-Hunt, Charles p.243

Anarchism/Alternative

Anti-Slavery International p.247
Bishopsgate Institute p.248
Freedom Press Bookshop p.63
Housmans p.75
Marx Memorial Library p.264
Nutri Centre Bookshop p.104
Pathfinder Bookshop p.111
Porcupine p.214
Stepping Stones p.140
Watkins p.158

Antiques & Collectibles

Alfie's Antique Market p.239
Bloomsbury Auctions p.226
Camden Passage Market p.240
East West Antiques and Books p.240
Kelly, Don p.243
Portobello Road Market p.242
Spink p.138
Spitalfields Market p.244

Arabia/Middle East/Islam

Agape Arabic Christian Centre p.8
Al Saqi Books p.9
Call to Islam Bookshop p.41
Dar Al Dawa p.50
Dar Al-Hikma p.51
Dar Al-Taqwa p.51
Darussalam p.51
East London Book Book Shop p.57
Fine Books Oriental p.180
International Islamic Dawah Centre p.78
Islamic Cultural Centre p.260
Maghreb Bookshop p.88
Pendleburys p.195
School of Oriental and African Studies Bookshop p.124
Trotter Books, John p.207
Zainab p.164
Zam Zam p.164

Archaeology

British Museum Bookshop p.3, 38-39
Egypt Exploration Society p.254
Graves-Johnston, Michael p.218
Institute of Classical Studies p.285
Museum of London Shop p.98
Trotter Books, John p.207

Architecture/Building

Amwell Book Company p.167
Architectural Association Library p.247
Artwords p.12
Building Centre Bookshop p.3, 40
Chelsea College of Art and Design p.280
Civic Trust Library p.253
Courtauld Institute of Art p.4, 49
Design Museum Bookshop p.54
Fielders p.59
Geffrye Museum p.256

Subject Index

Subject Index

Military/War

Earlsfield Bookshop p.176
Imperial War Museum p.76, 258
National Army Museum Bookshop
p.99, 265
RAF Museum Library p.270
Under Two Flags p.148

Music

All Flutes Plus p.9
Archive Books and Music p.168
Argent's Printed Music p.10
Barbican Chimes Music p.14
Books and Lyrics p.171
Boosey and Hawkes p34
Brittens Music p.5, 34
British Library p.398
British Music Information Centre p.250
Chappell of Bond Street p.5, 43
Christian Books and Music p.45
Dress Circle p.55
English Folk Dance And
Song Society p.254
Farhangsara p.59
Guildhall School of Music &
Drama p.282
Hobgoblin p.74
Horniman Library p.258
House of Yesterdays p.212
Kensington Chimes Music p.82
Music Room p.98
Owen Books & Music, Wesley p.5, 159
John Price p.221
Rose-Morris p.120
Royal Academy of Music p.285
Royal College of Music p.287
Schott Universal p.124
Teerans Booksellers p.144
Travis and Emery p.207
Trinity College of Music p.287
Wimbledon Books and Music p.161

Natural History

British Geological Survey p.36
Charles Russell Rare Books p.202
Horniman Library p.258
Maggs Bros Ltd p.191
Natural History Museum p.102, 268
Royal Geographical Society p.272

New Age/Esoteric

Atlantis Bookshop p.13
Inner Space p.4, 77
Mysteries p.4, 99
Nutri Centre Bookshop p.104
Stepping Stones p.140
Watkins Books Ltd p.4, 158

New Zealand

Kiwi Fruits p.83

Photography

Amwell Book Company p.167
Artwords p.12
Classic Camera, The p.3, 47
Hayward Gallery Bookshop p.71
Magma p.88
The National Portrait Gallery Bookshop
p.101
Photo Books International p.3, 112
Photographer's Gallery
Bookshop p.4, 112
Shipley p.4, 125-126
Silverprint p.127
Tate Modern Shop p.143
Walther Koenig p.83

Poetry

Ash Rare Books p.216
Enterprise (readings) p.323
Keats' House p.301
Owl Bookshop p.108
Palmer's Green Bookshop
(readings) p.109
Lance Pierson p.321
Poetry International p.328
Poetry Society p.324
The Poetry Library p.269
Torriano Meeting House
(readings) p.325
Troubador Coffee House
(readings) p.325
West End Lane Books p.160
Ulysses p.208

Politics/Philosophy

BBC Shops p.15
Black Gull p.169
Blackwell's, Charing Cross Road p.18

Psychiatry/Psychoanalysis/ Psychology/Psychotherapy

Science

Spain/Spanish

Sport

Swedenborg (Emmanuel)

Theatre

Subject Index

Order our other Metro Titles

The following titles are also available from Metro Publications. Please send your order along with a cheque made payable to Metro Publications to the address below. **Postage and packaging is free**.

Alternatively call our customer order line on **020 8533 7777** (Visa/Mastercard/Switch), Open Mon-Fri 9am-6pm

Metro Publications
PO Box 6336, London N1 6PY
metro@dircon.co.uk
www.metropublications.com

London Architecture
Author: Marianne Butler
£**8.99** ISBN1-902910-18-4

London Theatre Guide
Author: Richard Andrews
ISBN 1-902910-08-7 £**7.99**

Museums & Galleries of London
3rd ed Author: Abigail Willis
£**8.99** ISBN 1-902910-20-6

Bargain Hunters' London
3rd ed Author: Andrew Kershman
£6.99 ISBN 1-902910-15-X

Veggie & Organic London
Author: Russell Rose
ISBN 1-902910-21-4 £6.99

London Market Guide 3rd ed
Author: Andrew Kershman
£6.99 ISBN 1-902910-14-1

Food Lovers' London 3rd ed
Author: Jenny Linford
ISBN 1-902910-22-2 £8.99

Guide to Cookery Course
3rd ed Author: Eric Treuille
£7.99 ISBN 1-902910-17-6